The Secret Dreamworld
of Andrea Cooper

The Secret Dreamworld of Andrea Cooper

A Woman's Journey Home to Her Heart

Susan M. Tuttle

Advance Praise

"A captivating and deeply insightful book that takes readers on a remarkable journey of self-discovery and healing. *The Secret Dreamworld of Andrea Cooper* is a powerful testament to the human spirit's capacity for healing and transformation. It is a must-read for anyone seeking to overcome the challenges of their past and embark on a journey toward a more fulfilling and authentic life."

—SANDY BROWN, author of *Porn Addict's Wife*

"Susan Tuttle's allegory could be the tender hug you've been waiting for to guide you through your 12-step journey and toward a reclamation of inner treasure that has the potential to light up the world. Andrea's story made me feel loved, understood, and unapologetically human."

—ERIN HEARTS, host of *Grace + Boundaries: Navigating Intergenerational Trauma with Erin Hearts*

Table of Contents

For those of us who feel something's missing
and long to find our way back home to our hearts and souls.

A Note from the Author

*Somewhere between sleepwalking through life and living awake,
there is a void. But there is also opportunity.*

Andrea has been sleepwalking her way through life. She's been denying what is, and accepting far less than she yearns for. By the time we meet her, she feels like she's let everyone down—including herself.

In the story to come, Andrea dreams of awakening to a voice, one who echoes her recurring thought that "something is missing." It's an invitation to a fantastic journey, accompanied by guides and traveling companions who remind her that she's not alone. Along the way, Andrea comes to several crossroads where a decision must be made and faces personal truths that threaten to open a Pandora's box of insurmountable pain. Will she remain asleep, or wake up and come home to her heart? Ultimately, Andrea must decide if she has the courage and will to persevere.

. . .

Dear Reader,

I wrote this story, a combination of allegory and insights from my own experiences, for all of us who've ever felt that something is missing.

What is that missing piece? Are you willing to do what is necessary to learn what it is? And are you willing to consider giving up some of what's familiar to find your way home?

Don't answer now. That's what this book is meant to help you figure out. As you read, remember that there is no right or wrong, good or bad, must-dos or don'ts. There is no one way to explore and discover. What there is, however, is an opportunity to find a new perspective, one that might lead to making peace within, doing life differently, and ultimately finding your way back home to your own heart and soul.

I hope that as you read this story, you'll become intrigued enough to want to begin the process of seeking and finding your truth. Maybe you'll consider trusting a power greater than yourself—one within yourself, or one of your understanding—to help you find your way. I thank my higher power daily for the gifts I've received, including the opportunities to shed old perspectives and the curiosity to seek new ones. I'm grateful to have been given the space and the healing to write this book and share my message.

May the words written on these pages help you begin or add to your own personal healing journey. One that will take you home to yourself.

CHAPTER 1

It's Time to Wake Up

The clock stops ticking
The hands are still
Time is measured by units, minutes, hours, days
Time is of the essence, it's precious
Time is sometimes wasted, borrowed, or taken advantage of
Time is space, a void, indefinite yet infinite
We have nothing but time
Yet we are running out of time
It's time to wake up

Tick tock … tick tock … the clock is ticking, but the hands are still. Andrea is dreaming. Her eyes twitch back and forth, and her brain shudders just for a moment. The dreamworld offers a place of rest, but also opportunity—here Andrea's most secret thoughts and feelings run free.

At 7:00 a.m., the hands on the clock start to move again. Andrea wakes up, stretches her arms wide, and then yawns. She feels like part of her is still in the dream, and she is preoccupied by a message she heard there: Something is missing. She has the sense that this isn't the first time she's dreamed this, but she shakes it off. Throwing one leg at a time over the side of the bed, she gets up and gets ready to go about her day.

As she runs her errands, she muses about missing pieces. Her life's pretty simple. She thinks about her daily routine, her exercise, her business contacts, her friendships, her children, and her grandchildren. She resists thinking about James. She's been increasingly at odds with her husband, but she tucks any thoughts about that away. *My life isn't so bad*, she tells herself.

But her denial doesn't last. By early afternoon she's back to thinking about James. Thoughts and images flash by—things feeling out of control, tempers flaring, hurtful words spoken. The heavy mood and tone in their home. *Toxic*, she thinks and then immediately tries to convince herself otherwise. *This is all normal for couples who've been married as long as we have, right?* Tears come to her eyes, and she wipes them away. "Everything will be fine," she murmurs out loud.

And so Andrea goes about the rest of her day as if everything is fine. She focuses not on her marriage but on her schedule for the week, noting the yoga classes, lunches with friends, a few business and networking meetings—all this on top of her housekeeping responsibilities.

"My week is full," she says to herself. Keeping busy is a means of escaping her reality, though she's not fully aware of that yet.

The day flies by, and it's almost dinner time. She dreads this. Sitting in silence at the dinner table with James feels so lonely. Making idle conversation has become a chore, one she's begun to despise. But all long-married couples go through this. It's a slump, right? She continues to accommodate.

After dinner James heads off to his favorite chair, tucking his nose behind the newspaper and nursing his evening Jack Daniels on the rocks. Andrea forces herself to walk over slowly and kiss him on the head. "Goodnight, dear."

James grunts a slight acknowledgment of her presence and kicks his recliner back one more notch.

Andrea makes her way upstairs to their bedroom, completes her nightly rituals, and crawls into bed. She falls into a deep sleep, into that imaginary world that is so different from her regular world. It is peaceful and serene. Then there it is, the message that "something is missing." She can't tell if she can hear it or see it or is just somehow aware of it, but suddenly she finds herself drawn into a dark, seemingly empty space. Is this where she's supposed to find what's missing? In this dream, she's eager to do so. She is suddenly aware that in her waking life, she is not.

The 7:00 a.m. alarm goes off, and Andrea is abruptly pulled out of her dream just as it seemed she was figuring something out. She feels a slight irritation at that, but as soon as she gets up and starts going about her day, she's able to dismiss the message, her loneliness, and her true feelings. For now, her discomfort is her friend.

• • •

Later that day, Andrea finds herself in the paper goods aisle at the grocery store in front of a magazine rack. One of the magazine covers reads, "Feel Like Something's Missing? Then It Is!"

Ugh, that message again. It haunts her. She picks up the magazine and looks at the table of contents. "Come seek the adventure of a lifetime," it reads. "Explore faraway places where you'll be free from your mundane life, see page 44."

That, she thinks to herself, *is exactly what I need.*

She imagines herself exploring these faraway places, a map in one hand and a blue drink with a pineapple and a cherry hovering on top in the other. The map is filled with colorful lines and landmarks, and it all seems intriguing. She often dreams about finding someplace that will bring her joy, peace, and harmony. She smiles at the thought as she tosses the magazine into her basket and continues her shopping.

• • •

That evening Andrea notices her journal on her bedside table for the first time in months. She is about to reach for it when a cool breeze fills the room and ruffles the pages. Then she sees it: "Something is missing," written in her hand at the top of page one. She pauses and puts a finger to her lips, perplexed. Did she write that down before she started dreaming about it, or after? She can't remember.

It comes to her that she put her journal here to help her set intentions. "If you write a question down at night before you go to bed," someone told her, "you'll have the answer in the morning." She turns to the next clean page and writes, "What is missing? How do I find out?"

She closes the book and lies down. Maybe this time, her dream will tell her what she wants to know. *But do I really want to know?* she thinks. *Wouldn't I then need to do something about it?* Eager and conflicted, Andrea waits impatiently for sleep to come. As she lies there, she hears the hypnotic sound of the clock … tick tock … tick tock …

The alarm goes off. Gah! Has she even slept at all? She reluctantly heaves herself out of bed and takes herself through her morning routine: exercise, a hardboiled egg with some fruit, a few business-related calls. It all feels normal. It all feels ... ordinary.

By mid-afternoon, the lack of sleep catches up with her. *Just a twenty-minute catnap,* she thinks as she lies down on the sofa. Andrea grabs her favorite blanket from the top of the couch, a vibrantly colored throw hand-knit by her nana and soft as her love. Snuggling under the blanket, Andrea falls into a deep sleep, leaving her ordinary world behind.

$$\bullet \quad \bullet \quad \bullet$$

Andrea is dreaming, though she doesn't know it yet. She finds herself walking in the park and talking to her friend Teresa on the phone. There is a part of her that notices she's just wandering about, barely aware of her surroundings. She is only dimly aware of the birds singing, the bumble bees humming and buzzing about, the radiant sun shining, and the striking blue color of the sky. The clock in the background strikes noon, but she's too distracted by Teresa's incessant chatter to hear it.

Something is missing. This idea, not the chime of the clock, is what penetrates the hypnotic rise and fall of Teresa's voice. Though nothing has changed, she's filled with the sense that everything is about to. Her steps shorten, and her breath turns shallow—she's almost gasping for air. Her heart begins to audibly pound. Andrea abruptly tells Teresa that she needs to go and disconnects before Teresa can answer. She decides to rest on a nearby, rickety wooden bench whose frame seems held together only by the dreams of its previous visitors.

Something is missing. There it is again, growing louder. She thinks about the emptiness of her life and for the first time sees a space opening up, a frightening void. It's the space between who she is now and who she yearns to be. For the first time, she considers that this dark, scary space isn't the ending as much as a pause before a new beginning. There is some peace in that. She hopes she remembers that when she wakes up.

Then that oddly familiar inner voice speaks up. "Leave the dream now," it says, "and you will end this opportunity for change. Life will continue in your ordinary world. But if you recognize the power of where you are right now and the opportunity it can provide, you will be shown a new way of being."

Andrea is moved by the message. Looking around her, she sees that the sidewalk is now a stream made up of vibrant colors. She steps toward an empty room and enters cautiously. The door behind her remains open. Inside the room she sees a glowing message above a faint outline that might be a door that stands before her.

"In order to walk through the next doorway," it reads, "you must close the door through which you entered."

She looks around, hoping to find someone who will tell her what to do. She hates to be alone, especially in a strange place. Clearly, she needs to close the door behind her in order to walk through the next, but she's afraid the door in front of her is a figment of her imagination. She's even more afraid of what's on the other side of it.

The image from page 44 of the travel magazine pops into her head: "Explore faraway places," it says. Telling herself to be brave, she reaches back and firmly closes the door behind her. To her surprise, the new door doesn't open. There appears to be no handle or knob. She begins to feel around for it. Fear and panic set in; beads of sweat form on her face and neck. What if she's stuck here? Why did she close the other door?

Trust, whispers that quiet inner voice. "Trust" is not a word that has historically been in her vocabulary.

Andrea fights down her fear and stops frantically running her hands over the outline of the door. Instead, she takes a deep breath and reaches for where a doorknob would be if she could see one. Miraculously, she feels her fingers close around an invisible knob. She turns it, and the door opens.

There is nothing but light, but Andrea can sense a familiar presence, someone soothing and calming, and a feeling of joy rushes through her body. She has not yet crossed the threshold, but she knows that somewhere on the other side is where whatever is missing can be found.

She can hear the strains of Fleetwood Mac's "Go Your Own Way" playing from somewhere up ahead. She knows it's there to remind her that this is her journey, and hers alone. She hesitates for a moment, one foot in the air. And as she does so, the threshold abruptly vanishes.

Andrea wakes with a start, feeling as if she has fallen through midair. She's on her own couch, Nana's blanket on the floor. She is shaken. How can a simple door be so powerful? As she slows her breathing, she hears the sound of the clock—tick tock … tick tock. A simple reminder that whatever is happening in dreamtime, here it's just an ordinary day.

> *Help me embrace the void. Help me relax into the void.*
> *Help me walk toward the void. Allow it to bring forth*
> *what it will and may my hands be open.*
> —paraphrased from MELODY BEATTIE

Reflections for This Chapter

Integrate your thoughts by going through these activities now or coming back to them later. I invite you to listen to "Go Your Own Way" by Fleetwood Mac as you do so.

Can you think of a time when you had a dream and wondered about its meaning or message? Journal about a dream you remember and any messages brought to the light. There are no right or wrong answers.

Can you think of a time when you felt a void in your life? If yes, describe what it felt like. What sensations did you feel? How did you react or respond? Draw a picture if you'd like. Remember, there are no right or wrong answers.

If you've never felt a void in your life, have you ever felt like you were in a space between two worlds, in a limbic state? If so, write about that limbic state, or draw a picture.

CHAPTER 2

Staying Curious

Curiosity and questions will get you
further than confidence and answers.
—MAXIME LAGACÉ

The clock is ticking, and Andrea feels very worn out from her dream. She tries to remember the details, but she can only recall bits and pieces. "Damn it," she says. Her right hand's frustrated fingertips tap her forehead in hopes of jogging her memory. She remembers talking with her friend Teresa and then abruptly hanging up.

She wanders into the bedroom and opens her journal to the page where she wrote down her intention. Eager to fill the pages even with the little she remembers, she writes. As she does, some of it comes back to her. She remembers being curious about the door, as well as standing alone on the precipice of ... something. She remembers wanting to leave her ordinary life behind in order to find what is missing and then questioning herself. She remembers that inner voice encouraging her to step forward. She remembers not quite crossing the threshold.

One of the last things she remembers is the conviction that the doorway represents an opportunity for her journey to begin, the journey to those places where those missing puzzle pieces might be found. And then the threshold vanishing—just like that.

Weird, she thinks to herself, and then wonders if she'll pick up where she left off when she goes to bed tonight. She wonders if she really wants to pick up where she left off. *Am I really ready to explore all this, this secret dreamworld of mine?* she thinks. She doesn't know, and in true Andrea fashion, she shakes off the thought as quickly as she allowed it to enter her mind. *Everything is fine.*

That afternoon she meets up with a few friends for a late lunch and shopping. The conversations are shallow. The women are talking about reality TV and makeovers. *Boring,* she thinks to herself. She drifts off for a moment, remembering the in-depth conversations she used to have with her friends at the precinct. Even James.

"Andrea! Earth to Andrea!" It's her friend Samantha, snapping her fingers and calling her a space cadet. "Just kidding," Samantha says without a trace of remorse. This reminds Andrea of the way James makes fun of her and then tells her he's only kidding. She looks up at Samantha and tries to laugh it off.

When she gets home she makes dinner, then sits down with James. *Another silent night,* she observes, seeing James glowering and shoveling food into his mouth. She finishes her dinner, feeling sad and alone with her thoughts. At least there isn't a blow-up. James quickly retires to his beloved chair and plants his nose in his golf magazine. Andrea clears the table, cleans up, brings James his Jack Daniels on the rocks, and says good night. He mumbles what might be a thank you and takes several quick sips of his nightcap.

Andrea hurries to her bedroom and her journal, where she rereads what she remembers of her naptime dream. Maybe it will inspire her to pick up where she left off once she's asleep. She lies down amid small but enticing waves of enthusiasm and trepidation. *What if I don't like what I find? Maybe it's not a good idea to step back into the dream.* She turns over in bed. *But maybe it is …*

Andrea opens her eyes and decides to write down another intention in her journal. This time, she is more definite: "I intend to seek what is missing and do whatever it takes to find it." She props herself on her pillow and flips through the travel magazine she bought. She closes her eyes, thinking about those faraway places, and drifts a bit. Here in her bed one moment, in a world full of exotic plants and interesting animals the next.

She slips deep into a sleep that feels almost impossible to wake from, her body falling freely out of her ordinary life into her dreamscape. There is a shaft of light emanating from a crack in a doorway. Will this light lead her back to the threshold? Andrea remembers feeling uncertain about crossing that threshold, about leaving the safety of the box-like room for what lies outside it. *The void!* she whispers to herself.

She has a sense that this is the space between who she is and who she wants to be. *But who is that?* she thinks. Slipping deeper now, Andrea picks up her dream from where she left off during her nap. She can see her hand reaching out for a knob that is now fully visible and sturdy. It comes to her that once she opens the door and passes over the threshold, she will be passing from one level to the next, from her earthly self to her spiritual self, the version of herself who is willing to seek and find the truth.

Taking a deep breath, she opens the door and steps over the threshold into the light yet seemingly empty space.

Limbo, she thinks. Just like her waking life, in her ordinary world. She's been in real-life limbo for a very long time. So has her marriage. She and James barely speak, and when they do, they either have brief exchanges that end up with him insulting her, or they engage in toxic screaming matches. None of it is loving.

Is it James's drinking that's the problem? When he drinks, that's when the accusations and insults fly. He tells her how unappreciative and ungrateful she is. He asks her why she can't just be happy with what she has, like the other wives. He yells at the top of his lungs and sometimes he throws objects at her.

Andrea begins to tremble. She is still standing in the void, this limbic space, but she can see a vision, sort of like a movie, of her life playing out before her. She and James are in the kitchen, where so many of their altercations take place. James is reminding her of how lucky she is, asking her to be appreciative and grateful for what she has. She sees herself responding defensively, telling him that she's appreciative and grateful—but also lonely.

"Lonely!" James's voice booms, and the veins in his forehead stand out. He shakes his finger at her as if she were a child. "You have everything, you ungrateful bitch. How can you even say you're lonely?"

Dismissing her feelings. Minimizing her loneliness. Trying to make her feel guilty—and succeeding. The guilt Andrea feels wars with the message that something is missing. The void, this space between what she is and what she could be, is a space of internal conflict. But for the first time, even as she feels nervous about finding the truth, she also begins to feel curious. With clarity, she sees that by navigating this path with curiosity, the answer to that internal conflict might be revealed. The void, she's just beginning to see, is a magical place of opportunity where new beginnings can be created.

As she stands in limbo, wondering what else might be revealed, she sees a montage of scenes, visualizations, flashbacks, snapshots. More real events from her awake, ordinary world. She becomes aware of a voice—not her inner voice but a masculine voice that is outside of herself, from beyond herself.

"Savor the scenes that are about to be revealed to you," the voice intones. "Write what comes up for you in your journal."

She is surprised to find her journal in her hand.

"Be present to your time here," the voice (*he?* she thinks tentatively) says. "All that you see and experience here will assist you in preparing for your real-life journey ahead."

"What journey?" Andrea says out loud. "Where am I going?"

"The path will become clear soon," he says. "You will be shown more of the truth as we journey through the void."

Andrea breathes in deeply, trying to accept what's happening. "Who are you? Why can't I see you?" she asks.

"I am an archangel, sent to guide you. You will be able to see me soon enough, but for now it's important for you to try to trust and focus on my voice," he says.

Holy what? Andrea thinks.

"I will be helping you see your truth."

"How?" Andrea asks.

"I will take you through many scenes of your life," he says. "All I ask is that you be present to the opportunities there. See with fresh eyes."

Why should she trust this guy? she thinks. *Do I really want to see what happens to me? Do I really want to be fully aware of the truth?*

"The choice is yours," the angel says as if Andrea has spoken aloud.

Andrea considers this. She hasn't wanted to look too closely at her life for a long time now. But seeking her truth within a dream seems safe.

"Let us take a look at your marriage again," the angel suggests. "See what more there is to be discovered."

Andrea isn't sure how to do as the angel asks. But she finds that all she has to do is think about her marriage and scenes from the kitchen begin to play out before her. Watching, she finds it easy to rationalize. James doesn't physically abuse her. He doesn't cheat on her. Okay, so he drinks a bit, but so do a lot of people. "He's not so bad," she says, thinking of some of her friends' husbands.

But then the scenes flying by resolve into a single visualization. Andrea sees herself standing in the kitchen on a night she remembers quite well, a scene she will never forget. She remembers that this ends with her heart breaking.

James is irate, agitated, yelling. Objects are flying, cabinet doors slamming, glass shattering. In an instant, Nana's mosaic bowl, the one made up of vivid blues, greens, and yellows, lies in pieces on the hardwood floor.

"That isn't all happening by itself," the angel says gently.

Andrea forces herself to remember, and this time the scene plays out accurately. James is the one slamming the cabinet doors, throwing things, as he paces angrily about the kitchen and shouts accusations of ingratitude at her. James is the one who smashes Nana's bowl to the floor.

Andrea sees the dismay on her face and remembers how heartbroken and despondent she felt. Even now, she can feel the waves of overwhelming sadness flow through her body as she watches herself in the past, where tears are rolling down her face. She watches as that version of herself wipes the tears away as fast as they come, silencing her emotions and pushing them away.

That's a familiar tactic, she thinks. *One that helps dismiss what is and then helps justify why staying is my only option.* But as soon as she has that thought, it threatens to crumble away. "Our relationship isn't perfect, but whose is?" she says aloud. "Every marriage has its issues, right?" Her mind races and her denial deepens. It feels like a relief to not really know what she thinks or feels.

"This is not easy," the angelic voice says. "But the more you allow your truths to come forth, the more the void will provide an opportunity for growth. Keep going."

Reluctantly, Andrea continues to visualize what took place that horrible night. Even here, safe in the void, she's shaken by James's bellowing voice. She can feel herself trembling inside and out as he yells at the top of his lungs, "Damn you, why can't you just be appreciative?"

She sees herself in a fetal position on the floor next to the shattered bowl. James towers over her. "See what you made me do?" he roars.

From the void, Andrea murmurs, "He's a good man, overall. A good provider. He's loyal. He'll be different tomorrow. And I still love him. I think."

But her body tells the truth. She tenses up as she watches herself get to her knees and start picking up the shards of Nana's bowl. She can feel the words "I think" pour out of her, like water out of a faucet. She finds herself voicing the difficult questions she cannot bear when she is awake. "But do I? Do I still love him? He drinks, he's mean, and I don't like how he speaks to me."

Tears are running down her face even in the dream, but this time she doesn't sweep her feelings under the rug. This time she feels her loneliness and pain.

"He drinks more times than I'm willing to admit," she murmurs. "It feels so painful, I can barely stand it." She watches as the version of her in the visualization tries to sit up in order to lean against the cabinet. She remembers how difficult that was. When she'd finally sat up, she'd put her head between her hands and allowed herself to sit with the pain as her tears flowed freely to the floor.

Standing in the void, Andrea's body shakes as if it is trying to wake up.

The voice of the angel speaks, warm and compassionate. "There is more, Andrea," he says. "It is not quite time to wake up. You need to finish visualizing so you can begin to process your truth and heal."

Andrea reaches out as if she can see this angel.

"You will see me when the time is right," he says. "For now, notice what happens in your body when you and James are in conflict. Notice what takes place in your heart and soul. It may be difficult, but it is important."

Andrea knows that she can no longer sit in denial, but that scares her. Denial has been her friend.

A new scene plays out before her. James is sitting at the dinner table, drinking heavily. He's barely eaten, and even though it's a dish he's liked plenty of times before, he begins to attack her over it. "You, Andrea, are the worst cook I know," he says with deceptive coolness. "Your skills are nonexistent. You're a lousy wife. You're an embarrassment." His volume starts to rise as the insults keep flying.

For the first time, Andrea can see herself and how she reacts in these moments, and realizes how small and meek she becomes, almost as if she doesn't exist. She just takes it. She always takes it. She tells herself it will get better, that it will be different tomorrow, but it never does and it never is. It only gets worse.

This visualization ends with James banging his hands on the table like a child having a tantrum, and she sees herself covering her ears as she did as a child. His yelling reminds her of her mother's shrieks.

She looks up as if she can see the angel and says, "My body shakes, my throat gets tight, the insanity sets in, and then my emotions shut down. This is what happens to me each and every time, and it's getting worse."

"Yes," the angelic voice says. "Feel it, but do not dwell there. Sit quietly for a few minutes. Acknowledge to yourself the work you have already done in becoming aware."

Andrea doesn't entirely understand what's happening. Her body is still noticeably shaking, her vocal cords are making a humming sound, and she finds herself moving her hands as if she's warding off toxic and evil spirits. She does this for a few minutes and then looks up and tells the angel that she is ready to move forward, ready to face her truth.

"Then we shall continue with the next visualization," he says. "See these for what they really are: snapshots of your truth."

Andrea feels the weight of this place, this limbic state she has been living in. She is beginning to see the insanity of telling herself it's not that bad and it'll all be fine. She wants it all to be just fine, but it will never be just fine. Her dream is turning into what feels like a nightmare as the truth begins to unfold.

The angelic voice encourages her one more time to allow the process to flow and not to fear the truth. He acknowledges how difficult this is and affirms her for the steps she has taken thus far because they have taken courage. "It is okay to vacillate for right now," he says. "No decisions must be made today."

This helps Andrea feel like she can breathe. She nods.

The angel encourages her to visualize a scene with her children. "Let us see who you are when you interact with them," he says.

Andrea thinks of her children, and she flushes with a mixed sense of—what? It seems to be a tingling feeling of embarrassment and shame. She realizes that she feels judged by her children, which feels paralyzing. But she follows the angel's suggestion and finds herself flashing back to a year or so ago when she actually thought of leaving James and was planning on telling her parents and her children about her plan.

The scene unfolds before her. She is about to have lunch with her son Ben and daughter Sophia at her favorite restaurant, Shake It Up. Ben is thirty-two years old. He is a man of few words, but when he speaks his voice is soft and calm. She loves that about him and wishes she were more like him. He loves his mother, but he has a difficult time trusting her. Sophia is thirty years old and quite the opposite of Ben. She is sassy, like her mom, and a bit loud—especially when she's angry or passionate about something. She, too, loves her mother, but struggles setting healthy boundaries with her. Both Ben and Sophia care deeply for their mom, and they want to see her happy.

Andrea spots her children sitting in their favorite booth. She is feeling brave. She is about to acknowledge her truth.

"I've been thinking," she says to her children. "I've been thinking of leaving your father. We have been—"

Sophia interrupts, "Are you kidding me? A woman at your age on your own? You can't afford that. That's crazy."

Ben follows. "Mom, you need to think this through. Dad can't be alone. He needs you. He loves you. He …"

Andrea in the visualization and Andrea watching herself both tune out for a minute as the kids rail at her. Guilt and shame overpower any courage she needs to say what she wants to say.

Andrea watches the flashback unfold as her children look her straight in the eyes and say in unison, "Are you insane?"

The all-too-familiar thoughts fill her head. Andrea loves her children, and she knows they love her, but their opinions hurt her, and their words upset her. She is left feeling empty, as if she has no value. She feels small just as she does after she and James argue.

Her children don't come around much anymore. They have no idea of the hell she is living. She makes a decision: it's no longer safe to talk about her circumstances with them.

There is an awkward silence.

She watches as the waiter takes their orders, refills their water glasses, and pours their iced tea. "Lemon, anyone?" the waiter asks.

The food arrives, they eat, and conversations about nothing flow as if "everything is fine." As Andrea watches this scene from the void, she realizes that this day took place a year or so ago, and yet here she is today with nothing having changed. She still feels empty and alone. She is no longer close to her children, as she once was. *What happened?* she thinks.

She remembers her children coming home from grade school, so happy to see her. She remembers them hugging and kissing her, and the three of them sitting at the kitchen table, dipping chocolate chip cookies into a glass of fresh cold milk.

19

"Don't tell your father, it's our secret," she would say, and they would laugh. She remembers that this ritual lasted well into their later school years. *They trusted me*, she thinks to herself. But she began to realize that they actually did start to lose their trust in her early on. She was overprotective, occasionally irrational, not always forthright. As they moved into adulthood, her anxiety and need to control grew more consuming within her. She didn't withhold her opinions, and her kids found her meddlesome. Their relationships became even more strained.

Now adults, her children still see her as meddling, irrational, and controlling—shortcomings that don't invite trust. Andrea yearns for her relationships to be different with her children, yet she understands the distance that has been created over the years which has been partly her doing. But she's lost faith in herself, and she remains cautious in all of her relationships. She tells them that everything is fine, so no wonder they are convinced she's crazy. And still, they do not know the hellish state she lives in.

"Mom—Mom," her son says in the visualization. Across the restaurant table, Andrea snaps to and smiles reassuringly. She pays the check, they kiss one another on the cheek, politely say their goodbyes, and head toward their separate cars and their separate lives. *Will they ever know my truth?* Andrea wonders.

Coming out of the visualization, Andrea sees herself for who she has become with her children: a doormat, a martyr, a victim. Worst of all, she feels like a stranger around her own family. She recognizes how she succumbs to her fears and abandons herself. As with James, she quietly disappears into the background.

"It is easy to fall deep into the trap of believing 'everything is fine,'" the angel says. "I want you to continue your thoughts about your life, Andrea, because soon those visualizations will help create new thoughts, and those new thoughts will lead you to your truth."

"That's what I'm afraid of," Andrea whispers. She wonders if she'll ever have the strength and courage it takes to step out of the void and into a new way of being. But it does feel easier here, in the dream, and she is beginning to allow herself to see the truth with each flashback. Breathing in deeply, exhaling slowly, she decides to stop questioning and go with the flow of the dream.

"Stay in curiosity," the angel says.

Andrea looks up, hoping to see the angel materialize, but instead she sees a vision of an enormous wooden box with a large brass lock. *Could this box hold the answers to my questions?* she thinks. She wonders if there's a map inside to help her steer her way out of the void, and where she can find this box. Is the hunt part of her journey? Is the box hidden in a faraway place?

The angel replies, "Yes, indeed it is, Andrea, and we will embark upon a magical journey in order to find it."

For the first time, Andrea feels almost giddy. A treasure hunt! Then she wonders if she's being silly.

The voice of the angel assures her that she's not being silly at all, in fact, quite the contrary. "This secret box does indeed hold some of the answers to your questions, Andrea, but the journey to find it could be arduous," he says. "There is a path that will take you to the hidden box. Is this a journey you would like to embark upon?"

"Can you tell me more?" Andrea asks.

"It's an incredible journey made up of many miles and scenarios like the ones you just experienced," he says. "It will be difficult, tiring, and require a lot of effort at times. But in the end, it will all be worth it. It is ultimately up to you if you are up for the expedition."

"But is this real, or am I still asleep?" Andrea asks. She fears she might feel all of the feelings she feels in her dream while awake. That's something she's avoided most of her life.

The angel assures her that she is still asleep, deeply asleep. "In order to travel down this path, you will need to trust, Andrea," he says. "You will need to act with courage, exercise patience, and have a willingness to take risks."

All of these points frighten Andrea, but she feels deep down that she needs to take the risk.

Going on this journey is central to her one day moving out of the void, out of this limbic state she lives in. It would be a giant step toward moving away from feeling paralyzed and toward self-care.

"I'm in," she says simply.

"Excellent," says the angel. "So you accept my invitation?"

Without hesitation, Andrea accepts the invitation. She hears the song "Life Is a Highway," the version by Rascal Flatts, and suddenly she's no longer worried about where she's going.

In Andrea's bedroom, she is getting ready to wake up from this deep sleep. She will carry with her the feeling of safety, of being in the care of an angel. There is silence until the sound of the clock returns. Tick tock … tick tock … the clock strikes 7:00 a.m., and Andrea begins to awake.

Sometimes all you've got are the questions you are asking.
—SAH D'SIMONE

Reflections for This Chapter

Life is a highway, so hop on and enjoy the ride. I invite you to listen to "Life Is a Highway" by Rascal Flatts as you integrate your thoughts by going through these activities now or coming back to them later.

Andrea has allowed "the inner critic voice" to determine how she feels about herself. Often what James and her mom have to say about her holds sway over how she actually feels about herself. These beliefs keep her from doing things for herself—until the day she says, "No more."

Have you ever felt that other people's thoughts about you mattered more than your own? What things have you not done for yourself because someone told you that you can't? Journal here. (This activity comes from *52 Lists for Calm*, by Mora Seal.)

Today, you have the choice to say "no." List some of the things people in your life have told you that you can't do. You also have a choice to do something different. Compile a list of 10–15 things you have believed and carried ... things you believed you couldn't do.

Now look at your list and ask yourself who is actually stopping you from doing these things. Hint: It is not the person who told you no. You are the final decision-maker, and you are the one in control of your thoughts and actions.

Review your list and circle any of the things you've been told not to do that align with your values—and that you might want to do. Plan to do one or more things on your list that feel positive and safe to you. Remember, you get to create your life on your own terms.

CHAPTER 3

Runnin' Down a Dream

Dreaming permits each and every one of us
to be quietly and safely insane every night of our lives.
—WILLIAM CHARLES DEMENT

Tick tock ... tick tock ... the clock strikes 7:00 a.m. and Andrea wakes up from her dream. She is filled with a mixture of hunger and fervency; she can barely lie still. Her journal is open to the page where her intentions are written. *Time to fill up these pages,* she thinks as she sits up and writes down everything she can remember. It all feels so real. She remembers the angel's invitation to embark upon a journey, a journey that may be arduous but one of self-care and love. She smiles with excitement at the thought of seeking her truth.

Her smile quickly turns into a grimace as negative thoughts sneak in and begin to plant seeds of doubt. *Do you really want to go on this tiresome journey, Andrea? If you do, you might be opening Pandora's box, not some mysterious secret box. Then what? Don't rock the boat. You have a good life. Appreciate what you have. You are so unappreciative. This higher power stuff is all hogwash. You don't really believe in it. Who says you're worthy of the love and acceptance this higher power claims to offer?*

"Enough!" She yells out. Feeling a little shaken by the negative, almost hateful thoughts in her head, she finds the strength to dismiss them for now, so she can write more positive thoughts in her journal. As she writes, she remains aware of a struggle between the voice that supports her in taking care of herself and the voice that tells her she's undeserving.

It's a beautiful day, so after she's done running errands, she decides to tackle her unkempt backyard garden. But when she gets outside and takes one look, she sighs. *Too much work,* she thinks, and meanders over to the swing that hangs from a gigantic, elderly oak tree. It's one of the most majestic trees she's ever seen, and every day it brings her joy.

She swings back and forth, thinking about the dream journey that might lie ahead. She's intrigued, she thinks it's ridiculous. She's excited, and yet she's dismissive. Her old friend denial shows up, and she begins to justify why life is not so bad with James. Self-doubt joins in, and it's easier to slip back into the complacency of pretending everything is fine.

When she heads back into the house to start dinner, she finds James waiting in the kitchen, drumming his fingers on the table. She can sense his annoyance but has no idea why he's agitated. He announces that he won't be eating dinner at home tonight, that he's meeting up with some guys.

Andrea is surprised—he hasn't gone out with the guys in months—but she lets it go and nods her assent. She'd rather have the house to herself. Once he's dressed for an evening out and has left, telling her not to wait up, Andrea heats some frozen mac and cheese in the microwave. James would sneer, but this is one of her favorite solo meals. She steams some broccoli to go with it.

Andrea settles into her favorite chair, turns on Netflix, and stuffs herself with her comfort food, feeling content and somehow free. She loves watching the kinds of miniseries James hates, then takes herself off to dreamtime and whatever awaits her there.

As she slips under the covers, she reaches for her journal and writes down her intention of returning to her dream on the next empty page. The travel magazine is as she left it, turned to page 44, so she picks it up and begins to read where she left off. Her mind drifts off to one of the faraway places as she drowsily listens to the sound of the clock.

Tick tock … tick tock … the clock has just struck 10 p.m. when an enormous BANG! startles her fully awake. She can hear James downstairs. He's slamming around, opening, and closing cabinets and drawers and muttering profanity to himself. She can tell without even seeing that he's looking for his favorite rocks glass. "Are you okay?" she calls.

She can hear him mumble something, but she can't make out what it is. Sighing, she heads downstairs. As she passes the console table near the kitchen, his phone rings, vibrating against the table's polished wood.

Wow, it's late for someone to be calling, she thinks, glancing at the phone. On the screen she sees a familiar name. Her entire body tightens, her heart accelerates, and anger courses through her blood. She feels enraged, humiliated. She loses her mind.

What happens next turns into a blur. Moments after it's all over, Andrea can't say what just happened. Her mind veers away from what threatens to be pain and shame, and she makes her way in a trance-like state back to bed. *Everything is fine,* she tells herself. *Isn't it?*

Bang! The front door slams shut for the second time that night.

Andrea lies in bed and remembers her silly fantasies about angels and dreamland. How foolish it all seems. Facing her truth right now is a terrible idea, anyway, far too painful. Tears streak her face. Her eyes are already swollen from the crying she did downstairs. Her nose is red and raw from blowing, and her body feels weak from carrying the burden of her shame.

On this night, there is no escaping to a faraway place, no running down her dream. Her negative thoughts, self-doubt, and despair render the invitation to embark on that journey, at least for this night, null and void.

. . .

The next morning Andrea wakes up from a restless night's sleep only to find her journal on the floor. Its empty pages are wrinkled, and the intention she wrote down the night before has been scratched out. She doesn't remember much. She and James were screaming at each other, doing the dance they always do when they are at odds. But there's a different feeling to it, one she can't quite put her finger on. She stares into what feels like empty space. *The void*, she thinks.

A knock on the bedroom door startles her. It's James. Andrea calls out cautiously, asking what he wants. He cracks open the door and asks, surprisingly humbly, if he can come in so they can talk. *It will all be fine,* Andrea thinks to herself. And as their conversation proceeds, it is fine. Until it isn't.

. . .

It is much later, nighttime, when she opens her journal and boldly writes her intention on top of the next empty page.

With so much teetering on the brink of loss, she is more determined than ever to find what is missing and to do whatever it takes to find it. She closes her journal, lays her head down on her pillow, closes her eyes, and says to herself, "Tonight, on this night, I accept the invitation." The clock strikes 10 p.m. Tick tock … tick tock. Silence.

Andrea falls freely away from her ordinary life into her dreamscape. This time, before anything else comes to pass, she hears the angel's voice. He consoles her by acknowledging her broken heart and the devastation of recent events. His voice is strong, fatherly, and meditative.

"Breathe deeply," the angel says. "Inhale to a count of seven, hold to a count of seven, then exhale to a count of seven." As Andrea complies, he suggests she do this seven times before opening her eyes.

When the breathing counts end and her eyes open, Andrea sees him—a beautiful, almost perfect creation. The angel stands tall, aglow with light. His eyes are chocolate brown, his wavy hair is long and well-kept. He looks athletic—*can angels be athletic?* she thinks distractedly—and his skin is tan with a hint of olive.

Are all angels this easy on the eyes? Andrea is embarrassed by her thoughts, but she finds comfort in his presence. This is an actual archangel standing before her in his OluKai sandals! His impressive wings are widely spread, and he radiates warmth. His voice is hypnotic, but in a comforting way.

She gathers her composure. "Um, hello."

The angel smiles at her. "I am Metatron, Highest of Angels," he tells her matter-of-factly. "I am known to be the guardian of heavenly secrets and a mediator with humans. I watch over children in heaven and on Earth."

Andrea nods as if she is taking this in, but she is dumbstruck.

"I also help people who need help starting a new project—including a new way of living," he continues as if all this is normal. "I am here to help you discover what you've hidden deep down inside. I am here to guide you on your journey."

Andrea needs more time to absorb all this. "Why can I see you now?"

"I thought it best not to give you too much to absorb right away. Aside from that, I did not want to be a distraction."

"Oh," she says faintly because he is a bit of a distraction. "So is this journey you speak of about to start?"

Metatron's voice is gentle. "We must have a contract, you and I, before we begin our journey together. You will need accountability if you choose to embark on this journey, and I will be one of many who will help you hold yourself accountable."

"Who else will I be accountable to?" Andrea asks.

"Yourself, of course, and me. But you will also encounter many other guides as you travel this path of growth, change, and healing. I am but one of them. We are all part of a plan designed by a power greater than ourselves."

"God? The Universe? Who is this higher power?" Andrea demands. "And why should I trust you or it?"

"Excellent questions, Andrea. You will discover more as you go. You will have an opportunity to learn how to open your heart again, how to trust again. I know that trust is something with which you have struggled."

Feeling teary, Andrea pulls her hands in close to her heart.

"We will take things slowly, I promise," he says. "I am here to guide you, but the choice of whether to take this opportunity to learn and grow is ultimately yours."

Trust, Andrea thinks. That feels more dangerous after what just happened with James.

"Trust can be something we grow together," says Metatron.

She allows herself to consider this, to hold onto the thought of growing trust together. It is then that she's able to surrender some of her resistance.

A strange energy force guides them to the door from her kitchen leading to the lush grass of the backyard, where her garden lies. Andrea finds herself standing with Metatron next to the tree, the one she admires and adores, the one with the swing she sits in when she wants to lose herself. She begins to feel a sense of safety, surrounded by these things she loves. She exhales, and her body relaxes a little more.

A gentle breeze whisks through her hair. The birds sing their morning song. Andrea begins to feel some relief from the burdens she has been carrying. A new kind of energy shines through. *Being in nature helps me clear my mind,* she realizes. *Maybe it will also help me soothe my soul and heal.*

"Being one with nature is an incredible way to connect with one's soul," Metatron affirms. "To feel rejuvenated, calm, and free."

Andrea realizes that she's been so caught up in her limbic state of mind that she's forgotten the time she's spent hiking, biking, and gardening. All of it was a regular part of her everyday life—until it was not. She wonders if she'll have the opportunity to invite nature back in. Perhaps that could be a step toward a self-care plan.

"All in due time, Andrea," Metatron says. "All in due time."

What else have I stopped inviting into my life? she wonders. She begins to formulate a list: dates with James, in-depth conversations about the mysteries of life, frequent visits with her grandkids, lunch with Sophia, breakfast with Ben, Zumba, hilarious happy hours, shopping trips with friends. *I used to love to do these things,* she thinks. *What happened to me?*

She paces back and forth in the backyard and kicks a pile of weeds out of her way, thinking about all she's let fall to the wayside. Painting, growing vegetables, writing blogs. She remembers that she used to enjoy playing board games and cuddling with her cat, sitting in front of the firepit and watching the flames. The most painful memory of all is how she and James loved to dance in the moonlight under the stars by the firepit. She sits in her favorite chair on the patio and begins to drum her fingers on the table as she considers all she's let go.

Andrea thinks about how she barely sees her children or her grandchildren because she doesn't want to meddle in her kids' lives. How she waits to be invited, and then becomes upset when no invitations are forthcoming. She thinks about how she works out at home since COVID because she is scared to death to go back to the gym.

She stands up again and begins to pace, thinking that while part of her would love to break out of her routines, there's another part that thinks it sounds exhausting. She picks up a snail from the patio and softly tosses him into the overgrown weeds nearby, so she won't step on him. *That wouldn't be harmonizing with nature, would it,* she thinks wryly.

It's not like she doesn't have friends or interests! She thinks about Teresa and a few of her other close friends. She thinks about how much she cherishes her friendships. She considers that perhaps it's due to the fact that she can't slow down enough to make the time to chat with less pressure.

Her days are filled with activities and outings; it's in the evening when she feels most married and alone. Most evenings she sits at home binge watching Netflix and reading self-help books. Not a bad thing, she considers, but lately there's no end to it. It's as if she feels broken, like she needs to fix herself. "I miss the things I used to love to do," she says out loud and plops herself back into the chair.

Metatron speaks, startling her. She'd forgotten she wasn't alone. "Notice that the space between, the void, as you call it, is showing you who you are today: the *nurturing you* and the *neglecting you*. But there is a great opportunity here to change and grow. To choose differently."

Tears well up and begin to roll down Andrea's cheeks. For the first time in a while, she feels the loss of not just her relationship with others, but herself. She shakes her head and gathers her thoughts. She knows what Metatron says is true, but a huge part of her just wants to believe that she's fine and that this dream is nothing more than that, a dream.

"Of course you are fine," says the angel. "You do not need to be fixed. What you need is healing, to create anew, and I am here to help you. This dream is more than just a dream, Andrea, but deep down you already know that. So if your intent is as you have stated in your journal, then it is time to let go of your resistance, and it's time to let go of that old belief that 'everything is fine.' It is time to move forward—if that is what you choose."

Andrea knows he is right. She looks up just as a gusty breeze blows through, bringing with it the poignant fragrance of flowers. In awe, she watches as an orange and black Monarch butterfly lands on her hand. And then the most beautiful blue and purple dragonfly passes by and perches itself on one of the branches hanging from the wise oak tree. There is healing here, she can feel it.

Just then she senses movement in the handsome old oak tree at the center of the yard. The leaves flutter, and then one very large branch takes a sudden dip. Andrea stands and approaches the tree and sees that there's an oddly shaped object dangling from one its gnarled branches. The strange shape begins to unfold in front of her. "It's a scroll," she says to Metatron.

"It's an invitation," he replies. "It also contains a contract. Do not be afraid, Andrea. I have been down this road before. I know the way. Let me guide you on this part of your journey."

Is she still asleep? She pinches herself to check, then wonders if that even works. She has so many questions, almost too many to ask. Maybe it's better to just go with the flow of the dream, to allow the angel to guide her.

She reaches out and carefully plucks the scroll from amidst the leaves, half-expecting something weird to pop out. But no, it appears to be just as Metatron said: an invitation and contract, with a date and spaces for her and Metatron to sign at the bottom. Instinctively she knows that they represent a life-changing opportunity.

"You need to be sure this is what you want, Andrea," the angel says. "Read carefully, and please take your time."

Contract

I, Andrea, am committed to transforming my life. I understand that I will get out of this journey as much as I put into it. I understand that it is up to me to surrender what keeps me sleepwalking so that I can exchange neglect for nurturing. I acknowledge that a lot will be asked of me. I will enter with an open mind and heart. I will seek avenues that will help me exchange old beliefs and perspectives for new ones, and I am committed to identifying blocks, removing stressors, and creating new goals based on my new beliefs. I agree to fully participate to the best of my ability. I will be honest with myself and my guides even when the going gets rough. I will be accountable to myself and to my guides. I will recognize and celebrate successes and the gifts that present themselves during the transformation process. Above all I will breathe, relax, be present, stay curious, ask questions, learn lessons, laugh, cry, get angry, find joy, and enjoy the ride down the highway of life.

Andrea doesn't hesitate. "This is what I want," she tells Metatron.

He presents a pen, and she signs the contract, agreeing to travel the highway of life with her angel by her side. She is open to all that is available. Almost, anyway. For the first time in a long time, Andrea feels a glimpse of hope and what it is like to be awake—even though she knows she is still asleep.

"This is so weird," Andrea says. "I feel the skeptic in me wanting to judge, my ego wanting to dismiss, and a frightened little voice planting the seeds of doubt. But the real me? The real me wants the journey, and for today, I'm not attached to any outcome. I don't know how I got here, but I'm ready to get where I'm going."

Somewhere in the background, she can hear Tom Petty singing out "Runnin' Down a Dream" as she presents Metatron with the signed contract.

Today I will participate fully in my life
and be unattached to the outcomes.
—SAH D'SIMONE

There are no particular reflections for this chapter, but you can think about any dreams you are runnin' down. I invite you to listen to the song "Runnin' Down a Dream" by Tom Petty before reading Chapter 4.

The Skeptic

EGO
I can badger, I can bully
I can persuade, I can manipulate
I can deny, avoid, and comply
I am in control
I carry out my will, and everything is fine
I am still searching for peace within ... through my ego

SPIRIT
I can admit, I can accept
I can be courageous, I can be wise
I can be humble, I know my limits
I am not in control
I learn to "let go," to "surrender"
I find my inner peace within ... through the spirit

Andrea thinks: *First there was peace, and then there was a battle between my ego and the spirit.* And her negative thoughts show up like demons in the night. They bring negativity, fear, anger, resentment, and pain. They deplete Andrea of her energy and raid her joy. They steal her breath in the night, making their way deep into her mind and seeping into her heart and soul.

She shivers and shakes as she tries to dismiss the demons, but they still visit from time to time.

Andrea is ready to go on her journey, but her demons remind her of the old beliefs she used to hold and the ones she still carries. She can feel her ego wanting to get in the way, wanting to bully, manipulate, and control. She has a fleeting thought that even though Metatron and other guides will be on this ride with her, she can surely find peace within her own ego self and do this alone. See? She is fine and everything will be fine.

When she snaps out of her denial, she can admit that she's not that courageous, and that it wouldn't be wise to do this alone.

The ego pushes back. The spirit prevails. The ego pushes back again.

Seeking to distract herself from this inner battle, Andrea considers the fact that she may feel this push/pull throughout her adventure and accepts this fact. She understands one of her desires is to feel less of that push/pull cycle. Her aim as she lets go of her ego is to welcome in the concept of a power greater than herself. Deep in her thoughts she realizes that this is not going to be easy and that it will take commitment and dedication. She will need to learn to trust. *Then I will be able to conquer in the battle within*, she thinks. She shakes her head, knowing she needs to put this battle to rest for now since it's time to collect a few items to take along with her. She will need some clothes, of course, and toiletries. Her journal and a fine ballpoint pen are a must. Her phone, for sure, so she can take pictures, since no one in their right mind will believe her when she shares her experiences.

Metatron interrupts her thoughts. "You will need trusting partners with you. You can't do this alone. I see that the demons are trying to fill your ego with negative thoughts and ideas. They're trying to distract you and throw you off course."

Andrea sighs.

"Are you ready to explore the concept of a power greater than yourself, or are the demons too loud?"

Andrea lets out a nervous laugh, "About that. I'm not sure about this spirit guide stuff. I'm not religious, so this talk of a higher power makes me uncomfortable."

"Andrea," Metatron says quietly. "You are experiencing the battle within, the one between ego and spirit. It's leading you to skepticism. This has been an ongoing internal battle within you for decades, and now you have been presented with an opportunity to reevaluate your old beliefs. Perhaps to exchange them for new ones. This is part of the challenge."

Andrea has not relied on anyone but herself and her ego for a very long time, and starts to tell the angel so. But she can hear her cynical tone, the tone James hates, and cuts herself off. That's her ego speaking, she realizes.

"I'm sorry," she says. "I might need some help with all this."

"I'd like you to take a look at one of your memories," Metatron offers. "It is a rather intense conversation with James about your relationship. It will clarify things for you."

Andrea agrees with some reluctance—she knows what she is about to see will only bring the truth, or at least some of it, to light. *And am I ready for that?*

Metatron asks her to close her eyes and allow the visualization in. She can see herself in the kitchen with James, trying to explain to him that she's lonely, that it feels like something's missing.

"Everything's fine," he says.

Andrea watches herself yell, "So why do I feel like something is fucking missing?"

"You're fine, Andrea!" James snaps. "Just be grateful and content like every other woman in our circle of friends. Why can't you just be happy and appreciative like the others?"

Andrea watches herself flush. She remembers that she felt ready to explode. She was and is so tired of being told she's fucking fine. She watches herself, hears her snarkiest voice yelling: "I don't feel fine, James. Our relationship is not fine. You are not fine, James. You drink too much, you're an angry man, and you're a mess."

Antagonistic, Andrea thinks. *Truthful too.*

She watches James's rage, and then the two of them sling harsh, nasty words back and forth. The room gets small. She feels small. She is exhausted. She takes it. She always takes it.

He wins!

The visualization ends abruptly. "What are you feeling, Andrea?" Metatron asks.

"I feel like I'm losing the battle, and I'm heading straight toward the gates of hell," she says. "My ego thinks she's winning because the meek me feels guilty and crawls into a hole of shame. I get scared, Metatron, and then I give my power away. My ego tells me that everything will be fine. But it's never fine."

"It is in times like these that you need spirit to lean on," he says simply. "Your ego has been running the show for quite some time. But now you have the opportunity to do something different."

Andrea exhales sharply. "I want for things to be different," she says, "but I'm not sure I can commit to leaning on this spirit. I'm anything but religious, and it just seems foreign and out of reach for a person like me."

"The spirit, this power greater than yourself, wants you to know it is here for you," Metatron tells her. "The spirit, this entity, this power loves you just as you are."

Andrea tears up. "I have a story to share, may I?"

Metatron nods encouragement.

"I grew up in a fairly religious home," she says. "We celebrated all of the holidays and traditions. We attended temple regularly. My brother and I went to Sunday School and Hebrew School. Our family didn't talk about God or the Bible, but my brother and I were taught Bible stories from the Torah, and we knew the characters."

"Which stories do you remember?"

"Oh, we were fascinated with the story about Moses and the burning bush, and how Moses led our people to Mount Sinai, where they waited many days for his return," Andrea says. "And then there was King David, a character we learned to love and hate. We thought he was a bit scandalous and mischievous, which made him seem relatable somehow."

Metatron gives her a clear-eyed look. "But there's more," he prompts.

"We were also aware of what took place in the ten days between Rosh Hashanah and Yom Kippur," Andrea says with some discomfort. "It was the test of time."

"And what did that, the test of time, mean for you?"

"Each year, the question remained: whose name would be written in The Book of Life?" Andrea says. "I was afraid of this God and his Book of Life, but I had respect until …"

Metatron is quiet.

She looks down, gathering her words. "I believed in those stories. I loved our family get-togethers during the holidays. We honored all the traditions, rituals, and practices. And even though I was afraid of God, I respected God." She swallows. "Until the day my brother's life was taken from me."

Metatron takes her hand. She's grateful, but she can barely feel it. She sees, as clearly as if a video began playing before her in midair, a day from her childhood unfolding. It's the holidays, and her mother is cooking up a storm. Andrea breathes in the aroma that came from her mother's kitchen as if she were there. She watches her mom, full of life, teaching her and her brother how to cook and talking about passing down her recipes to them and so to her grandchildren. The vision fades.

"My mother loved the holidays then," she says wistfully. "She was a good mom in those moments. Until. Well, you know."

Metatron listens quietly, patiently.

"It was a beautiful spring day, purple blossoms everywhere," Andrea remembers. "Jacarandas are one of San Diego's most spectacular trees. The air was warm, and also crisp—just full of life, it was a glorious afternoon …"

She trails off and looks at the oak tree without really seeing it.

"Please, go on," Metatron says.

"The phone rang," Andrea says. "There was an accident, they said, a terrible, tragic accident. Greg, my brother Andrew's best friend, had a brand-new car, and they took it out for a spin. Andrew was riding shotgun."

She can hear Metatron breathing quietly beside her. Unconsciously, she syncs her breath with his.

"The scenery on that road is breathtaking," she remembers. "The Jacarandas along the streets, the poppies at their feet. But they were going too fast. Greg lost control of the car."

Andrea is plunged back into the accident she never witnessed but can't stop imagining. The car going over a steep, jagged ledge. Loud noises, pungent smells, the sound of sirens. She can see first responders scrambling their way down the bank, crushing the poppies in order to save lives. A medical helicopter overhead.

Metatron quietly reaches for her hand.

"Andrew and Greg were flown to the hospital. We didn't know any of it because Greg was unconscious, and my brother was unrecognizable." Her voice catches, but she wants to finish the story. "Greg survived, though he was paralyzed from the neck down. He was just seventeen. Andrew was DOA."

She looks up at Metatron and realizes that he knows all this. Of course he knows it. "I can see my mother's heartbroken face like it was yesterday. I can still feel her rage. I can see my Nana's sorrow and feel her misery. I can see my father's look of horror and disbelief, and I can feel him disconnecting from the world."

"What about you?" Metatron asks.

"Oh, I felt nothing," she says. "I was numb. I was never shown how to grieve the death of my brother. So I didn't, really."

"You were twelve," says Metatron. "Almost thirteen."

"The day my brother died, that was the day I stopped believing in God. My mother did too. Every day from then on, she swore at God. She hated God, and she told me that God and the Torah were full of shit."

She glances at Metatron, expecting him to look pained, but he appears to be listening without judgment.

"My mother blamed God and my father, neglected me, damned the world, and got lost in a bottle," Andrea says. "Me, I made peace with the idea that God didn't exist. And that is when the battle between my ego and the spirit began."

Andrea stands up and begins moving aimlessly about the yard. Metatron accompanies her.

"After Andrew died, my mom became an angrier person—verbally and emotionally abusive. She lost her zest for life—in

43

a way, she died too. My father took her abuse and pretended it was okay. We never talked about it. We just decided that 'everything was fine.'"

"You must have begun to doubt that everything is fine, or you would not be here," Metatron says. "This is a step toward healing this place in you. To open yourself back up to the spirit."

Andrea feels a surge of discomfort and stammers her words. "But—but I can't. That Book of Life, I still fear it. And that is where I live, with that fear."

"That is not a place where you must continue to dwell."

"I let go of the idea of a power greater than myself long ago. Why would a higher power want anything to do with me?" Andrea asks. She has a huge lump in her throat and can barely speak. *Is this the "something" that is missing?* she wonders. *Is this why I feel so alone?*

"You are far from alone," Metatron answers, though she is sure she didn't speak aloud. "This journey is about exploring and discovering what is missing, Andrea, not religion—unless you want it to be. It's about spirituality. And if and when you are ready, ready to say goodbye to the ego and hello to the spirit, I am here for you, the spirit welcomes you."

Andrea swallows hard as she imagines getting ready to say goodbye to her ego and hello to the spirit.

"When you feel ready to re-examine what you have been told, and when you are ready to let go of those old beliefs that have kept you captive, I am here for you," Metatron says. "When you are ready, I can share with you a myriad of ways you can define this power greater than yourself, designed for you and for you only."

Andrea looks up with tears in her eyes and says, "I am not sure I can fully invite a power greater than myself in quite yet, but I do feel a sense of gratitude, and I know I'm not alone. I'm interested in hearing and receiving what it is you have to share."

Metatron spreads his wings and tucks Andrea inside, cradling her. "Just breathe," he whispers. "You are not alone."

Andrea feels the lump in her throat begin to loosen, releasing some of the emotions that have been stored up and neatly packed away for decades. She takes a deep breath and sheds tears for her losses. As she cries, a bright light appears, bringing with it a source of energy that holds the secret ingredient for healing, peace, and grace. Within minutes, a cool breeze blows, and the faint sound of the clock ticking can be heard in the distance. As the clock chimes, Sheryl Crow sings "Every Day Is a Winding Road" somewhere nearby.

"Every day is a winding road," Andrea whispers to herself. "And I think I'm finally ready for the ride."

> *Re-examine all you have been told.*
> *Dismiss what insults your soul.*
> —WALT WHITMAN

Reflections for This Chapter

Integrate your thoughts by going through these activities now or coming back to them later. I invite you to listen to "Every Day Is a Winding Road" by Sheryl Crow. Take it all in as you travel down your own winding road.

Was there a time you stopped believing? Was there a time you stopped practicing your faith? Was there a time you questioned the spirit, God, or a power greater than yourself? What feelings and emotions come up?

If you stopped practicing your faith, did you ever restore it? Write about your experience. If you haven't had this experience, have you been witness to someone who has? Share your thoughts.

Can you think of the time when you first practiced your faith and/or believed in God or a power greater than yourself? What was that like for you? What memories do you have? Can you picture your place of worship? How about family gatherings during the holidays? What smells, tastes, sounds, etc. come to mind? Write about it or draw a picture.

CHAPTER 5

First You Must Learn to Breathe

*Breathing is meditation; life is a meditation.
You have to breathe in order to live, so breathing
is how you get in touch with the secret space of your heart.*
—WILLOW SMITH

The clock remains still, which makes it easier to hear Andrea's breath: soft, smooth, steady. Andrea flips back her hair, takes a deep breath, and opens her heart to new possibilities. She has a sense of peace, of feeling connected for the first time in a long time.

But then the negative voices chime in, just as Metatron warned they would. They take the form of tiny little demons of doubt, demons that take over her thoughts and zap her energy. She can feel them invading her space, and already she begins to feel depleted.

"Tell me about them," Metatron says from beside her.

They feel malevolent, evil. They have wiry white and gray hair, their large bloodshot eyes glow in the dark, and they wear black capes that twirl with each undignified step they take.

They make tasteless hissing sounds mixed with giggling as they slither, slide, and swish about, spewing negative thoughts one right after another. She can feel the heat of their breath on her face, and it smells like a combination of moth balls and Bengay.

"Gross," Andrea says out loud, but the demons laugh and swirl around her like shadows. They whisper that she is not worthy of this higher power's acceptance and love. She gasps.

"Andrea," says Metatron, "those dirty little demons are real and part of the spirit world. But you do not need to carry them with you anymore. They can be vanquished by good energy and thoughts. I will show you how. It all starts with your breath."

Andrea shivers in the sunlight, eager for the day when she can discard these demons. She makes shooing motions with her hands, trying to get them away from her.

Metatron invites her to sit in her swing under the gigantic oak tree. "Here are your journal and a pen," he says. "Take some time to write about the demons. Consider how they have served you and why they may no longer serve you now."

Andrea turns to an empty page and writes "Demon" at the top. As she writes, her pen flies across the page, almost as if it were moving on its own. She writes: *These nasty little demons of mine, oh so familiar. Oddly, they comfort me at times, like an antiquated yet recognizable blanket. But the majority of the time they suffocate me to the point where I cannot breathe. I want to rid myself of these nasty creatures, I need to find a way to make them vanish.* Andrea's demons have been with her for some time, so there is a lot to say. She's afraid that if she stops writing, they will come back and take her from her dream into a nightmare.

"As long as you are open to exploring the good, these demons will not be able to inflict their evil upon you," Metatron says.

Andrea exhales a huge breath of relief.

"That's right, that's right, breathe into the rhythm of your heart," Metatron says. "Let's start by taking in your breath to a count of seven, holding, and then exhaling to a count of seven."

Together, they repeat the process a few times. It helps Andrea relax enough that within moments she is no longer thinking about the demons—or seeing them, for that matter. For now, she is able to feel some peace. She feels pulled to write down what she can remember of the aftermath of her brother's accident.

It's hard. Her body shakes as she writes, and her handwriting is wobbly. She writes about her mother drinking herself into oblivion. She sees for a second time her dad telling her it was fine. "FINE," she writes, and then whispers, "It was not fine—it was never fine."

Andrea closes her eyes. She is overcome by the realization that there was never space for her own anger, confusion, and grief. The only way she was able to express her feelings was to leave her belief in God—in any kind of higher power—behind, and she knows now that her life has not been the same since.

Andrea opens her eyes. "Is it normal, Metatron, to feel all this anger and grief after all these years?"

"Very normal," he says.

Andrea writes in her journal in big bold letters: **I am ready to get my life back.**

"If you are ready, I am ready," Metatron says. "Let's go back to your breath. It will help you connect with that secret space in your heart." He offers her a soft, pink blanket.

Andrea takes it gratefully, noticing that it smells like vanilla and spice. A welcome change from the putrid dankness of the demons.

Metatron tells her to get into comfortable clothes and a relaxing position.

"But ..." she says.

"Look inside your bag."

And there, in a bag she hadn't noticed, was a pair of clean pajamas. And just like that, she feels cared for and refreshed. She no sooner pulls out the pajamas than she finds herself already wearing them. "That's convenient," she says. She was wondering about how to disrobe in front of the archangel.

Metatron smiles. "Before we begin, you will need to give yourself permission to seek an image of a safe and sacred place. Can you do that?"

Andrea nods and finds her place under the tree. She sinks into a comfortable position, wraps herself in the soft, fragrant blanket, and lets out a sigh of pleasure. "I'm ready," she says.

"Think of a sacred space where you can bring your deepest, darkest secrets and thoughts," Metatron says. "Fill the space with whatever comes to mind. It is yours to do with as you wish."

She thinks of a meadow, and it feels familiar. "I am in a meadow, and it's filled with lush grass, and there's a small stream whose banks hold little yellow and white flowers that look like daisies, but they're not."

"Beautiful," Metatron murmurs. "What else do you see?"

"I see ladybugs nestled in between the petals. I see dragonflies. They are known to be good omens and they symbolize transformation and change. I see butterflies in a myriad of colors flying about and—look!—the bees are busy making a hive," Andrea says. "They all have one job, and that is to protect the queen. Yes, they're working together to protect and nurture their queen."

Metatron nods.

"There are some larger animals here," she says, "but I can't quite make them out. Why can't I see them?" She pauses, then says in surprise, "There's an oak tree, just like this one, just like the one in my backyard. I like it, it feels very peaceful. Can I stay here?

"We need to leave the meadow for now but please know it is your sacred place and you can visit it at any time during your awake life too. You can visit when you feel anxious, upset, or even when you just want to be present while you meditate," Metatron says. "It is your sacred space."

Andrea opens her eyes and smiles. The meadow is safe, but she also feels the comfort and safety in her own backyard under the great oak tree.

"From this safe space, consider a power greater than yourself and take a moment to imagine what this divine energy might look like. Envision whatever form, shape, or direction this power takes on. You must create in order to relate," Metatron says.

"I feel like this is going to be awkward," Andrea says. "What if I can't think of anything?"

"It is okay for you to feel uncomfortable," he reassures her. "There is no judgment here. Simply embrace the peace of your sacred space and begin to breathe in and out."

Somewhere in the distance, Andrea hears a drum beating rhythmically, hypnotically. She soaks up the beat, breathing in time with it, and tries to see this place she is creating as a space where she'll be able to let go and surrender her ego. A sacred space in her heart where she will have an opportunity to meet a power greater than herself.

She thinks about the God of her past. The God who judged and controlled all of humanity, and who wrote the names in The Book of Life. This is not who she wishes to see.

"He took my brother and my mother from me," she cries out. "I hate this God, this almighty God. This God has been dead to me for a long time."

Metatron takes Andrea under his wings and says, "What you are feeling is real, but what you envision and what you have been holding onto needs healing. I am here to help you heal."

Andrea breathes in time with Metatron. Inhaling one, two, three, four and holding; exhaling one, two three, four. They do this six times while she relaxes into her breath.

"I will not let anything happen to you," Metatron whispers. "Trust is significant. I want to help you create an image that is relatable to who you are today, not one you resented back then. Let me help you let that old image go."

"I have carried that image for a lifetime. I'm scared to let it go," she says. "Maybe I'm scared to let go of my anger too."

"Close your eyes," Metatron says. "I can help you access your own imagination and lead you to your own wisdom."

Andrea does not feel wise, but she does as the archangel asks.

"Envision your sacred space, this place where you can rest and breathe, this place where you feel safe."

She smiles, just a little.

"You are enough," Metatron says gently. "You are worthy. You are strong and wise. You are fully alive. May the light shine within you."

Andrea begins to slowly slip into a meditative state within her dreamscape. Her breath slows, and although she doesn't know it, her heart rate calms too.

In her sacred space Andrea curls up next to the tree. Its branches are curiously smooth and refined, not rough at all. She feels like hugging the trunk, so she does so. She loves this tree. She feels connected to it, though she doesn't understand how or why. She feels very much at home in this sacred meadow under this magnificent tree.

"Now that you feel content and safe," Metatron says, "breathe deeply and envision opening your heart."

She breathes slowly, rhythmically. She pictures her heart opening like a rose, its petals unfurling delicately.

"There is a power within you," the archangel tells her. "A power both of yourself and greater than your human self. A source of energy, guidance, and positive change."

Andrea nods slowly.

"This partnership between yourself and spirit is one you create," Metatron reassures her. "What and how it looks is up to you—it is personal. There is no judgment. Open your eyes."

She does so and finds Metatron is handing her a pair of 3-D glasses.

Andrea laughs. "What's this?"

"Let us imagine that we are watching a movie." Metatron puts his own glasses on. He looks as ridiculous as it is possible for a winged angel in multicolored glasses to look, but she dutifully follows suit.

"Oh!" Andrea breathes. "Everything looks so different! Sort of magnified and magical at the same time."

Together, she and Metatron look into the sky. After a moment, an image of an old, wise wizard floats by, alongside the clouds. "He looks like Gandalf," Andrea laughs.

The wizard smiles and nods. "Good day," he says in a deep, resonant voice whose vibration she can feel coming up through the ground.

"It tickles," she laughs.

Another figure drifts by, one she thinks resembles Dumbledore from the Harry Potter books. He is wearing a cape, and its movement creates a welcome breeze.

Dumbledore is followed by several small rays of light, each of which feels slightly different to Andrea, but they are all warm and friendly.

"Guardian angels," says Metatron.

Andrea grins. She likes imagining that her higher power could come in the form of a ray of light. She continues to watch, and she sees several different animals—jungle cats, a bear, a raven, a small herd of deer.

"These are spirit animals," Metatron interjects. "Quite wise and powerful."

They prance and gambol before Andrea, then disappear.

"One's higher power may take the form of a teacher like Jesus, Buddha, Muhammad, Mother Nature, or Father Sky," Metatron tells her. "Or it can appear in the form of a goddess like Volva of Seidr or Aurora of Gamma," he says, adding, "also known as Viola and Aurora."

Andrea watches as each of these beings appears, in awe of their beauty and healing power. She is able to sense their positivity and fluidness. One by one, each teacher and goddess acknowledges her with a smile and then walks over a small bridge that crosses the stream. She can feel a rush of energy in her heart.

"A higher power may reveal itself as a symbol," Metatron says, and they watch as the Star of David, a Latin cross, a mandala, and the Tree of Life appear in and then fade from the great blue sky.

So many choices, Andrea thinks.

"I have known individuals to choose a word, or phrase, or lyrics from a catchy song that represent a sign that their higher power is amongst them," Metatron tells her. "The point is it's your higher power, so accept whatever form presents itself to you. If it feels uncomfortable that's okay too. Perhaps you will simply start and end with the breath."

Metatron takes off his 3-D glasses and holds out his hand for hers.

She places her glasses in his palm and whispers, "Thank you for being patient. Thank you for being here with me and for not allowing me to do this alone."

Metatron smiles and says, "From this day forward, you will never be or feel alone again. This is a spiritual experience, not a religious one—unless you want it to be."

"I understand," Andrea says. And suddenly, she does.

"I want to take you through a body scan. This is a great time, as you close your eyes, to visualize the meadow, your sacred space," Metatron says.

"A what?" she asks.

"It is simple," he tells her. Lie down and relax."

She does so.

"I want you to start at the bottom of your body, at your toes, and work your way up," he says. "Take a deep breath and wiggle your toes."

Andrea laughs as the grass gently tickles her feet.

Metatron asks her to allow the sensation to rise up her calves. "Breathe," he says. "Feel into your feet, your legs, your pelvis. What do you find there?"

She squirms a bit. "My hips, my pelvis, there's a tight feeling there, almost like a cramp," she says.

Metatron asks her to be with this and breathe until the discomfort softens. They breathe in and out together, and she notices once again the sound of a distant drum.

"And now your heart," he prompts.

Andrea winces. "It aches so," she cries out. "It feels like my heart is breaking."

"The first step of healing is awareness," Metatron says.

Together, they breathe once again and finally, the ache lessens. The angel asks Andrea to move her awareness to her neck and shoulders.

She feels a pull, and lots of tension. "Really tight," she says. "And sore to the touch!"

Metatron once again encourages her to breathe with him. In time she feels some relief—the pain has miraculously been released. He asks her to move from her shoulder and neck areas to her face, which actually feels relaxed and tension-free. And then to the top of her head, where she feels tingly and oddly comforted.

"Before we close this practice, I would like for you to sit for a moment before opening your eyes and acknowledge where you feel pain free and where you feel tension," the archangel says.

Andrea says, "Okay."

"Place your hands on your heart, and as you breathe, imagine taking it in so it lands in your heart center," he says.

Andrea can feel her heart center as she breathes in and out to the sound of the drum. The sound of the drum is slowing down, and so is her breath. She finds comfort in this. As her breath slows and she exhales, she sees black smoke moving out of her body. Perhaps the black smoke is a representation of her negative thoughts, old beliefs, and those dirty little demons? Whatever it represents, it has been released. She realizes she's releasing some of the things that no longer serve her.

Inhaling, she imagines a ray of light. And from that ray of light, she receives the power of strength, compassion, love, and wisdom, all things that serve her well. As she opens her eyes, a rush of safety and relief moves through her body. She's able to make the connection between the importance of the breathing exercises and helping her find this sacred place in her heart. She has the means to participate in this creative exchange between good and evil, between her ego and the spirit at any time. She is no longer powerless.

Andrea breathes in deeply, arms open wide, and lets out a big breath, a lion's breath. As she absorbs the beauty of her sacred place, she thanks the heavens above.

Metatron raises his eyebrows as he watches Andrea experience this part of her journey. "This is your journey Andrea, but I need to remind you that you are not in charge. You will be guided, and each guide serves a purpose. That means that on this journey, you will be riding shotgun. You are the passenger. Do you understand what this means?"

"I think this means it's time for me to let go of my ego," Andrea says slowly, "and that it's time to stop allowing my emotions to run the show. I think it means that it's time to allow my guides and my helpers to take the reins, that it's time to let go of control. Am I correct?"

"Excellent," Metatron says. "You are about to embark upon the adventure of a lifetime, Andrea, so sit back and enjoy the ride."

The song "Hymn for the Weekend" by Coldplay plays softly in the background as they get ready for the unknown.

Today, I will look to my Higher Power as the source
for all my needs, including the changes I want
to make in my recovery and life.
—MELODY BEATTIE

Reflections for This Chapter

Integrate your thoughts by going through these activities now or coming back to them later. I invite you to listen to "Hymn for the Weekend" by Coldplay. This is a beautiful melody to listen to as you engage in the following meditation practice that includes guided imagery.

Andrea needs guidance to help her relax in order to create that sacred space within her heart. Metatron uses specific tools such as breathwork, meditation, and guided imagery—also known as visualization—to assist her.

The use of breath work, guided imagery, body scans, and meditation can help each of us relax into our heart space. These are great tools to put into practice within your own life. Let's play and practice.

Have you ever had to face something so challenging that your body became tense or it shook uncontrollably? Here's a practice you might use to help you regulate your emotions and stay present in the moment.

1. Lie down somewhere comfortable and close your eyes. You can find a drumbeat used by Native American cultures or any other music you find soothing and/or relaxing.

2. Begin by breathing slowly and naturally. Begin to scan your body. You can use the example outlined in Chapter 5 starting from your toes and working your way up to the top of your head.

3. Start by envisioning someone or something that embodies compassion, wisdom, and power. Then breathe in and visualize a ray of light.

4. As you inhale, count to seven and hold ... tense your muscles and take in the things that serve you.

5. As you exhale, count to seven and hold ... and gently release any tension. As you release, envision your exhale as dark smoke, the things that no longer serve you.. Notice how your body reacts and responds.

6. Breathe mindfully for several moments, then repeat this process. Observe the parts of your body that begin to relax. You can also include affirmations like "I am strong," "I am willing," and "I am deserving."

7. Continue to breathe mindfully for several moments and relax.

Once you have completed the meditation, take some time to reflect, then think about the questions below. I invite you to use your journal to respond to them. Feel free to write about anything else that comes up for you.

Where does your body often hold tension? How can mindful thinking help release tension?

As you scan your internal environment, what are you noticing most about yourself?

Do you feel more attuned with yourself, with your heart space? Why or why not?

CHAPTER 6

A Quick Reality Check

Our truest life is
when we are in dreams awake.
—HENRY DAVID THOREAU

Dusk offers a time to reflect upon the day that has passed and the day to come. An in-between state not unlike the one experienced by Andrea, who is still traversing that place between waking and sleeping. She sits in her backyard—at least, as it appears in her dream—beneath the beautiful, old oak and writes in her journal about all that has happened so far. *What a gift it has been, what an experience. But is any of this even real, or is it all a bunch of bunk?*

Metatron reaches over and touches her shoulder. She notices that he's been tidying up. "Just a few loose ends that need to be cleared up before introductions are made," he says.

"Is it almost time for me to meet some of the others?" Andrea is both cautious and curious.

"Yes," says Metatron. "Each guide who travels with you will be representative of a life experience that you will revisit. No need to feel confused, worried, or scared. Each guide will introduce themselves and explain their purpose. You will see."

Breathe, breathe, breathe, Andrea thinks to herself. Then she chants aloud: "Inhale one, two, three, four, five, six, seven, and hold ... and now exhale one, two, three, four, five, six, seven." She repeats this several times. She takes in the largest breath of all and exhales with a hum that helps relieve her anxiety.

"Excellent breath work," the archangel says. "Keep practicing. You are going to come to appreciate it as we travel. Come now, I want to show you something."

Andrea walks across the lawn behind Metatron, feeling the grass beneath her feet. *Am I still asleep?* she wonders. Near the firepit, she notices several shiny ceramic bowls with little pouches of herbs. Next to that is a pile of sticks and a second pile of colorful yarn in every shade imaginable. *These weren't here earlier*, she thinks.

Metatron responds to her thoughts in that disconcerting way. "No, they were not. And yes, you are still asleep."

Andrea ruffles her hair, giving her scalp a scratch. "What is all this for?"

"All of this is designed to help you heal so that eventually you can wake up and live the life you want," the archangel says.

She hears a melodic sound coming from behind her, almost like wind chimes but more delicate. Turning around and looking back at the old oak, she sees that there are small, black hearts hanging from the branches. They are steady and calm even in the breeze.

She opens her mouth to ask what on earth this means when she's startled by another sound, a soft *thwump*. And just like that, a scroll drops from a particularly twisted branch.

The scroll has some writing on it. Andrea crosses over to it and reads aloud, "Why do you feel something is missing? Answer: because something is missing."

She remembers the travel magazine. *Duh,* she thinks, and then sighs.

Then she notices a second question on the scroll. "When did you first feel this way?" she reads. She turns to Metatron. "Well, I guess we're going to find out."

"You are correct, we are going to find out," he says, guiding her back to the blanket under the tree. "I want you to return to your sacred place, to your place in the meadow. Can you do that?"

Andrea hesitates. "I don't know if I'm ready to deal with all those feelings," she confesses. "I'm not comfortable with them." She can hear herself falling into her old familiar patterns of denial and avoidance. She remembers to breathe.

Together, she and Metatron get comfortable under the tree and begin to practice the breathing and visualization techniques from the day before. And just like that, two deer also appear, pleased and proud. It's a black-tailed doe and her fawn.

"These are your guides for this next part of your journey," Metatron says. "The doe is here not only to guide you but also to teach you a valuable lesson, one you missed as a child," the archangel tells her.

The doe walks up to Andrea and rubs her nose against Andrea's hand. The deer's nose is wet and it tickles. Andrea laughs happily with childish delight. The fawn then places one of the black hearts from the tree at Andrea's feet. On the front of the heart is the question: "When did you first feel like something was missing?"

Before Andrea can ask if she's supposed to answer the question, the heart flips over so the back side is showing. There it is written: "You began to feel this way at birth."

Andrea gasps and puts her hands to her face. *How did they know?* she thinks. This is something she's known all along but been too afraid to admit. She has felt unlovable since birth, and this is one of many reasons why she feels something is missing.

The doe speaks, surprising Andrea. "It's time to heal this place in you. Let me show you the way."

Andrea trails after the deer with Metatron following behind as the song "Sweet Child O' Mine" by Guns N' Roses begins to play. It is the beginning of their journey together.

Today, I will tell myself I'm loveable,
I will do this until I believe it.
—MELODY BEATTIE

There are no particular reflections for this chapter. However, I'd love for you to listen to "Sweet Child O' Mine" by Guns N' Roses before reading Chapter 7.

CHAPTER 7

First Stop, 456 Reality Road

There is no such thing as a perfect family.
Every family is unique with its own combination
of strengths and weaknesses.
—AUTHOR UNKNOWN

"Just follow the light." It has grown dark, and now Andrea can see that there are little black hearts paving the way on the brightly lit path.

"So many black hearts," Andrea says softly. "Why?"

Before the doe can answer, Metatron speaks up. "All in due time," he says.

Andrea notices she's carrying something that resembles a travel bag. Rifling through it, she discovers that it holds all the items she set aside for a journey when this whole thing started—and a few new things. One of the additions is a picture of her and Nana baking cookies. She remembers finding it in a drawer a few days ago. *How did that picture get into this bag?* she wonders. *How did any of it?*

"The picture is a symbol of what is to come," Metatron says.

"Where are we going?" she asks.

"We are taking you to 456 Reality Road, the home you were brought to after your birth," he says.

Andrea feels a wave of anxiety. She has mixed feelings about returning to 456 Reality Road. She starts to practice her breathing routine, repeating the exercise several times as she finally settles into her breath.

"Good job!" Metatron says. "It is here that I leave you in the hands of the black-tail doe and her fawn. They will guide you on this part of your journey. Remember, you are not alone; you are never alone. You are safe. I will be back soon enough." He places his hand on her face, smiles gently, and then vanishes into the light.

"I am not alone. I am safe," she says aloud.

The path comes to an end, and she looks up to find they are standing before the house on Reality Road. Andrea lived here from the day she was first brought here to the day she left for college. She looks at both deer, hesitating.

The fawn touches her nose to Andrea's hand and the doe says, "Today, you will receive some very special messages from your nana."

She and her fawn lead Andrea to the sliding glass door at the back of the house, through which they can see the kitchen. It looks just like Andrea remembers it.

"Close your eyes and breathe," the doe says.

Andrea and the deer breathe deeply and in sync, matching the beat of a drum that has started playing softly in the background.

Before long, Andrea senses an energetic shift and opens her eyes. The doe and her fawn join her. Right there in the kitchen, they can see five-year-old Andrea with her nana. Nana is bouncing around the kitchen with her rolling pin in one hand and a recipe card in the other. Andrea is laughing and getting ready to mix the batter. Together they roll out the dough and begin to use several cookie cutters. Laughter fills the room.

"Nana," Present-day Andrea whispers. "She made me feel human and loved."

They watch for a while. Five-year-old Andrea's happiness spills over to the grown version of Andrea now watching. She can even smell the sugar, the flour, the dough. "I used to love to bake," she says. "Why don't I bake anymore?"

"Perhaps you will again," says the doe.

In the kitchen, young Andrea is gazing wistfully at her reflection in the metal mixing bowl. Suddenly she blurts out, "Nana, why don't I look like Mommy, Daddy, or Andrew?"

Nana sits down in what present-day Andrea knows is her favorite chair in the kitchen and invites little Andrea to sit on her lap. Nana loves her up, cuddles her, and smothers her with lots of kisses.

Five-year-old Andrea giggles, and then there's a "ding" signaling the oven is up to temperature. The kindergartener pops up. "Can I?"

Nana shows Andrea how to put on the oven mitts and together they cautiously open the oven door. Together, they carefully place the cookie sheet in the oven. Nana sets the timer.

"Good job," Nana says.

As the cookies bake and their sweet aroma begins to fill the air, Nana and Andrea cuddle together in Nana's chair. Nana's hazel eyes are clear, her voice tender and sweet. "The story goes like this," she tells Andrea. "One bright sunny day, a beautiful baby girl fell from the sky like an angel. That little girl was you, Andrea, you are shiny and bright. You were brought here by the angels, and your job is to shine on those who might have lost their light."

Little Andrea's green eyes grow huge, and she begs her nana to go on.

"Your mommy and daddy were very happy with your brother, but they wanted a second child so much they could hardly stand it." Nana puts a hand to her heart. "They prayed for a baby to come. But it didn't happen. Your mommy and daddy became very sad, and they would look at each other with empty eyes and broken hearts."

Present-day Andrea looks at the doe and her fawn and says, "I felt their sadness, even years later. They had so much sadness over their infertility problems, and then later Andrew's death, and of course their own personal demons. Sadness was an emotion I was familiar with, and so it's the emotion my five-year-old self-identified with most."

"I know," says the doe.

"Your mommy spent a lot of time in her room alone, and your daddy took care of Andrew," Nana tells young Andrea. "Your daddy would tell himself that everything was fine, but deep down he knew it was not."

The little girl nods. *Already, she knows what it's like to live like that*, present-day Andrea thinks.

"Your mommy lost her light, Andrea," Nana says. "Your daddy was losing his too. And that's when you came into their life and shone the light that was missing."

"How, Nana, how?"

"One beautiful autumn day," Nana remembers, "a neighbor was visited by angels who brought her a beautiful baby girl, a baby girl who came from a soul family of light bearers."

"Then what happened?" young Andrea asks with excitement.

"She realized she wasn't going to be able to take care of this beautiful baby, so she arranged for another angel to bring the baby girl to your mommy and daddy. And that baby girl was you," says Nana, giving her a squeeze.

This feels so surreal, present-day Andrea thinks. *It's like I'm back there.*

"The day you were handed to your parents was a day the angels sang," Nana tells young Andrea. "A day there was light again. It was the light that everyone remembers, Andrea. You are the light."

Five-year-old Andrea bounces on Nana's knee in delight. "What about Andrew?"

"Well, your brother was a little confused at first," Nana laughs. "He didn't know what to make of you. He made these silly faces at you, but he also made kissing noises while standing on his tippy toes and peeking inside your bassinet. You cooed and smiled, and you warmed everybody's hearts with your light."

Young Andrea smiles with satisfaction and pride.

Nana pulls little Andrea closer to her heart. "Andrea, this is the reason you don't look like Mommy and Daddy. It is because you came by way of the angels, and angels always look different than the mommies and daddies."

Five-year-old Andrea pauses, a little confused, then giggles and says, "Okay." She prances around the kitchen holding a flashlight like a microphone and bursts into song. She sings and dances herself into exhaustion. Collapsing into a chair, she looks up at nana and says, "I have another question, Nana."

The timer goes off. The cookies are done.

Present-day Andrea squirms as she watches. She knows what's coming. She does a quick body scan and notices that the area around her heart hurts. She picks up the picture of she and Nana baking together, holds it close to her heart, and breathes.

"Nana," says five-year-old Andrea in her piercing little voice, "Nana, Mommy doesn't love me the way she loves Andrew. Sometimes it feels like she's mad at me, but I don't know why. Is she mad at me? Does she hate me?"

Present-day Andrea's eyes fill with tears as she watches Nana pause, struggling to get the words out. *I know what that feels like*, she realizes. *That lump in the throat.* It keeps her from speaking when she's caught off guard or when there's a difficult conversation to be had. Maybe that's how it felt to Nana too.

Nana places a plate of cookies on the table with a tall glass of milk. "Come now, let's sit at the table. I want you to listen carefully, can you do that?"

Five-year-old Andrea nods.

"Your mommy and daddy loved you and Andrew so much, they wanted to have another brother or sister. So they asked the angels for a third baby. But the third baby never came. They were so sad and disappointed. It isn't your fault, Andrea, that their sadness grew. It was never your fault."

Five-year-old Andrea doesn't understand. But she nods wisely.

Present-day Andrea looks over at the doe. "I always thought I was the reason for their sadness," she says. "I thought I disappointed them somehow."

The mother deer's brown eyes are full of tenderness and compassion. "Your five-year-old self couldn't understand. But now you have a second chance. It's time to let go of the self-punishing thoughts and embrace the truth."

"I would really like to let this go," Andrea agrees. "How?"

"Do you remember playing with your dolls?" the doe asks.

"I remember—oh!" Something flashes by. "I remember telling my dolls that no one loved them. Did I really?"

"Yes, you told them that," the doe responds. "Nana would intervene and tell you that you loved your dolls and your dolls loved you."

Andrea smiles. "I remember now."

"You were working through why it felt like your parents didn't love you as much as Andrew," the doe says.

"I just wanted to feel loved!" Andrea cries out past the lump in her throat.

"It felt to you like nothing you tried worked," the doe says, "and so you gave up and turned inward."

"I really thought something was wrong with me, that I must have been born wrong," Andrea says slowly. "I thought I was unlovable and unworthy. And I've been carrying those old beliefs ever since."

The doe and her fawn nuzzle her shoulder gently by way of comfort as Andrea tries to untangle the past. She peeks back into the kitchen, where she can see how much her five-year-old self adores Nana and hangs on to her every word.

"I love you so much," Nana says.

Five-year-old Andrea smiles, touches Nana's face, and tells her, "I love you too, Nana."

The vision of Nana and five-year-old Andrea quietly fades.

Andrea is quiet for a moment, realizing that she lost a piece of her heart and soul at five years old. "I want it back," she says.

"That is why we came here," the doe says. "It's time to let this go. Surrender the false beliefs that no longer serve you. You deserve love and being loved."

Andrea takes a sharp breath in.

"Your parents loved you the best way they knew how," the doe continues. "It wasn't perfect, but they did love you. And now it's time for you to love yourself.

"I don't know if I know how."

The doe asks, "If you could speak to your five-year-old self what would you tell her?"

Andrea pauses and says, "You are the light, and no one can take that away. I am so sorry for the pain and for the burdens you carried. I see how hard you tried to be perfect, thinking that would win their love. You need to know that you do not have to seek perfection in order to receive love."

The doe and her fawn's ears twitch.

Andrea continued, "You are a beautiful child of God, who loves you just as you are. I want you to let go of what I passed on to you, what you learned early in life. You never, ever have to give your heart and soul away again in order to feel loved. You are enough and you deserve to exist."

"That's beautiful, Andrea," the mother deer says.

"I would ask her to forgive me for placing all of those burdens on her. I would tell her I am so sorry, sweet child o' mine, please forgive me."

Present-day Andrea looks over at the mother deer and her fawn and says, "Then I would give her the biggest hug and kiss ever."

The mother deer and her fawn look at Andrea with admiration. "One of the biggest lessons on this road trip is for you learn is how to forgive so that you can learn how to re-parent that little girl inside so that you can learn to love and accept yourself just as you are today," the mother deer says. "You too are enough, Andrea."

Andrea whispers to the mother deer and her fawn, "Thank you."

They leave the back porch on Reality Road and return to Andrea's backyard, where Metatron awaits them. Andrea sees him out of the corner of her eye and smiles. She now understands why the black-tail deer and her fawn were her guides for this part of the journey. Their mission was to provide the comfort and nurturing her parents could not give her. They were also used as a vessel to provide visualizations of her time with Nana, who was able to help her five-year-old self understand the means to love and be loved. And just as important as what they guided Andrea to, the doe and fawn were themselves models of what the love and trust between a mother and child is supposed to be like: nature and life itself acting on instinct and knowing to create loving care.

Andrea thanks them both again.

"Now wrap your arms around yourself and tell yourself that what was once a part of you can now be released. It is time to let go of these old beliefs and fallacies even the ones that tell you that you are not worthy and that you should not exist," the doe says.

Andrea does as the mother doe suggests.

"It's time to live the life you deserve," the doe continues. "You are in charge. You can now parent yourself."

Andrea holds herself tighter and gives herself a gigantic hug, allowing her body to feel the serenity and peace she yearns for. The loss was real, and the grief is present. She knows she's carried these false beliefs for far too long, and she feels ready to say goodbye to them.

Andrea turns to both deer and to Metatron. "Thank you for teaching me how to talk to my inner child, how to re-parent her, how to love her," Andrea says, "I am so grateful—and absolutely exhausted."

Metatron thanks the deer for their work. He encourages Andrea to breathe and rest. The song "Here," by Kari Jobe, quietly plays. Andrea's false beliefs, her burdens can be seen leaving her body as black smoke she exhales. A gust of wind carries them away, back to her backyard where she will rest under the great oak tree. This wind provides a sense of peace, serenity, and light. Andrea rests peacefully under the tree in her backyard, where she feels safe and protected, as her dream continues. In dreams, as in love, all is possible.

Today, God, help me open myself to the process of grieving my losses. Help me allow myself to flow through the grief process, accepting all the stages so I might achieve peace and acceptance in my life. Help me learn to be gentle with myself and others while we go through this very human process of healing.
—MELODY BEATTIE, *Language of Letting Go*

Reflections for This Chapter

Integrate your thoughts by going through these activities now or coming back to them later. I'd like to invite you to listen to "Here" by Kari Jobe as you do so. The melody is soft and beautiful.

Andrea has carried around the belief that she's unlovable for decades. After experiencing many painful events in her life, she's finally willing to let go of some of her old beliefs.

Can you think of a belief you've been carrying around, one that has led to painful life experiences? Are you willing to grieve whatever it is you carry and then let it go? One way to start the process is by writing thank-you and good-bye letters. You can also do this exercise after reading Chapter 8.

Thank-you Letter

Identify the belief you've been carrying and name it. Tell the belief you remember the first time you felt that way and briefly write about that time. Then write about how that belief served you and how it may still be serving you today. Thank that belief for serving you for so many years, for acting as a coping mechanism, as a protector. Let it know that somewhere in your life, knowingly or unknowingly, you learned to trust it as an emotional and spiritual guide. Thank it for all it has done for you over the years, as this old belief did, after all, help you survive.

Good-bye Letter

This letter is you getting ready to dismiss any old beliefs you might still be carrying. These beliefs have been longtime friends that kept you safe and protected, but in a false way. Andrea believes she has to be perfect in order to be loved. Her people-pleasing has been a way to earn the love of others.

Write about what you experience when you buy into old beliefs. What does it feel like to carry these thoughts around? When you're ready, tell these beliefs they no longer serve you and that you no longer need them to feel protected and safe.

Let them know you're ready to walk away, to take the risk to enter a brave new world filled with joy, fulfillment, and truth. Be sure to tell those old beliefs that you are choosing to leave them behind so that you can live the life you envision and desire. You are worth it.

CHAPTER 8

Back to 456 Reality Road

*Better to get hurt by the painful truth
than comforted with a lie.*
—KHALED HOSSEINI

Time has its own flow, its own beauty and grace, especially in a dream. Andrea is back home under the tree in her backyard and is feeling some urgency to write down all of the details of her visit to 456 Reality Road. She combs through her bag, hunting feverishly for her travel journal.

"Found it!" she yells, realizing no one is there. *I'm alone, but I know I'm alone,* she realizes, *and it feels okay.* She finds her pen and makes a few quick notes about her most recent visit. There's a lot to unpack.

She writes, feeling grateful, safe, and comforted by the beauty and stillness. The rolling hills that surround her are covered with brightly colored perennials as far as she can see—butterfly weed, gaillardias, geraniums. She reminds herself that she wants to get back to gardening.

As she writes, she pictures many acts of abandonment. Her mother slithering away into her bedroom to find comfort in the bottle. Her father becoming smaller and smaller as he endured her mother's rages, then telling Andrea that "everything is going to be fine" as he quietly snuck off to his big leather chair and his face behind the newspaper.

Metatron comes and stands beside her.

I remember feeling sad and alone even then, watching my parents slip away as they disconnected from themselves and me, Andrea thinks to herself.

"The day after Nana heard you tell your dolls no one loved them, she had a very serious talk with your parents," Metatron says.

His voice is so gentle that Andrea doesn't startle. But she's surprised Nana intervened. "She did?" she asks.

"Your parents sought out professional help, and some healing began," he tells her. "There was a time you all became a family again. The years between the time you were five up until the time you were twelve were mostly good ones. Your mother was happy, present, and attentive. She did not drink heavily, only on occasion. She taught you so many things. She taught you to bake, to garden, to paint, and she taught you to love life. She took you and Andrew to museums, art shows, and to concerts."

"I remember," Andrea says quietly.

"You saw your first concert with her," Metatron says. "You were twelve. You thought going to see Kiss with your mom and brother was beyond cool. You idolized Gene Simmons and his tongue tricks, ones you tried to practice at home."

Andrea snickers as she remembers practicing in front of the mirror.

"Your father could finally exhale, relieved that he was no longer the enemy," Metatron continues. "He and your mother actually took steps to heal their relationship."

"I remember that after they came home from a night out alone, they would look relaxed with one another," Andrea says. "My dad looked at my mom with adoring eyes, and she'd touch his face with affection. Those are good memories."

"Your dad loved your mom even when she was struggling," Metatron says.

"He taught me to play softball and Andrew baseball," Andrea remembers. "We'd take long hikes on the beach or in the mountains. I adored the times we went fishing and grunion hunting."

"Ah, grunion hunting," Metatron says.

Andrea laughs. "Chasing those little creatures up and down the beach was wild. We weren't allowed to dig holes on the beach to trap them. We had to take them by hand. Tricky, because they were really slimy and slippery." She grimaces. "Yuck!"

She thinks about the full or new moon, and how the sky was so enchanting each time the grunions ran. She feels a surge of joy, but then the last grunion run where they were all four together stops her short. It was the night before the accident, the one that took her brother's life. The one that broke her mother's spirit. The one that changed her life forever.

"That was a terrible day. I am so sorry," Metatron says. "But know also that the four of you were a family and enjoyed life together as a family. It was not perfect, but it was better than it ever was. You were happy in those years until that horrible day."

Andrea smiles. It feels good to remember some of the good things.

Metatron takes her under his wings in comfort as the black-tailed doe and her fawn approach. The doe carries another black heart, which she carefully offers to Andrea.

It reads, "When your brother died, those hurtful messages got stirred up again, the ones that told you that you were unlovable, unworthy, and undeserving. It was then you began once again to feel alone, and your loneliness turned to anger."

"I remember feeling so angry, scared, and disoriented," Andrea says, her eyes filling with tears. "It felt like I was filling with darkness." *So much anger, so many outbursts, too many to count,* she thinks to herself. She hangs her head, heavy with shame.

The doe nudges Andrea's hand with her wet nose for a moment with compassion and then whispers, "Andrea, it's time to return to 456 Reality Road. It's time to heal this place in you."

Metatron steps forward. "You were just a little girl, so when you did not know what to do with your anger, it became a part of you. Are you ready to visit this part of you? It could be painful."

Andrea tries to swallow past the familiar lump in her throat. She can't tell if it's harder or easier now that she knows something of what's coming. She tells herself to breathe, relax, inhale, count ... hold ... exhale. She repeats this seven times.

"It is time," Metatron says.

The hands on the clock continue to stand still, as time is not measured in this place. Time is space, a void. Indefinite and infinite.

Metatron and the two deer count with Andrea. Their voices are strong and soothing.

"You are worthy," Metatron says.

"You are loved," the doe says.

"You are safe," says the fawn.

As the dream continues the doe and the fawn guide her back to the path that leads them to 456 Reality Road. Andrea's nerves are jangling as she gets ready to enter her childhood home for the second time.

This time, Metatron and the two deer guide her to the front porch, where they can see inside the living room's picture window. As they watch, they see a younger version of Andrea in the room. She appears alone, but then a shrill scream breaks the silence. "NOOOOO! Not my baby boy!"

Andrea's father is trying to console her mother, who pulls away abruptly. "This is all your fault!" she shrieks.

Standing on the front porch, Andrea shudders as she and her teenage self watch her mother self-destruct before their very eyes.

"You gave him permission to go and now, now he's dead!" her mother cries out. "This is all your fault, and I will never forgive you, you bastard. I hate the sight of you!"

Andrea's mother throws a glass vase at her father. It falls short, shattering into tiny pieces at his feet.

"That's what my life feels like now, shattered," she sobs. "I will never be the same."

"And she wasn't," Present-day Andrea whispers.

Inside the house, they see Nana grab teenage Andrea by the hand and pull her away, whispering loving words even as Andrea tries to cover her ears. Present-day Andrea remembers that even though Nana was trying to shield her, she could still hear her parents raging. She can hear it now, and she watches helplessly as her mother wails, rages, and curses her father, using her most cutting go-to criticisms to wound him. *That's where I get it from,* she thinks. She feels some compassion for James. He is often a recipient of her rage.

"I blame you and God for taking my son!" Mom yells. She slams the bedroom door shut.

"It was like she died too," Andrea tells Metatron and the deer. "I lost both my brother and mother on that beautiful spring day."

"Because you did," Metatron answers. "You have carried that pain for a very long time."

The four witnesses on the porch take in a breath together and then place their focus back on the visualization. Andrea sees herself walking—no, tip-toeing—toward her parents' bedroom a few days after her brother's death. As teenage Andrea cracks the door open, she and present-day Andrea can hear muffled whimpers, almost inaudible. The room is dark and dirty, and it reeks of alcohol, body spray, and sweat. Teenage Andrea draws back, her nose wrinkling.

"I can smell that room even now," adult Andrea says. "That poor child."

The doe says, "No child should have to go through what you did. But you are stronger than you think, and you will heal."

They watch Andrea's mother jolt up like a lightning bolt, yelling and cursing at God. She looks at thirteen-year-old Andrea and shouts at her to get out. Words of hatred spew forth, leaving teenage Andrea shocked into speechlessness. She appears frozen in place, staring as her mother comes undone, until Nana grabs her one more time and leads her to safety.

"No wonder I feel so scared and uncomfortable when someone yells at me," Present-day Andrea says. "No wonder I want to crawl into a hole. No wonder James has the effect on me that he does, and I on him."

Metatron and the deer nod in affirmation.

"Your mother was bitter, resentful, and overpowered by grief," Metatron says. "She did not have the tools she needed to deal with her grief, and so she took the only path she knew to numb her pain: drinking. She was unable to cope with your brother's death and the guilt she carried."

"It's so easy for me to fall into a place of anger and bitterness and resentment," Andrea says. "Is this why that feels so normal and familiar?"

"You shut down your most vulnerable emotions to protect yourself, Andrea," the doe responds. "Anger, bitterness, and resentment became the only feelings you knew. They helped you cope; they helped you protect your heart. You were thirteen, and you did the best you could."

Metatron speaks up. "You never stopped wanting to share and shine your light. But it took the form of feeling responsible for fixing your mother's loneliness and your father's helplessness."

Andrea nods. "After that day, my mother rarely came out of her room. I missed her so. I was desperate to find ways to connect to her in any way I could."

The fawn nuzzles her hand, and she runs her fingers over its sweet, fuzzy head. "There were times my mom would actually say hello and call me "dear." Very rarely, she'd blow me a kiss. But most of the time, my mom would turn away as if I didn't even exist."

"This taught you that you couldn't trust anyone, and that you were undeserving of both love and even your place here on Earth," Metatron tells her. "We need to heal this place in you."

Andrea is beginning to see that her mother's hatred of God and everyone around her had spilled over into Andrea's own spirit. She began to see the world as an unsafe place. She remembers that as the days, weeks, and months went by, it became harder and harder to make the effort to even be around her mother.

"It got to the point where I couldn't stand looking at her," Andrea says.

"You internalized those feelings, Andrea," Metatron points out. "You began to feel shame, and to blame yourself."

Andrea's eyes fill with tears as she watches her thirteen-year-old self go from confident and happy to depressed and withdrawn. She sees for the first time the damage her mother's choices and actions did. She sees that her mother's abandonment, neglect, and overall treatment toward her sent the message that she was worthless, undeserving of love. She sees the impact of this on her adult life.

"I carry my mother's shortcomings inside me," she says. "I've been treating myself the same way my mother treated me."

This turns out to be the one of most difficult parts of spiritual awakening thus far. She feels a wave of anger. "I don't like these realizations," she snaps. "I'm not comfortable accepting my mother's shortcomings as my own. I didn't ask for this, I was a child."

Metatron and both deer sit with her pain and discomfort until Andrea can start to come to terms with a portion of her truth. As Andrea begins to decompress, she says, "I think I've been living in denial because the pain has been too deep. I've buried these memories for so long that I'm overwhelmed by the feelings that are emerging."

"Yes," the doe says.

"I've been sleepwalking most of my life because it's given me a false sense of comfort. It's been okay with me to live in denial, but I'm beginning to see that may no longer be an option," Andrea says.

"It's not," the fawn says.

"I'm not quite ready to give up all my denial," Andrea admits wryly, "but what I can take away with me from today is that I need to start taking care of myself so I can heal these places. This sleepwalking, this denial, have kept me stuck in this limbic place for too damn long."

They all take a deep breath together. "We support you in taking steps to take care of yourself, Andrea," Metatron says. "And this ends this segment of the visualization. There is much to process."

"For so long I felt responsible for my mother's grief and sadness, for so long I wanted to protect her," Andrea sighs. "But my mother kept rejecting me repeatedly. This is so very painful. Will the pain ever stop?"

The doe steps close beside her. "It was not your job as a child to protect your parents," | she says. "It's the parents' job to protect their children."

The fawn nods. "When your brother died, the guilt they placed upon themselves for not protecting him became insurmountable. They couldn't live with it, and it was you who suffered most. Your parents did not protect you, Andrea, and for that I am so sorry."

"I see that now," Andrea says.

"You have an opportunity today to re-parent that part of you," the doe says. "To learn healthy ways to cope, to protect your heart, to set appropriate boundaries, to love. You have a chance to learn how to love yourself and to forgive those who have hurt you."

Andrea thinks about all the years she questioned why she was alive and why Andrew died, trying to make sense of her existence. All the years she spent trying to escape the pain, unable to heal those aching memories. There was only one place she could escape to when all hell broke loose. She sits up straight.

"What do you see, Andrea?" Metatron asks.

"I see a porch swing, like the one I use to love to swing on with my nana."

"A porch swing like the one over there?" He points to the other end of the porch.

Andrea is ecstatic. This swing represented hope, hope for a new day. Together they walk toward the swing, and she sits down. "It was here I would look for the rays of light as I prayed for the angels to come down from the sky. I just wanted my mother to get better, to love life again, to love me again. I hoped they would come down from the heavens and teach my mother how to love me the way she loved Andrew."

Her eyes open wide as a wave of truth hits her. Her mother really didn't love her the same way she loved Andrew. *She never did,* she thinks to herself. *It wasn't my imagination.*

"That day my mother rejected me, I prayed for the angels to come and take me away," she says. "I remember telling the angels that I wasn't worthy of my mother's love and asking them to please take me back. I hoped and prayed they would come for me."

Metatron and the deer are still.

"I watched for the rays of light, but they never came."

"The job of the angels was never to rescue you Andrea, their job was and still is to guide you," Metatron says. "But on that day when you felt they did not hear you, you stopped believing in them. And the angels wept."

"I regret that decision," Andrea says, allowing the swing to sway gently back and forth. Her tears begin to flow. Within moments, she can see rays of light beaming down from the sky. "Look," she says.

"We never gave up on you, Andrea," Metatron whispers in her ear. "You gave up on yourself. But now you have a second chance. The angels are rejoicing."

The doe and her fawn are moving through the front yard, each step spreading the energy of kindness, love, hope, nurture, and gratitude. Andrea breathes it all in as she swings back and forth on the front porch of her childhood home. She feels the warm rays from the angels on her face, and a sense of tranquility comes over her.

· · ·

Andrea opens her eyes and feels the peace that surrounds her. "There is more to see when you are ready," the doe says.

Andrea gets up from the swing and positions herself in front of the picture window that stands before her. "Ready," she says.

Metatron smiles and says, "Let us look in on 456 Reality Road for the last time—at least on this leg of your journey."

Andrea sighs with relief, but she can feel beads of sweat trickling from her forehead into her eyes. As she wipes them away with one hand, she uses her other hand as a visor and leans in. There she sees her thirteen-year-old self and Nana, sitting on the couch and playing a game of gin rummy. She smiles. Nana takes care of her, loves her. Nana is her rock. Andrea smiles with adulation. Seeing her sitting on that couch just reminds her how much she misses her even today.

Playing cards was one of their favorite things to do together. She watches how Nana talks and talks, using her gift of gab as a means of distraction. Then she throws her cards down and says, "Gin," just like that.

Andrea giggles as she watches Nana and teenage Andrea banter back and forth. "I loved my nana so much, and I know how much she loved me," she says. "Why wasn't it enough?"

The two deer and Metatron meet her eyes with compassion.

"Dad loved me too," she says, "in a different way. It was easier to see when he had moments of feeling free of Mom's judgment." She pauses, then blurts out, "We never talked about the elephant in the room. My mom behind a locked door drinking herself into oblivion."

"That must have been very painful for you, Andrea," Metatron says.

In the visualization, a second game of gin rummy starts and ends quickly because now it is thirteen-year-old Andrea who yells out "Gin!" Nana grins. She tells Andrea she's becoming a gin rummy master, and gives her a great big hug.

Present-day Andrea watches all this unfold and says, "We never talked about it, none of us, we never talked about Andrew or his death. There was one rule in that household and that was to never further upset my mother." She watches the scene for a moment in silence, thinking, *What the fuck ... she was past being upset, she was dead inside. How much further could we have upset her?*

"I was so enraged," she tells the deer and Metatron. "I used to yell out that I was still alive. I never understood why that didn't seem to mean anything."

"I do not know Andrea, but you are enough," Metatron emphasizes.

Inside the house, Andrea's father walks into the room as Nana clears their mugs of tea and heads to the kitchen. Andrea can hear him ask her teenage self about her day.

"Dad mostly just carried on as if nothing was the matter, as if nothing had happened and everything was fine," Andrea murmurs. "I knew things were not fine, but each time I came home from school and he asked me how I was, my safest answer would always be to say that I was fine. My dad wanted to believe I was fine, and I wanted him to believe it too."

"And yet you were not," Metatron says. "But we are here now to create change so that you can heal these places in you. This part of the visualization is coming to an end, Andrea."

Present-day Andrea watches her dad smile and hum his way to his chair. He sits, hiding behind his newspaper, until *Jeopardy* comes on the TV. She watches as he and teenage Andrea watch *Jeopardy*, *Wheel of Fortune*, then *Law and Order*, together pretending that everything's fine. In the background, she can hear her mother yelling, a prelude to crying herself to sleep.

"I can see how my young self buried her thoughts and feelings, and how she used television as a means to escape her reality. She stuffed most of her feelings away along with tiny pieces of her heart."

Tears well up in her eyes as the vision fades, leaving thirteen-year-old Andrea lost in a TV fantasy world and holding onto the one emotion she knows best: anger. Andrea looks up at her guides. "I keep thinking of that box, the one you showed me. Is that where my emotions are hidden away? Where is that box, anyway?"

"Finding the box is part of your journey, Andrea," Metatron says. "But first we must make room for fourteen-year-old Andrea, who is also suffering from trauma along with raging hormones."

With Metatron's encouragement, Andrea once again looks into the picture window. Inside the house, Andrea, now one year older, is crying in Nana's arms.

"I remember this day," Present-day Andrea says. "I just got my period, and my mother was nowhere to be found."

Nana tries to calm teenage Andrea, holding her tight. "Welcome to the sisterhood, dear."

Teenage Andrea pulls away. "What the hell does that mean?"

"You're a woman today," Nana says, ignoring the snark. "From now until your fifties or so, you'll bleed each month for five to seven days. It's natural and normal."

"It's gross," teenage Andrea says.

They watch as Andrea's father comes into the room and awkwardly hands his daughter a pink pamphlet with the words "About Your Period" on the cover. "Um, maybe read this," he says. "You could ask me questions, if you have any?"

Teenage Andrea grabs the book, rolls her eyes, and walks away.

"He meant, 'Please don't ever have any questions, and for the love of God please don't seek me out,'|" Andrea says to the doe. If deer could smirk, Andrea could swear this one does.

"It wasn't all bad," Andrea remembers. "Every month when I got my period, I'd say to Nana, 'Welcome to the sisterhood,' and Nana would wink. We never really talked about it, but I remember that ritual felt comforting."

Inside the house, teenage Andrea has reappeared, dressed and running late for school. She glances in the hall mirror. "I hate the way I look," she says. "I'm so fat."

Nana and her father exchange a look. "Ready, dear?" her dad says. "Oh, and by the way, you look beautiful today."

Teenage Andrea takes a breath, shakes off her ugly mood, and switches gears. "Thanks, Dad. Let's go."

Present-day Andrea says, "I was a mess. I was angry at my brother for dying, my mom for checking out, my dad for not standing up to her—I was even angry at Nana for loving me, sometimes. But she never gave up on me. Nana loved me, pimples, greasy hair, rages, and all."

"When did anger shift to perfectionism?" Metatron asks.

Andrea looks down at her lap. "Even at my angriest, I still wanted to fix everything and everyone. I thought if I fixed myself ..." She shakes her head.

The doe nuzzles her hand, urging her to continue.

"I thought if I could just get it right, my family would be happy. I tried to please my parents, Nana, my teachers, my softball coach—everyone in my life. But I think I lost myself somehow. Did I?"

The doe gives her a level look. "People-pleasing is a way to try and control the world around you. And for a while, being a high achiever seemed to relieve some of the rejection and loss you were feeling. It made it easier for you to pretend that everything was fine."

Andrea shifts uncomfortably. She can see that she's still confusing busyness for happiness.

"But on the whole," the doe continues, "your anger was continuing to fester, and it found a home in a dark space within."

Andrea is present enough to recognize that she still carries that anger today.

"When you can get in touch with your anger," Metatron says, "your body will be able to release it. It is there you will find peace."

"Nana told me something like that. To let it out. But when I found a way to release some of my resentment, I was betrayed," Andrea says.

"Let us watch," Metatron says.

Inside, it is a different day. Teenage Andrea is just home from school, and it is clear she's distraught.

"What's wrong?" Nana asks.

"Something awful happened at school today," teenage Andrea blurts out. Her hands are shaking.

Nana takes her hand and squeezes it. "Everything will be fine," she murmurs.

"Everything will not be fine!" teenage Andrea yells. "Nothing is fine!"

"Can you calm yourself enough to tell me what happened?" Nana asks.

"My stupid health teacher," teenage Andrea says shakily. "She was teaching us healthy ways to cope with our feelings. She said it would help to write them down, maybe even write a poem. So I did."

"How lovely," Nana says.

"It was *not* lovely," teenage Andrea snaps. "She said she liked my poem, Nana. She complimented me on my writing. I felt really proud. I'm so stupid!"

"You are not stupid, Andrea," Nana says.

"The teacher reported me to the counseling office," teenage Andrea cries. "I had to go down there and sit for hours! But I wouldn't say a single word. I couldn't. I was too angry. I trusted my teacher, Nana!"

Nana takes her hand. "I am so sorry you feel betrayed, Andrea."

Teenage Andrea hands Nana the poem, who reads it aloud.

ANGER

I am suffocating, I am drowning, I am in a black hole
I am scared, I am lonely, I am being held in bondage
I feel guilty, I feel shame, I feel disconnected
Anger, it's a part of me
Exaggerate, drama queen, shake it off
Everything is fine, you will be fine, let it go
I am suffocating, I am drowning, I am in a black hole
I do not see the way out
Anger, it's a part of me

"This is a beautiful poem," Nana says. "And you have a right to be angry—at the world, and at your teacher. She should have talked to you before reporting you to the counseling office. She should have talked to me or your dad."

Teenage Andrea sniffs and wipes her face with her hand.

"You and I will no longer succumb to the belief that everything is fine," Nana promises. "We'll fix this together. And I'm sorry, Andrea, please forgive me. I love you, sweet child."

"I love you too," whispers teenage Andrea. She hugs Nana as the vision fades.

Present-day Andrea holds quite still, feeling the memory of that day. "But we didn't fix it," she says. "We stopped saying everything was fine, but I kept right on pretending and people-pleasing. I knew how proud Nana and my dad were for all of my accomplishments. They were my private cheering squad, but I was so determined to get away from my mother I just left them behind."

Metatron asks, "Is there something you would like to say to young Andrea? You can pretend she's right in front of you."

Andrea feels self-conscious. But she says, "I am so sorry for the pain you carried, for your losses and feelings of loneliness. I see how hard you tried to build connections to people who just weren't available. You worked so hard to prove you deserved to exist."

"You are beginning to connect the dots," Metatron says. "This is good."

"Can you help me learn new ways to cope?" Andrea asks.

"We can. It will take time. Can you be patient with the process?" Metatron gives her a searching look.

"I would like to think so," Andrea replies.

"It is time to leave 456 Reality Road for now," he says. "Are you ready to go and face what's next?"

Andrea nods. A gentle breeze blows, and she watches a sheer translucent curtain cover the picture window. Andrea feels sleepy, and as she closes her eyes, she says, almost chanting, "I am strong, I am a survivor, I am safe, I am … exhausted."

"Rest," says Metatron. He picks her up and carries her. "Let us return to the oak tree in your backyard where you feel safest."

Andrea sighs.

As he carries her back down the well-lit path, Metatron says, "Remember, Andrea, everybody hurts sometimes. But you have an opportunity to heal your hurt, exit the void, and enter a life of abundance. You are a light bearer, and your light will continue to shine even in the darkest of times."

Back home under the tree, Andrea sees that some of the black hearts have turned white. The song "Everybody Hurts," by R.E.M., plays softly. The clock remains still, but soon it will begin ticking again.

Today I allow myself to purge painful memories.
Today I notice that voice of suffering pulling me
away from my potential to live, laugh, and love.
—SAH D'SIMONE

Reflections for This Chapter

Integrate your thoughts by going through these activities now or coming back to them later. I invite you to listen to the song "Everybody Hurts" by R.E.M. as you do so. The words will reflect upon the theme of this chapter, but remember, there is hope for a new day.

One of Andrea's old beliefs is that she's not worthy of her mother's love or her own existence. She never feels like she's enough. List the things that you believe or have believed about yourself, things that you feel shy, scared, embarrassed, or ashamed about. Things that might be difficult to admit or express.

You deserve the space to express whatever is inside of you. The longer you keep it in, the more potential it has to become something powerful and negative. The quicker you can get it out of your body physically—by writing it down and allowing it to exist—the lighter you will feel. If you're uncomfortable seeing your most private thoughts in a journal, it's okay! Feel free to write it on a separate piece of paper in order to feel safe. The important thing is to get your feelings out. (This activity comes from *52 Lists for Calm*, by Moorea Seal.)

CHAPTER 9

Next Stop— Addiction Lane

Children are gifts if we accept them.
—KATHLEEN TURNER CRILLY

Something feels different. Andrea wakes and begins to write about what took place on Reality Road in her journal. She remembers Nana telling her that children are gifts, whether they're a parent's natural child or brought in by the angels. *Sadly, some children like me do not receive this message from their parents that they are gifts. And like me they spend a lifetime trying to prove their worth,* Andrea thinks.

After a moment, she pauses and looks up. Her backyard feels dank. She feels a sense of the void, that empty space in between. "Why?" she says aloud.

The black-tailed doe appears beside her. "You've told yourself for years that you don't belong, that you shouldn't exist. These lies have held you back from embracing the truth: that you are a gift. You do have the right to exist, and I am here to help you nurture this wound."

"It's true," Andrea says. "I see myself as strong, as a survivor, but the harsh reality is I still don't believe I deserve to exist."

"You are strong, and a survivor," the doe says. "But there is more healing to be done. It's time to go deeper."

Andrea can feel perspiration spring out on her forehead.

"Breathe, Andrea. It's so important to breathe." Metatron appears in front of her. "Reach into your bag. There is something you need to see."

Andrea warily reaches into her bag and her fingers close on a newspaper clipping. *Where did that come from?* She pulls it out.

It's a local newspaper clipping from 1979, the year she was a college freshman. The headline reads, "Andrea Cooper Is the One to Beat." The article goes on to talk about Andrea's statistics—batting average, on-base percentage, homeruns, runs batted in, and number of hits. Andrea smiles sadly. "I remember this article. I was the one to beat until …"

"Until that horrible day," Metatron finishes. "We need to pay a visit to Addiction Lane, Andrea. That is why the atmosphere feels dank and musty. That is why this part of the meadow feels like a void."

Andrea wants to sink into the moss beneath her feet.

"This was a dark and painful time in your life, and I am wondering if you feel ready to heal this place in you," the doe says. "You will have another guide for this next part of your journey if you choose to go forward, but know that we will always be with you in spirit, and you can call upon us at any time."

Andrea smiles with gratitude in her heart.

"You do have a choice," Metatron says. "You can surrender these old beliefs so that you can learn to treat yourself as a gift—to yourself, to others, and to the Universe. Or you can choose to forgo this part of the journey."

Andrea is at a crossroads that feels oddly familiar. She can stay here in this part of the yard within the void, or she can make her way forward to the giant oak tree that she can see in the distance. The sun glances through its thick branches.

She looks at the mother deer and her fawn and thanks them softly for their nurturing, parenting, kindness, and care. "I know I need to go," she says, "but I am scared. I feel so vulnerable so raw. I feel like if I don't go, I'll just continue to spiral down into that black hole of 'something is missing.'"

"It is your choice, Andrea. It always has been," says the fawn.

"I don't want to sleepwalk anymore," Andrea pleads. "I don't want to feel like I did when I was in college—lost, sad, desperate. Please help me heal this place in me."

The two deer begin their breathing practice with Andrea: in to a count of seven, hold for seven, out for seven. Together they breathe, pause, and start again. They repeat this seven times as they walk together toward the giant oak tree. Andrea is aware of her fear, anxiety, and resistance, but she continues to move forward.

She feels a slight gust of wind and looks at the great, giant, old oak ahead. *She is waiting for me,* she thinks. She notices that the tree appears to have a pulse, like her own heartbeat, like the vibration she feels from the earth below her feet. She can feel them all sync up.

The flow of the wind carries her silky, soft blanket closer to where she is sitting. The blanket finds its resting spot and settles on her lap, waiting to be wrapped around her. *Become one with the tree,* she thinks—and wonders where that thought came from. *I am safe here, under this tree. I feel the harmony and strength from the tree, the calmness it provides, and a balance in nature. I am so grateful.*

"I read once," Andrea says, "that trees teach us about being more human and help us master the difficult art of seeing others and ourselves as we truly are. I think that is what this journey is about. I think that's why it's so important for me to feel connected to the great oak tree and the earth it buries its roots in. Is it?"

The fawn walks toward her and nudges her blanket, and the doe helps Andrea wrap her beautiful blanket around her. They all sit quietly under the tree, listening to its wisdom.

Andrea holds her article in one hand and her travel journal in the other. She thinks about the thoughts and memories that came up for her revisiting Reality Road. She feels drawn to taking out her pen and jotting something new down. "Each experience provides me with a pathway to healing," she writes. "Each experience provides me with an opportunity to feel the feelings I once tucked away."

She looks up to find Metatron standing next to her. "It feels good to write it all down," she says. "It feels like a second chance, one where I get to write my new story."

Metatron smiles. "It is time to meet your next guide. A teacher of sorts who will be the one traveling with you on this next part of your journey."

She feels a wave of nervousness.

"It's time to trust, Andrea," the archangel says. "You don't have to drive this journey. You'll be riding shotgun."

Andrea laughs. "Ah, yes, let go of my ego, embrace the spirit, I know."

"Take a deep breath, and exhale the word 'trust,'" Metatron prompts. "Practice extending trust to that power greater than yourself that lies within yourself."

Andrea gets up from under the tree, breathes, and whispers, "Trust." As she exhales, she feels a soft breeze blow through her hair and senses a new energy in this part of the backyard.

"Andrea," says Metatron, "I am pleased to introduce you to Tara the tigress, who is a yogini guardian for humanity. She will be your guide for this stretch of your journey."

And there she is. A majestic, gleaming, eyes glowing. She very slightly inclines her regal head.

Andrea takes a step back. "I'm taking the next leg of my journey with ... this ..."

"Tigress," Metatron says calmly. "She is a goddess of peace, prosperity, and long life. But before she can extend those gifts to you, she must first help you face what really happened on Addiction Lane."

Andrea is stricken. He is asking her to relive one of the darkest places of her life, characterized by perfection, people-pleasing, coping mechanisms, pain, and substance abuse. "I almost died there," she says faintly. "You want me to go back there with this ... wild beast?"

"I prefer the term 'spirit animal,'" the tigress says mildly. Her voice is surprisingly pleasing.

Andrea startles. The deer spoke, after all, why shouldn't the tiger? "I'm sorry," she says to ... Tara, was it? "I'm just scared at the idea of having to plunge back into that darkness again in order to find what's missing."

"You must travel to Addiction Lane to confront the events and emotions that led you to that dark place, Andrea," Metatron says. "When you do that, you can begin to heal. Tara is perfect for this part of your journey. She is not only a yogini guardian for humanity but also a goddess of peace, prosperity, and long life. You need her."

"So, this is the only way to find my way back to my heart to my soul," Andrea says slowly. "This is the way out?"

"I can help you heal your heart as well as return you home to your soul," the tigress says.

Andrea looks up at the blue, protective dome of the sky and finds some serenity in such a wonder. "I know I need to face my demons, and this is one of the biggest demons that needs facing."

She takes a step forward, looks the tigress straight in her soft, amber eyes, and breathes deeply. Then she extends her arms and invites the tigress in.

"I am ready to trust the process and the path. I am calling upon your wisdom, boldness, and power as a guide, Ms. Tigress. I am placing my life and trust in you."

Andrea looks at Metatron and the two deer.

"We will always be with you, Andrea, in spirit," says the archangel. "You are never alone. But on this part of your journey the tigress will be your guide. She knows how to help you overcome all obstacles. Ready?"

Andrea gives a thumbs-up and then says, "Wait—obstacles?" Before she can ask more questions, she is swirled into another realm, leaving her fears and the meadow behind. *Where are we?* she wonders.

"We are on the Skyway of Life," says Tara the tigress. Apparently she can hear thoughts, too, just like the archangel.

Andrea has no idea how fast they're moving, but she can feel a descent. *That's weird,* she thinks, *my ears are popping.* And then they arrive, whatever arrival means. She catches her breath, clears her throat, and shakes off what feels like spritzes of moisture from the air. Then she glances at the street sign in front of her and freezes. There it is, in front of her dorm. "Addiction Lane," she whispers.

"Move-in day," the tigress says softly. "Remember?"

Andrea turns expectantly toward the dorm, but there in front of her is what looks like a drive-in movie screen. "Wow," she says. "I mean, what the hell?"

"This time in your life was very painful," Tara says. "You experienced a lot of loss, and you may feel a lot of emotions revisiting it. We will be watching on this screen so that you feel safe."

They make their way across the street to a park Andrea doesn't remember being there. It's quickly apparent that it wasn't when she sees, in addition to the normal swings and slides and shrubs, many animals milling about. The tigress leads her to a picnic bench attached to a table covered with a red checkered cloth. There is food and drink laid out on top.

"We might be here for a while," the tigress says.

Andrea takes in a large breath and exhales with a humming tone, trying to calm herself.

"I will be by your side at all times," Tara says. "Remember, our purpose, our focus, our aim is to heal this place in you."

And with that, they turn toward the screen and watch Andrea move in.

"There I am," present-day Andrea says. On the screen, her seventeen-year-old self is meeting her roommates for the first time. "I remember how free I felt."

"You had carried so many burdens, so much sadness, and so much anger," the tigress agrees. "You thought this place would be a fresh start. We are here to make sure that this time you get one."

The tigress and Andrea watch college Andrea dancing excitedly around her bright, colorful dorm room with her roommate, Maddie. "I love this room!" she squeals.

On screen, college life unfolds. College Andrea is relaxed and joyful, feeling free of the drama and trauma of Reality Road. Present-day Andrea and the tigress watch as college Andrea makes friends, enjoys her classes, plays softball.

Present-day Andrea laughs. "There I am, admiring all the boys—some of them even admired me back." She watches, remembering. "And there I am, missing my mom and dad. I actually missed Nana the most."

"They missed you as well, Andrea," says the tigress.

Present-day Andrea is having fun watching her early college days, but she's all too aware of what's coming up. For a while, she'd been able to tuck away all the thoughts and feelings she hadn't processed from Reality Road. But her coping strategies ultimately won out, and people-pleasing, perfectionism, and negative thoughts began to creep back in.

Tara and adult Andrea watch silently as college Andrea slowly comes undone. Mood swings. Meltdowns. Trying too hard. Not trying hard enough. Then comes the day when the article comes out, the one that reads "Andrea Cooper Is the One to Beat."

Andrea watches her younger self read the article in the paper and struggle to take it in. She remembers that she started having trouble, even then, with ugly thoughts. The ones that told her she was a fake, that she had no talent.

She remembers that those little demons didn't stop there. Those pesky little demons slithered around her head, telling her that her teammates were jealous of her notoriety—in fact, they couldn't stand her. The voices told Andrea she was completely unlovable. They topped it all off by telling her she wasn't worthy of being acknowledged because she wasn't worthy of existing,

Present-day Andrea watches college Andrea look in the mirror and, instead of being proud of her accomplishments, silently berate herself. *Sure, that reporter thought you were great, but you're such a loser,* she remembers thinking on that day. *Nobody even likes you. You're a mistake. You shouldn't even exist.*

"SHUT UP!" On the screen, her college self screams at the mirror. Then she flings herself onto her bed, where she curls herself into a ball on her bed and covers her ears, sobbing.

"That was an awful day," present-day Andrea says. "Something inside me snapped. I couldn't handle all that pressure of doing and being it all. Perfectionism is a slow death."

"It almost led you to your real death," the tigress murmurs.

"I know," Andrea says uncomfortably. "I remember what happens next."

She forces herself to watch the screen as Maddie, her roommate back then, notices Andrea's anxiety and mood swings and decides to get spunky, lively Andrea back by introducing her to the party scene. Maddie explains the different substances available—how much they cost, whether they're made from plants or are synthetic, what kind of high or effect each produces. Andrea doesn't care about any of it as long as she can experience the euphoria that lets her leave her ugly thoughts behind.

The action on the screen leaves freshman year behind and jumps right into the first semester of Andrea's junior year. Andrea isn't living with Maddie anymore. Instead, she shares a big apartment with two friends from the softball team and three other classmates. She and Maddie see each other at games and sometimes get high together, but they are not as close.

"I thought it was fine," present-day Andrea says to the tigress. "I thought I was fine."

"Yes," Tara says, "You have been persistent in trying to convince yourself and others of that."

"I was managing my grades so I wouldn't lose my softball scholarship," Andrea says.

"But the pressure became too much," the tigress says.

"Perfectionism," they say in unison.

They sit back and watch as college Andrea's partying increases. She's finding it harder and harder to say no to the drugs. Present-day Andrea winces in shame.

"We need to air all your dirty laundry, Andrea, so we can bring the truth to light." The tigress leans in.

Overhead, Andrea sees a small, fluffy cloud bright against the sky. From behind it, rays of light beam down upon her. She wonders if those are angels.

"They are here to remind you that you are not alone, and of the healing and the beauty that is to come," the tigress says.

On the screen, a beautiful fall day unfolds. The air is crisp, and the leaves are changing color. It is bucolic and yet it was on this day, Andrea remembers, that everything took a turn for the worse. On the softball field, the team has gathered around the bleachers and is watching the coaches whisper, look up, and whisper again.

"Girls, we have an announcement," says a coach. "There are going to be some changes for the new season, some new regulations from the NCAA."

"The National Collegiate Athletic Association," Andrea tells Tara.

"We've heard some rumors of steroids being used and even abused in some instances, and so we'll be starting drug testing …"

Watching, Andrea feels the panic she felt on that day.

"We have a new Athletic Director and things will be tightening up," the coach continues.

College Andrea is looking agitated. She leans over and whispers to Maddie, "How long does this stuff stay in my system?"

Maddie shrugs her shoulders.

Present-day Andrea watches her younger self panic, knowing

that college Andrea is feverishly trying to figure out how to game the system. She remembers that she loved softball and being an athlete back then. She loved her school, her teammates, her coaches. She couldn't imagine not being part of this family. But she also loved her drugs and the way they numbed her, so she didn't have to feel.

College Andrea is back in her apartment, rifling through drawers and looking for her stash. The phone rings.

Present-day Andrea tenses. She remembers this call. She watches her younger self answer the phone and then listen, her face going white.

"What's up?" asks her roommate, Jillian.

College Andrea lets the phone fall and drops to her knees, crying.

"That was the day my nana died," present-day Andrea says.

A montage of scenes take place on the screen. College Andrea locking herself in her room; unresponsive to her roommates knocking and asking if she needs help. Jillian calling her head coach Delilah and later, Delilah coming over to get Andrea up and showered and to make her eat. Delilah telling her that everything will be fine.

Present-day Andrea flinches.

"I'm going to get you excused from your classes and from practice for one week, Andrea," Delilah says. "I'm also going to get you some help. I think it's a good idea for you to see a grief counselor."

College Andrea looks up in surprise.

"Andrea, I need to ask you something," Delilah says. "I need to know if you're using drugs. The other coaches and I have noticed a change in you over this past year."

College Andrea scowls.

"We know you've been struggling. We know things at home have been difficult, and things here can be intense. Your behavior is changing. Your grades are slipping. We're here for you, Andrea, we care about you, and we suspect you might –"

"How dare you!" Andrea is in a rage. "You need to leave now." She turns to her roommates and screeches, "And you! You all are nothing but a bunch of snitches and hypocrites!" She marches back to her room mumbling, "Rats—you're all a pack of rats."

She slams the door, turns the lock, slams the bolt home, and yells, "I'll show you!"

Delilah checks in over the next few days, but Andrea's roommates hide the truth. She's not eating, she's not sleeping, she's lightheaded, she's exhausted but can't seem to stop moving.

The scariest part of all is when she begins to hallucinate. Present-day Andrea and the tigress watch in dismay as college Andrea babbles about "the bugs," scratching at things that aren't there. Her roommates are frightened and don't know what to do.

Present-day Andrea's eyes fill with tears. "She's in so much pain. My heart hurts for her," she tells the tigress.

On screen, college Andrea is spewing words of hate, yelling about her mom, her brother, her father, and Nana. It sounds like gibberish. She stops for a moment and then cries out, "I love you Nana, why the hell did you leave me?" Then she screams, "I hate you God, you son of a bitch. You took my brother. You took my nana. I hate you." She falls to the floor, her body limp.

Present-day Andrea finds this excruciating to watch. The tigress encourages her to breathe and hang on for just a bit longer.

The roommates debate calling Andrea's parents, or the police, but finally settle on calling Delilah again. Young Andrea is still on the floor and barely breathing when Delilah bursts in and immediately begins CPR. "Call for an ambulance!" she yells.

The scene flashes to the hospital, where a doctor on duty comes out to the waiting room and tells Delilah and Andrea's parents. "She almost died," he tells the coach. "You saved her life, Delilah. We'll be keeping her on a 24-hour watch."

Andrea's parents have tears of gratefulness in their eyes, and they give Delilah a huge hug.

The doctor doesn't come out and call Andrea suicidal, but he does say that it's clear she's been abusing dangerous substances for a long time, and that she could have overdosed. He explains to Delilah and her parents that coming off these drugs sometimes causes psychosis. He recommends transfer to the hospital's detox unit.

Andrea's mother gasps. Her father consoles her.

And it is here that Andrea finally meets up with the consequences of her addiction.

The scene moves forward. Andrea has been in detox for a while and is beginning to feel somewhat more human. She has been moved to a private room where she's allowed visitors outside her family for the first time, and Delilah is sitting next to her bed.

"You've scared quite a few people, Andrea," Delilah says. "Your father, your mother, me, all of your coaches, your teammates, your teachers, your boyfriend. You've have been holding onto a secret, but the secret is out."

College Andrea can barely breathe.

"You have a lot of people who love and care about you, but they can't clean this up for you. You have to do it for yourself."

Present-day Andrea watches as her younger self shuts down during the family therapy sessions. Her young self closes her eyes in shame and self-pity. Eventually the three of them are able to talk openly and honestly, but there is still so much work to be done. Recovery and healing are on the horizon. She can now see what college Andrea cannot.

Later that week, another discovery: Delilah putting a picture of Andrea and Nana on the nightstand. As college Andrea drifts off to sleep, Present-day Andrea hears Delilah speak. It's as if a higher power is using Delilah as a mouthpiece.

"There is help available to you if you choose a path of healing, Andrea," says this power greater than Andrea herself. "It may be a painful path, but it will also be a path of exploration, discovery, and healing."

Delilah leaves the room, but present-day Andrea sees that the presence of a higher power remains.

College Andrea opens her eyes and sits up straight. "Wait. Who are you?" she asks.

A voice can be heard in the hospital room. "I am your divine power, Andrea. I am here to guide you and to help you heal. The choice is yours."

Young Andrea looks around suspiciously and then lays her head on her pillow. "Hogwash. Now go away."

"I never knew how that picture got there," present-day Andrea says.

"It was your higher power, Andrea," the tigress says. "Acting through Delilah."

"I can't imagine that this divine power still wants me in the kingdom," Andrea says.

"This is a new beginning Andrea, with more work still to be done," Tara says. "But, yes, this power greater than yourself wants you to feel connected, however that works for you."

College Andrea's time in detox continues to play out on screen.

"These days were some of my darkest moments," present-day Andrea says, "but I felt a source of energy steering me toward the path of healing. Was that my higher power trying to connect?"

"Your higher power has always been there for you."

On the screen, a nurse is explaining the detox process. "Detoxing is not always predictable or straightforward," she says. "The likelihood of you experiencing severe withdrawals is probable. You need to cleanse your system so you can live consciously. Do you understand?"

College Andrea rolls onto her side in disgust.

"Your life is a gift, Andrea," the nurse says. "You need to clean up, and you need help. You need me."

"I remember that," says present-day Andrea. "When I looked back over, no one was there. Was I hallucinating? Was the nurse this power greater than myself?"

"A little of both, Andrea, a little of both," the tigress said.

"It took me three full days to get through the worst of it," Andrea remembers. She can see now that a divine power intervened. A power greater than herself came in the form of a nurse who tried to prepare her and protect her from further pain.

"Wow," she says. "The invitation to believe was right in front of me. I wish I had accepted it."

Together, she and the tigress watch as the next four days are packed with intense counseling. Young Andrea is worn out mentally, emotionally, physically, and spiritually. Her parents arrive to take her home, and they have a few family counseling sessions. They are as grueling as the detox experience, but they are the beginning stages of healing.

On the screen, Andrea packs up her belongings to the sound of "Gold Dust Woman" by Fleetwood Mac. She picks up the photo of her and Nana. "I am a gift," she whispers, remembering how many times Nana told her that, seeing Nana's familiar broad smile. A sudden breeze lifts her hair, and she says, "Nana?" She flips the picture over, where a little black heart is printed right next to the date stamp.

Present-day Andrea smiles at the heart she never noticed before. "I think I can finally let go of the guilt I felt for leaving. I can see in Nana's eyes how she supported me going away to college. I can see through her smile how proud she was of me and how she only wanted me to be free and happy. She never wanted me to feel guilty or sad."

"That is truth," the tigress says.

"I've carried this sadness and guilt much too long. I think I can let it go. Maybe I can start to let go of my self-loathing too."

The tigress places her paw on Andrea's hand, acknowledging her courage and strength.

"Thank you for helping me see the ugly truth and the beauty behind it. Thank you for helping me find the path toward fully loving and respecting my body, my mind, my life, and spirit," says present-day Andrea. "Thank you for reminding me that I have been substance-free since that time in my life and what a beautiful gift that has been. Thank you for guiding me and helping me heal this place in me."

The velvet curtain closes over the big screen, and the sun casts its rays over the picnic bench. Andrea and the tigress sit quietly as the rays of light dance in the in-between. Time is infinite in this place.

Today, I will think healing thoughts.
—MELODY BEATTIE

CHAPTER 10

The Ugly Truth and the Beauty that Comes from It

You couldn't hide from the bad things and pretend they didn't exist, that left you with a dream world, and dream worlds eventually crumble. You had to face the truth. And then decide what you wanted.

—SARAH CROSS

"I feel like I just went through the spin cycle. Is this what hell feels like?" Andrea asks.

"Hell is when someone abandons their soul," Tara the tigress says. "You were definitely in a dark place, Andrea, but your soul was and still is alive. It is bruised, but not fully abandoned. It is my job to help you heal that place in you and to come home to your soul."

"Can we go back to my backyard where I feel safe?" Andrea stands up. "I think I need time to process before jumping into any more memories."

The tigress asks her to close her eyes, to breathe and relax, and they begin their ascension back to the skyway. The air swirls and eddies around them as if they are free-floating kites in a great and wide sky.

Within moments, they are descending, and Andrea finds herself thinking about her visit to Addiction Lane. Miraculously she is in her backyard within moments, breathing in the spring-fragranced air, and she finds refuge on her silky blanket under the tree. Her travel journal is wide open, waiting for the details of this last adventure. And so, she takes the time she needs to write about what happened on Addiction Lane. She writes: *This was the worst time of my life, the darkest of darkest of times. I see how the hate I had for myself turned into me abandoning and neglecting myself, then and now. I see how I abused my body because I hated myself, thinking it was okay to abuse my body the way I did. NO MORE! It is never okay to abuse my body, and I will never do that again. Today, I am working on healing and loving myself. I feel...* She pauses as she feels the heaviness. Her head hurts, and she puts the pen down to rest.

Tara sits beside her and reminds her to invite all of her spiritual guides in for assistance if she feels the need. "Each will bring the nurturing, the love, the energy, the wisdom, the serenity, and the strength you require," she says. "This is how you will remain empowered, Andrea. This is how your light will continue to shine upon the world."

Andrea smiles faintly. She wants to believe she is a gift, a light bearer, but she's struggling with the after-effects of the visit to Addiction Lane.

She looks up at the black hearts dangling above from the thick branches of the great oak tree. They still seem mysterious, but less ominous now that she knows the black doesn't represent evil, but rather the places she still needs to heal.

Across the way in her backyard, she can see shiny ceramic bowls, sticks, and colorful balls of yarn like the ones she saw before. She gets up to check it all out. "I've seen these before, something about rituals," she calls out to the tigress. "What exactly are these for again?"

"Rituals that will come later," the tigress says simply.

There's a rhythmic vibration Andrea can feel radiating from deep within the roots of the tree. It pulses in tune with the ceramic bowls, the fascinating sticks, the colorful balls of yarn. It aligns with the lush rolling hills, the brightly colored flowers, squishy mushrooms, and milkweed scattered about. *Become one with the tree*, Andrea thinks. She looks at the tree and says, "I receive a sense of power and strength from you, great oak tree. Your sturdiness provides a sense of safety and balance in nature. Your wisdom is everlasting. I feel alive and awake when I am near you. You provide me with the courage I need to move forward on my growth journey. Thank you!"

She notices the smell of smoke and looks back toward the firepit. She wanders over to the firepit with journal and pen in hand. She sits in a rocking chair that also seems familiar. Its cushion is thick and comfortable.

Andrea rocks back and forth. *I can't hide from the bad things and pretend they don't exist. I can't stay in pretend world because dreams eventually crumble, and it's time to face the truth.* She begins to write, and her pen moves rapidly across the page. The words are flowing, the tears are rolling, the ugly truth is running through and from her mind.

The tigress sits beside her and rests her heavy white paw on Andrea's hand. "Thank you for allowing me to accompany you on one of the toughest parts of your journey," she says. "I know it was not easy."

"It was certainly the darkest time in my life," Andrea says. "I never want to feel as bad as I did then. I almost died." She writes in her journal, *I never want to go back to that time, I only want to move forward and heal.*

"A part of you did die during that dark time," Tara says. "But I am here to help you reconnect to that powerful divine light within. There can be a dramatic healing breakthrough when you rely upon your spiritual connection."

"I still struggle with the concept of God, but I do thank God every day for not letting me die," Andrea says.

"You are a miracle in God's eyes, Andrea. You were given a second chance—one your brother Andrew did not get. You are alive, and you need to embrace that gift," the tigress says.

"I received a lot of help then," Andrea says, "and I've been sober and clean ever since. But I still feel lost and alone much of the time, like something's missing."

"I am here to help you find what is missing," the tigress says. "The answers are near."

"Is that why I keep seeing a vision of that big wooden box with the brass lock?" Andrea asks. "Does it have the answers to my questions? Does this box even exist?"

There is a small sound Andrea can't identify, and when she looks up, she sees the black-tail doe and her fawn before her. She smiles, happy to see them again.

The fawn gently places a black heart in Andrea's hand. The words on it read, "There is a wooden box, and it is hidden in the garden. Go and look for the box. But first you must find the key for the box, which lies deep within the soil. It's time to get your hands dirty. You must do this before you hit the skyway."

Andrea hands the black heart back to the fawn and heads for what looks like a garden. The two deer follow her toward the unattended garden, where she finds a small trowel and a bigger shovel. "We are here with you just for this time in the garden," the doe says. "Once you find what you need in order to move on, we will move on too."

The fawn approaches and lays one more item at her feet. It is a beautiful pendant whose engraving reads, "Always with you."

"As you go forward, you have an excellent guide in Tara," the doe says. "She is truly a legend."

Andrea's eyes widen.

"See how her black and gray stripes are woven into her white fur? Those stripes represent her mighty and powerful gifts," the doe tells her. "Her coat is full and soft for a tigress, not coarse. Her body is thick yet sleek, her muscles are strong. She exhibits lots of confidence."

"Something I could use right now," Andrea murmurs.

"I am also known as White Tara," says the tigress. "My presence indicates a boldness of spirit and a willingness to engage in your challenges and achieve inevitable success. So you, Andrea, are on your way to creating that success."

"Will you be guiding me alone on this next part of the journey?" Andrea asks.

"It is my practice to call upon higher spiritual guides for assistance when needed," Tara explains. "For example, your power greater than yourself and any others who have been witness so far. The powers and strength I carry will empower them to bring their light to the world through you."

Andrea listens intently.

"This will help you grow in your own spiritual advancement because our aim is to advance your level of consciousness as you heal. It is a team effort. No one source is better than another. We operate as one," the tigress adds.

"Ah," says Andrea. "I suppose I am open to whatever comes my way. By the way, I am just noticing now these numbers on your ankle. What do the numbers 333 stand for?"

"The repeated three symbolizes that all manner of assistance and support will be granted to ensure your attainment and safety. Safety is of utmost importance," Tara replies.

"Aw," Andrea says, "safety *is* of utmost importance. My nana told me about the importance of trust and safety, both things I have struggled with but am learning more about. On another note, my nana also told me I was born into a soul family of light bearers and how it was my job to shine the light," Andrea says. "Is this why you're here, to show me what this means?"

"First, let us find the key that unlocks the wooden box," Tara says.

Andrea looks around the neglected garden and sighs. Wishing the garden were more attractive, she begins to dig. And dig. So much digging—and sweating—that it makes her want to give up. Eventually she is so tired that she sits back to take a rest. But after five minutes pass, she dives back in, looking ferociously for that brass-colored key.

Finally, she shifts a huge hunk of dirt, and there it is! A brass key pops up from beneath the soil. "It's here. I found it!"

She keeps digging, and now she can also see the top of a box just below the surface of the soil. She begins to pull and yank the box from beneath the earth.

"Careful," says the tigress.

Nothing is standing in Andrea's way now. She brushes off the box and places it carefully on the ground. Letting out a big sigh of relief, she collapses to the ground.

"There it is," says the fawn.

Andrea receives a second wind and begins to thoroughly examine the box. She treats it like a capsule she might have once buried containing secrets from the past. Andrea twirls the box from side to side to see if there are any hidden messages written between the crevasses.

The tigress tilts her head with curiosity.

Andrea checks underneath the box to see if there is a date, but nothing is there. Nothing the naked eye can see, anyway.

"This box needs to be opened with care and love," the tigress says. "And you need to respect whatever happens once you do. Do you understand?"

Andrea carefully places the key into the delicate lock. Then she turns the key with a clicking sound.

The box begins to open on its own. Inside, there is a miniature box. The tiny box pops open, and out of the center of the box comes the most brilliant white light in the shape of a tiger. The numbers 333 are displayed, and the light amplifies from every direction. The light is a symbolic portrayal of the tigress's character; her boldness, confidence, and willingness to engage. The light is also representative of Andrea's journey: her search for knowledge, enlightenment, clarity, and healing. In so doing, she seeks to bring light to mankind, something Nana told her was part of her purpose. The waves of light move slowly through the air as well as through the tigress and Andrea, creating a tingling sensation.

"I feel the light," Andrea says. "It feels so powerful."

"The light is powerful, Andrea, it's an expression of its true meaning, which is a symbol of hope, goodness, and healing and strength."

In that moment, several black hearts fall from the tree. The doe and her fawn collect them and hand them to Andrea.

"No time to read each heart now," the tigress says, "but we will read each of them as we travel."

Andrea wonders which places of healing these hearts represent.

"We need to hit the skyway, as this will be a long journey," the tigress says. "Be sure to place the hearts in the wooden box. If you would like, we can read some of them along the way."

"Excellent," Andrea says with enthusiasm. She has been waiting for this moment for a very long time.

"Be sure to place the wooden box carefully in your bag and keep it close to your heart," the tigress says. "It is an item that cannot be lost or misplaced. Are you ready?"

"I am," says Andrea. She walks toward the tree, expecting to be led into a meditative state, but then notices that her animal guides are standing still. She looks back at them with a question in her eyes.

"Jump on," says the tigress, a quick gesture of her magnificent furry head over her shoulder indicates that Andrea is to climb onto Tara's back.

"Jump on wh—ooh, wait, Tara, no!" Andrea squeaks.

"Just jump on and hold tight," the tigress says. "This time you will witness the ascension and the eloquence hidden in the Skyways. You will see firsthand what divine power is capable of."

Andrea hesitates.

"This leg of your journey will be a combination of ugly truth and the beauty behind it." "NOW JUMP ON!" says the tigress.

The doe and her fawn say their farewells as Andrea grips her pendant and climbs onto Tara's back. The song "Truth to Power" by OneRepublic plays as they leave her backyard behind. A luminous beam of light swirls about them as they are lifted into the air. They become one with it.

I am not pretty;
I am not beautiful.
I am as radiant as the sun.
—SUZANNE COLLINS

Reflections for This Chapter

Integrate your thoughts by going through these activities now or coming back to them later.

This meditation is a great one … powerful … strong … like the light Tara the tigress shares. I invite you to listen to the songs from Chapters 9 and 10 before, during, or after you meditate. The songs are "Gold Dust Woman" by Fleetwood Mac and "Truth to Power" by OneRepublic. The words from each song are strong and powerful.

Find a quiet spot. Close your eyes and breathe … begin to inhale and count to seven, hold for seven, and exhale for seven. Repeat seven times.

- You see a brilliant white sun, and it shines a glowing white light.

- Waves of light begin to move through you, slow, deep, and healing.

- Out of the most luminous center of the sun, a solar tiger of white light stalks forth.

- You see the numbers 333.

- The light continues to shine to amplify itself, reaching far and wide into every dimension.

- There is not a barrier that can withstand it.

- The waves of light continue to move through you, slowly, powerfully, and deeply.

- You become one with the light.

Rest for as long as you need, allowing the process to soak into the depths of your soul. Be sure to ground yourself and hydrate. (This exercise comes from the *White Light Oracle Guidebook* by Alana Fairchild.)

CHAPTER 11

I Will Try to Fix You

*Life is like a wild tiger. You can either lie down
and let it lay its paw on your head;
or sit on its back and ride it.*
—UNKNOWN

"How are you doing, Andrea?" Tara asks.

"I was scared at first, but I love this ride in the great, open sky," Andrea cries out. "This is just an incredible experience. It's unbelievable—beyond my wildest dreams!"

"How so?"

"I don't even know where I'm going or what I'm doing," Andrea admits. "But so far, the ugly truth is leading me to the beauty that comes from it. Look at all this!"

"Show me what it looks like through your eyes," the tigress says.

"Oh!" Andrea is flummoxed. "I can't even begin to describe what I see, but I'll try like hell. So here beneath the clouds, we're ... suspended mid-stream. The sun is casting its rays through white clouds that look like castles in the sky. To the right I see pink clouds that look like cotton candy, and to the left I see puffy white clouds like cotton balls."

"Quite vivid, Andrea," the tigress says.

"Far down below us, I can see steep sloping hills, sharp and rounded ridges, and high jagged peaks. I see this massive body of saltwater covering most of the Earth's surface. The colors are beyond magnificent: blue, green, aqua, gray, dark blue, and seafoam green. There are red tides, brown tides, low tides, and high tides. There are other countless bodies of water—some of them are clear, bright, and calm. Others rage so quickly the color is a mystery."

"You are very observant," says the tigress.

"This is way better than any airplane," Andrea says. "From this vantage point, I can see all the land and all its inhabitants, from plants to animals—including humans, of course. Humans are the most unpredictable. Which I guess makes them predictably unpredictable."

"There is some truth to that." Tara laughs.

Andrea is intrigued by this new, higher perspective on the complexity of the human race. She considers her own family dynamics and wonders about her biological family, her ancestors. Complex indeed.

"I have felt loved, I have felt valued, I have felt success, and I have felt joy. I have also been lied to, betrayed, hurt, abandoned, neglected, and disappointed," she says.

The tigress lets out a supportive roar.

"I'm ready to surrender the burdens of my past, whether those burdens come from my ancestors, my parents, or my own domestication," Andrea declares. "And I will always cherish these moments in the sky with you, Tara the tigress. Where to first?"

"First stop: the police station where it all started," Tara says.

They glide down from the sky and make a smooth landing just outside the precinct doors. There, they find two comfortable-looking Adirondack chairs atop a large, black-and-white checked blanket.

"How old were you when you first started working here?" the tigress asks.

"I don't know, my mid-twenties somewhere. I lie about my age, and I've lost track." Andrea settles into the blue Adirondack chair with a pillow that says, "Change Starts with You." *No coincidences,* Andrea thinks to herself.

Just then the precinct doors fly wide open, wide enough for them to see right in.

"It looks like a scene from a play," Andrea says in wonder. "Is it real?"

"It's real," Tara says. "Let's watch it play out."

A younger Andrea comes into view.

"There I am," Andrea says. "Look how shy I was back then! Of course that place—so noisy, so much hustle and bustle. The hallways were full of testosterone, I wasn't used to that."

The tigress smiles.

"I was so young, but I made a great office manager," Andrea remembers, watching her younger self move about. "A lot of organization and admin, but sometimes I got to fingerprint people when they were booked. Oh, look, it's the holiday party!" She is distracted by the colored lights.

"Let's take a peek," the tigress says.

Holiday music fills the air, along with the smell of lasagna and garlic bread. The dessert table is particularly well-stocked and attracting attention. The alcohol flows, people are dancing and, it appears, having a good time. They can see twentysomething Andrea hanging in the back with her friends, taking it all in.

There is a small commotion among the young women, and the cause is soon apparent: a drop-dead gorgeous hunk of a cop saunters in.

"Wow, look at James," Andrea whistles. "Man, he was built. You could see his muscles through his shirt and his butt was nice and round and firm and—well, it was clearly love at first sight."

The tigress grins.

Andrea watches her younger self asking James to dance. He nods, and they share a dance under a garland-strewn disco ball.

"We danced all night," Andrea says to the tigress as they watch twentysomething James and Andrea swaying back and forth to Led Zeppelin's "Stairway to Heaven." "It was magical. It felt like a dream I never wanted to wake up from. I never thought a guy like James would be interested in someone like me."

They watch as James holds a sprig of mistletoe over Andrea's head and leans in.

"It was a great kiss," Andrea says. "My body tingled, my lips quivered, my legs shook, goosebumps all over … I felt safe, I felt protected, I was in love."

"And now?" the tigress asks.

She shakes her head and watches the precinct door close. Then she sits back comfortably in the Adirondack chair and draws the blanket over her legs and feet.

"Look up into the sky," Tara says. "That's where memories blossom and rich stories are told."

Andrea looks up at the dusky, darkening sky. "James and I were dating for close to nine months when we went to a friend's Halloween party. He was dressed as Superman and I as

Lois Lane. I really did feel like he was my hero. He asked me to marry him that night, and a few months later we married."

They sit in silence for a moment, watching as stars begin to appear in the darkening sky.

"A year after that, we had our son Ben. And two years after that, we had our daughter, Sophia. They've both given us grandkids now."

"Do I hear a touch of sadness?" the tigress says.

"We built a good life together, James and me. We raised our beautiful kids, and now we have the most amazing grandchildren. So why am I so damn unhappy? Why do I feel so alone? Why do I feel like my life with Superman has been one big disappointment?"

"No one can be Superman all the time," Tara says.

"James often tells me he feels like a disappointment," Andrea says, "and I basically agree. That's when he gets nasty and tells me I'm spoiled and perpetually dissatisfied. Am I?"

"We are here to address all of your old beliefs, including anger and discontent," the tigress reminds her. "Be patient, the answers will come."

Andrea lets out a sigh of distress. "James shames me for not being appreciative and happy. And when he does that, I feel even more dismissed and alone. It's been that way for a few years."

"What else has changed, Andrea?" the tigress asks.

"The drinking and raging are getting worse," Andrea says. "It just disgusts me when James is slurring his words and tripping over his own feet."

"I am listening," the tigress says.

"I took it for so many years, but that means that for years I was numb. I felt small and lost in the cacophony and chaos, just like when I was a child. But then …"

"But then?"

But then something clicked, and I spoke up," Andrea says. "I spoke my truth, and it felt damn good. I remember feeling alive."

The tigress raises her eyebrows.

"Everything I'd been holding in just came spewing out in a gush. I remember yelling—screaming!—at him, telling him I hated his lying, cheating, drunken, disgusting self."

"Did that feel good?" the tigress asks.

"It did! Until I realized how hurtful and unkind my words were and that I was raging just like my mother. I was so hurt that I wanted him to hurt. But that's not what people who are love do to each other. It's not who I am, but it's who I've become. A critical, angry bitch. James is right."

"Stop right there, Andrea," the tigress growls, not unkindly. "You have allowed others' words to beat you up for far too long. We are not here to substitute someone else's judgment for your own."

"Yes, thank you for giving me permission to feel, to express my ugly truth, and to just be," Andrea says.

"We will work on softening your tone and speaking your truth in love. But for today, we are here to bring what has sat in the darkness into the light. You have been suffering from what we call domestication," Tara tells her. "You clung to what your parents said or didn't say, and you formed agreements with yourself based on that."

"Agreements?" Andrea asks.

"Agreements are beliefs that become part of our internal system," the tigress explains. "This is how and where you learned to pretend, and to sleepwalk your way through life."

Andrea perks up.

"You were afraid of being rejected and hurt by the people you loved and trusted most. The fear of being rejected is the fear of not being good enough. This is something you carry Andrea."

"I've had my share of rejection," Andrea says.

"You have spent a lifetime unlovable and not good enough. As a result, you tried to please everyone who crossed your path—your parents, your friends, your colleagues, your children, James—even Nana," the tigress says. "But most of all it was the God you believed in; it was that God you tried to please most. And when you felt God had let you down, you began to give your heart away. The light within your soul began to wither."

Andrea's face is grave. "This feels like too much truth. I can't—I just—I feel really alone."

The tigress lets out a resounding roar. "You are not alone, Andrea. You were never alone, and you will never be unless you choose to be."

Then they hear a gentle voice speaking. "I am here, Andrea. I have always been here even when you could not see me. Can you hear me now, can you feel me now, Andrea?"

Andrea sits up straight up in the Adirondack chair. She doesn't want to miss this opportunity of encountering a divine power.

"Yes?" she ventures.

"Feel me, Andrea. Feel my love run through you, feel my spirit within you. I am your light, you are my light, you are the light, we are a team," says what she realizes is the power greater than herself. "You no longer need to be someone you're not; you no longer need to give your heart away in order to be loved. You are enough. Face what is yours in order to heal, so that you can take the steps toward loving and accepting yourself. Toward taking responsibility for your life."

The loving words are almost too much to bear; Andrea begins to cry. She relaxes back into the chair and puts her head on the pillow. She whispers quietly to herself, "You are enough. You deserve to be alive. You do not have to be perfect."

"Your image of perfection is one reason you reject yourself," the voice continues. "It is why you don't accept or love yourself, and it spills into your relationships with yourself and others. It's time to let go of the false beliefs, these agreements that cause you suffering."

Andrea listens with intent, but is having a difficult time absorbing and believing the words.

"It is important for you to understand that these agreements you made with yourself are bred out your life experiences and the trauma you suffered."

"I am beginning to see that now," she says with humility.

"If you want to live a life of authentic joy, you must find the courage to face the burdens you carry. It is then you will regain the power you have so freely given away. The opportunity to transform is yours, Andrea."

"I like that word 'transform,'" she says. "This pillow, it's the message I need for this leg of the journey. In order to transform, change needs to start with me."

"It's time to let go of the hell you have held on to so that transformation can begin," the divine power tells her. "It's time to surrender so you can create anew. I will always be with you Andrea; you need to trust that. You asked once if your answers are hidden away in the box. It is time for you to open the box."

The tigress encourages Andrea to take the wooden box out of her bag. Andrea does so, setting it on the ground at her feet.

When the box meets the earth, it opens for a second time, and out comes a burst of light. Each black heart that was stored in the box daintily floats up into the air.

Andrea's mouth opens.

The black hearts rise up one by one and hover overhead in a dark cloud. Each one is inscribed with one or two words: unworthy, bitch, too fat, too thin, unappreciative, addict, alone. The final heart simply says, "Existence?"

"These are the beliefs you have carried, Andrea," the tigress explains gently. "The ones that have kept you in pain and suffering."

Andrea is overwhelmed. From a distance, she can hear the tigress reminding her to breathe. *I can't breathe,* she thinks. *I can't breathe … it hurts too much.*

"Breathe, pause, and start again, Andrea," the tigress says. Andrea, inhales and counts to seven, holds for seven, and exhales for seven. "You have cobbled together a string of coping strategies, and you use them to stuff most of your emotions. If we are to move forward, you need to face what has been stored in the box. You can't afford to be selective."

"I've dealt with these old beliefs and coping strategies before," Andrea protests. "It's why for years I've been clean and sober from my dependency on drugs. I have not touched a drug since those early days. I do have an occasional glass of wine now and again, but I have never touched a drug. I am done with these old beliefs and coping strategies. They are in the past."

"You know that's not true," the tigress says, "or you would never feel that something's missing now. The truth is that each of these ugly thoughts have been creeping back in over the years, and you have been denying them. In fact, denial is one of them. You are on this journey to learn how to do it differently. And you are being given the tools to help you face more of your truth. But it is a choice, Andrea, one you will need to make. Change starts with you."

"I know," Andrea says quietly. "I understand, and I'm grateful for this journey. But that sure doesn't make it any easier to face my truths."

"Some of the patterns that developed based on the beliefs and agreements you made with yourself are still in play," the tigress explains. "It's the unhealthy patterns that have been inviting these coping mechanisms or coping strategies, if you will, back in."

"Everything you say is true, but it's still so hard to hear."

The tigress makes a soft purring sound. "Look."

Andrea opens her eyes to see a single black heart floating in front of her. It says, "Everything is fine."

"The one false belief you hold most tightly," Tara says, "and it is the one that keeps you stuck. Deep in your heart you know that everything is not fine. This belief only keeps you sleepwalking."

"Yes, I see that."

"These old beliefs keep you in an unhealthy place. The new agreements you create might challenge you, but they will also free you from the burdens you carry. It will take courage and a willingness to look deeper within, and a commitment to let go of these old beliefs and welcome in new ones."

"I have a lot of history with these old beliefs," Andrea says. "They're almost like old friends. But I know I need to let them go."

"There is a second batch of black hearts," Tara tells her. "They are your coping strategies. When you are ready ..."

Andrea starts her breathing sequence.

"That's right," the tigress says.

As she breathes, Andrea envisions herself releasing the pain and living a life full of joy and abundance. When she has exhaled her seventh breath, she opens her green eyes wide and, heart pounding, says, "I'm ready."

The box opens for a third time, and light surges from within followed by more black hearts. They look like shadows, but shadows promise that the light is near. Their messages include perfectionism, anger, denial, judgment, addiction, disassociation, and manipulation.

"I can see I use these as coping strategies when I feel hurt or disappointed," Andrea says slowly. "I've placed a lot of pressure on my Superman as well as my own Lois Lane to be perfect. And when we have not been, there's been a price to pay. We've made each other pay."

Tara the tigress nudges her gently. "None of what is being revealed is meant to make you feel worse than you already feel. It's meant to guide you to a safe place of healing, a place where you can be whole."

"I hear you, but right now all I can see are those awful words on these damn black hearts."

"The journey to wholeness takes willingness and courage," the tigress says. "Know that you can stop at any time, and I can take you home. I'll give you some space to decide."

The tigress moves away, leaving Andrea gazing pensively at the black hearts. She drops to her knees, recites the serenity prayer she learned in detox, and determines to call upon her higher power. She speaks aloud.

"I signed a contract at the beginning of this journey. I made a promise to myself and to Metatron that I would surrender what was not in my control, what keeps me sleepwalking, and what keeps me stuck."

A gentle wind blows through.

"I made a promise to my fourteen-year-old self to stop accepting that 'everything is fine,' but I've struggled with that. I need your help."

She can feel the tigress quietly watching.

"Today, I feel more deserving of this healing, no matter how painful it might be," she says into the breeze. "I'm ready and I'm grateful. For you, higher power, and for the deer, and for the tigress, and for Metatron. I feel your love, their love, running through me. I no longer want to reject that love. I don't want to abandon myself any longer."

Her higher power whispers, "You are loved, Andrea. I will not reject you. I will never abandon you, and at no time will you ever be alone, sweet child of mine."

The tigress closes her eyes and takes a deep breath. "That's right, Andrea, you will never be rejected or feel alone ever again. And soon you will meet two new guides to help you continue your exploration."

The tigress shows Andrea one last heart. It is yellow. Andrea looks up with a question in her eyes.

"It represents forgiveness," Tara says. "You are on a path toward that forgiveness. And there you will begin to find your true self, as well as your destiny. Are you ready?"

"I am," Andrea says. "I have to be. No—I want to be."

Tara kneels before her. "Then jump on—and don't forget the box."

"It's empty, isn't it?"

"Go ahead and put it in your bag. Here we go!"

With that, they soar off into the sky into the golden arms of the sun. As they coast along, the instrumental "We Can Begin" by C. Lanzbom plays on.

On this journey of life,
spirituality is the very sand which we travel.
—ROBERT W. CHISM

Reflections for This Chapter

Integrate your thoughts by going through these activities now or coming back to them later. I invite you to listen to "We Can Begin," by C. Lanzbom as you do so. It's a beautiful piece of instrumental music.

Can you think of any old beliefs or perspectives you're holding onto? Or can you think of any agreements you made with yourself when you were young, ones you still carry today?

Example: My first-grade teacher called me out in front of the class after I made a mistake on the assignment. I was only five years old, and I took on the belief that I was stupid. I am grateful I've been able to let that shame and humiliation go and stand tall in the truth that I'm not stupid. I just made a mistake.

I encourage you to look at your list of old beliefs, perspectives, or agreements you made with yourself and choose one or two you're ready to release. Take the time you need to ponder and, if so led, journal about the things you carry and how they have affected or still are affecting your life today.

Can you think of a time when you just didn't want to face the truth about yourself or a particular circumstance? If yes, journal about your feelings around what holds you back. Then write that lie on a piece of paper.

Next, visualize yourself telling yourself that this is a lie and that it's time to let it go. Do this as many times as you need to in order to be willing to surrender it. Then journal about your experience.

Last, take that piece of paper and perform your own ritual. You can burn the piece of paper outside in a safe, contained space, allowing the ashes to become one with the earth. Or you can tear it up, flush it down the toilet, and let it become one with the element of water. You choose! My hope is that it provides cleansing and healing.

One of the most courageous decisions you'll ever make is to finally let go of what is hurting your heart and soul.
—BRIGITTE NICOLE

CHAPTER 12

Celebrate the Goddess Within

The truth will set you free, but first it will piss you off.
—GLORIA STEINEM

These rooms and their four walls
So foreign yet so familiar
These rooms and their four walls
Filled with pain, suffering, anger, frustration, and tears
These rooms and their four walls
Filled with healing, freedom, calmness, satisfaction, and laughter
These rooms and their four walls
Where truth is spoken, where acceptance leads to change,
where self-love and humility begin.
These rooms and their four walls
What would these rooms and their four walls say?
These rooms and their four walls would say celebrating the
Goddess within is priceless

The tigress and Andrea are floating above a community building whose French doors open outward, revealing a large room with metal chairs set in a circle. Three of the walls are covered with a base of a soft Navajo white. The fourth wall has a mural on it that looks like a meadow, very much like the one Andrea describes as her sacred place. There in the center of the mural stands a sturdy, strong, glorious oak tree surrounded by lush green grass and bundles of yellow, white, purple, and pink flowers. The vibrant blue sky, puffy white clouds, and rays of sunshine complete the scene which helps the room to feel welcoming.

"Where are we? Andrea whispers.

"We are at a women's meeting taking place in the future," Tara says. "Soon, this room will fill with women who all struggle with the feeling that something is missing. This meeting is held once a week in a community building near your home."

"But—what if someone I know sees me, what if I recognize someone?"

"This is the future," the tigress repeats firmly.

The women begin to arrive. There are women from all walks of life and of all ages, from women in their twenties on up through women in their seventies and eighties. There are women from different ethnicities, cultures, and lifestyles.

"They share a very sacred spiritual journey," Tara notes. "Each of them seeks the goddess within. Shh, the meeting is about to begin."

A woman at the front of the room who appears to be the leader introduces herself, then asks another woman to read what she calls "the opening passage." The other does so, slowly and carefully, pronouncing every word clearly. Andrea can identify newcomers by their nervousness and intensity. Like her own. The veterans, on the other hand, listen with a sense of calm.

The woman reading the opening passage emphasizes that this meeting is a safe place of fellowship for women whose common purpose is to seek and celebrate the goddess within. She closes with a statement about being open to growing spiritually and to creating loving and healthy relationships.

Andrea is quiet, feeling the words resonate. Already she feels at home.

The leader explains that they will read three passages. The first passage begins, "Today, I am seeking the goddess within. At times I feel powerless, but today I seek empowerment." She reads a few more sentences and then passes the book to the woman next to her, who finishes reading the passage aloud.

The book is then passed to the next woman, who read, "Today, I am seeking the goddess within. I seek guidance to set me free from negative thoughts and feelings of insanity." She continues for a few more sentences and passes the book to the next person, who reads and passes it to the one after that until the second passage is complete.

The reading continues with the third passage: "Today, I am seeking the goddess within. Sometimes I look up to the sky for guidance. Sometimes I seek the elements and spirit animals. Sometimes I meditate and sometimes I pray. Most times I ask a divine power to show me what I need to see as I travel the path to find the goddess within."

Many of the women nod in agreement.

The reader ends with, "I know I cannot do this alone, so I ask for help from a power greater than myself, a divine power, one within myself and of my own understanding."

The words echo inside Andrea as she remembers the day Metatron talked to her about a power greater than herself. He had emphasized the importance of envisioning and connecting to a higher power of her understanding.

Andrea can feel that familiar lump in her throat. "There's something very comforting about this meeting," she tells Tara. "I think I want to find the goddess within."

"And you can, Andrea, and you will," the tigress responds.

"These women seem to feel a lot of freedom to ask for help, for guidance, for comfort. I'm scared though. I'm scared to seek the goddess within. What if I don't have one? What if she's crazy?"

"These what-ifs can be daunting," the tigress agrees.

"But this meeting shows me that it's okay to ask for support and guidance. I'm not alone, and can seek out likeminded people in my world."

"You can," says the tigress. "Shh, it's time for open sharing."

A tall woman stands in front of her chair in the circle. "Hi, my name is Rae, and I am seeking the goddess within. I would like to share."

"Hello, Rae," the women respond.

Rae says, "I love the idea of seeking the goddess, but I get caught up in my thoughts at times. Sometimes I tell myself 'I can't' when what it really comes down to is that I won't. I know that comes from a place of resistance or fear. Maybe both."

There is a slight murmur of agreement from the circle.

"I have worked at the same place in the same location for over thirty years," Rae continues. "I've felt safe in my routines. But recently, I found out there are going to be some changes at work, and that feels scary to me. I wonder what keeps this goddess from seeking and accepting change, especially big change?"

Andrea can see the women nodding their heads.

"On another note, I've been making some very positive changes since attending this meeting," Rae adds. "As I embrace

140

the idea of my body being a temple, I've started eating better. I'm making healthier meals at home."

There are smiles from the women in the circle.

"I've also taken up drawing. Sometimes I feel I'm not very good, but I have fun," Rae says. "And I'm writing poetry again, which I really love. These meetings have given me the courage and strength to take these small steps."

The women smile in support.

Rae continues. "It makes me wonder why I haven't taken more risks, why I haven't sought out more adventure and fun. I've always wanted to visit Puerto Rico, for example. What if I never get to go?"

Andrea shakes her head. She knows exactly how Rae feels.

Rae ends her share by placing her hand over her heart and making a promise to herself. She says, "As I continue to seek the goddess within, I will no longer use excuses about being too tired, or too busy, or too afraid, or too old. I will make every effort to leave the what-ifs behind."

Andrea sits up a little straighter.

"Today, I am making myself a promise," Rae says, "and that is to continue honoring my Inner Goddess by exploring my discomfort with change and taking risks. I will continue to ask my Inner Goddess what she wants and needs. Maybe one day I will even go to Puerto Rico, I think I would love it there. I will need some accountability from you all as I travel down this path of celebrating my Inner Goddess. Thank you for letting me share."

Andrea sighs heavily. "I didn't stay in the same job for thirty years, but I've stayed in an unhealthy marriage for thirty years."

The tigress is quiet, waiting.

"I don't remember the last time I asked myself what I really want or need. Maybe it's time for me to seek the goddess within. Maybe it's time to start asking her some questions."

Another woman introduces herself. "Hello, my name is Ruthie, and I too am seeking the goddess within."

"Hello, Ruthie," the women respond.

"For the past few years, I've been feeling disconnected from my relationships, including the one with myself. I've been feeling sad and lonely, and I've been closing myself off. It's like I'm losing parts of me, especially at work. And each loss is really wearing me down."

Andrea sees some of the women shifting in their chairs in discomfort.

Ruthie continues, "I plan to continue to attend these meetings on a more regular basis so I can learn to honor myself and the goddess within. If I can't honor and respect myself, how can I expect to receive that from others?

"Interesting!" Andrea says.

"I know that the goddess within is my higher power, a power greater than myself," Ruthie says. "At first I wasn't sure how to connect to her, but I love to walk in the woods, or on the beach, and when I walk, I do feel a presence. Perhaps that's my Inner Goddess, my higher power, trying to connect with me."

"Yes!" Andrea yells out, then winces. "Sorry," she says to the tigress.

"I am also practicing breathing and meditation exercises, and that helps me be more present. I'm exercising more, I'm participating in online group discussions, and I'm volunteering at a place where I can be creative and inventive. I feel like I'm on the road to reclaiming myself, and in that I am finding joy. Thank you for letting me share." Ruthie sits down.

Andrea bows her head. "I've lost myself along the way, just like Ruthie. I, too, need direction and guidance to find my way back to myself. I see myself in Ruthie. I want to be joyful again."

The meeting continues as more women share their experience, strength, and hope. Then the leader closes the meeting with a meditation and words of affirmation. She reminds the women to visit the tree if they feel so led before they go.

Andrea looks over at the tree painted into the wall mural and sees a box nearby filled with what look like little hearts. "No! It can't be!"

Just then the tigress tells Andrea to hold on, and they take off, soaring through the atmosphere. Andrea is quiet in her thoughts. She's thinking about this goddess within.

"I see the opportunity to explore my Inner Goddess if I continue down this path," she says. "But if I choose to forgo the rest of the journey, I risk falling back into my ordinary world where the opportunities for me to grow are few and far between."

The tigress says, "You are right where you are supposed to be," Andrea. "Take this time to reflect upon this dream, this journey thus far, and all it has to offer. Sit back and enjoy the rest of this ride. You will be home soon enough."

Andrea sits back and relaxes as she absorbs all of creation and its beauty. She and the tigress sail through the open skies, embracing the softness of the wind, the warmth of the sun, and the slight mist from the clouds. Andrea finds herself thinking deeply about her life in her awake world where she feels powerless so much of the time and struggles with that incessant feeling that something's missing.

"I already miss Rae and Ruthie," she says, surprised. "I feel like I've known them for a lifetime. It's like they and I are part of a sisterhood that seeks the goddess within."

The song "Sentimental Journey" by Hot Sisters begins to play quietly throughout the skyway. Andrea is engulfed in the beauty of the pastels that make up the skyway. She realizes that the skyway never gets dark, perhaps because it represents an ever-growing dream.

The greatest healing therapy is friendship and love.
—HUBERT H. HUMPHREY, JR.

CHAPTER 13

Relationship Row

There is no love without forgiveness,
and there is no forgiveness without love.
—BRYANT H. MCGILL

The tigress and Andrea soar through the sky, enjoying the scenery above, below, and in between. As they near their destination, the tigress speaks up.

"Our family relationships shape all the rest, Andrea. And you have a very complex family system. We need to explore more before you can fully heal. Remember, forgiveness is one of our goals. Continuing to develop your Inner Goddess is another. There is much more to learn in this place called Relationship Row."

"Can you tell me more about what I can expect?"

"You will have the opportunity to visit four of five houses on Relationship Row. The fifth, well, you'll see. You will see the parts of yourself that adopted unhealthy beliefs and perspectives, and how those defined all your future relationships.

"Like what?"

The tigress banks into a turn, passing a cloud. "Believing that everyone is inherently untrustworthy, for one. That plays a part in how you relate to yourself and others even today."

"How do I fix it?"

"We are not here to fix you; you are not damaged goods," Tara says mildly. "But as you reflect, explore, and discover, you'll have a clearer understanding of what happened to you and why you react and respond the way you do."

"That sounds like a lot," Andrea says.

"Together we can create a different story, a better story," Tara says. "One that does not fix, but instead one that blossoms. In that there will be softening, an acceptance, forgiveness, and relief."

"I want to mend my relationships, I do. But I've always struggled with allowing people to make mistakes and grow. I can be very unforgiving at times."

"You can be," the tigress says.

"I tend to hold grudges against those who've wronged me. I hold grudges against myself and have trouble accepting me as I am. I hold the biggest grudge against this power greater than myself, and I feel ashamed."

The tigress asks, "How so?"

"I know this power greater than myself has me exactly where I need to be, and it pisses me off. Damn it, what's holding me back from fully committing to it?"

"Trust," the tigress says simply. "When you can trust, then you will be able to surrender. Relationships are where we get to practice as we take our recovery show on the road. It's time to trust."

"Something happened back in the meeting room, something I haven't felt before. Could it be higher power at work?"

"It could," the tigress says.

"I feel as if I am growing a deeper connection with this power greater than myself even though I'm scared."

"You are being shown truth," the tigress observes. "It is what you do with that truth that matters."

Andrea reminds herself to stay present and enjoy the ride. Looking down from the skyway, she sees a scattering of tiny flowers through rolling, green hills. She sees cacti and other exotic plants and trees that look somehow right at home on the golden hills and in the mountains. She sees fruits, berries, cacao beans, and nuts available for all who wish to partake.

"Breathtaking," she murmurs.

The landing is bumpier than she expects. *I hope that's not an omen,* Andrea thinks. She sees a sign—Relationship Row—and a small row of houses. There are four of them—plus a fifth one that appears to still be under construction.

Andrea and the tigress make their way to the first house, which bears a sign that says "Family." It's a light gray two-story with white trim. Andrea feels a pang in her heart and a lump in her throat—this house looks a lot like the house on Reality Road. Through the windows, she can see an open kitchen with its laminate cabinets and countertops and a very bold tile backsplash. The avocado green appliances and cane-printed wallpaper were very stylish for the times.

"Look at all the fun cooking tools and utensils," Andrea says. |Someone likes to cook."

"Someone does," the tigress agrees.

Heading around to the backyard, Andrea sees a trampoline, batting cages, and a net for baseballs and softballs. There are striking planters and brightly colored ceramic pots filled with gorgeous, brilliant flowers placed strategically about. She spots pansies, morning glories, aloe, and other succulents. *Nana,* she thinks to herself.

"Can I go in?" she asks.

"Let's get a feel for each house on Relationship Row before you go in," the tigress says.

The second house has a sign that says, "Ben and Sophia: The Children." The house is blue with white trim, and its yard is framed by a driftwood fence. The front yard is thick with a ground cover studded with yellow flowers.

"Lantana," Andrea says. "Easy to grow."

"You like to garden," Tara observes.

"I used to spend a lot of time planting and gardening with Nana. I miss those days." Andrea takes in all the colors, the sense of warmth, comfort, and play. "This place reminds me of the beach house we used to rent when the kids were young. In fact, we rented one just like it a few months ago."

"So you did," the tigress says.

"That was the last time we were all together," Andrea says.

The tigress leads her to the next house, whose sign says "James."

"This can't be right," Andrea says. "Last time I saw James we were in our kitchen talking things out. Everything was fine."

"You will understand in good time."

The house is a tiny, ill-kept bungalow with peeling tan paint and rusted security bars on the windows. In the side yard stands a large tree, but its arms are thrown up not in invitation but in warning. The lawn has been neglected, and the weedy grass is pocked with gopher holes.

"I don't like the feel of this place," Andrea says. "What's happened to me and James? Tell me, please, did we—I can't—"

"I know this is difficult," the tigress says, "but this visit to Relationship Row is necessary to your healing."

They move on to the fourth house. "Wait, it's my house— our house," Andrea says. "This is where James and I live."

She takes in the familiar palm trees in the front yard and, as they walk around to the back, her pool, firepit, and comfy patio furniture. At the center of the backyard stands the giant oak. Andrea feels a little better just looking at it, but she also can't help but feel something's off.

"It looks like my house," she tells the tigress, "but it also feels empty, unoccupied. Like something's missing." She hears herself and covers her mouth with her hand. "I've always taken a lot of pride in this house. I've spent so much time decorating it, furnishing it, making sure everything is just so. That's the problem, isn't it? I've been paying more attention to material things than people."

"That is why we are here Andrea, to build awareness and to make the changes we are able to make. Be patient, dear one."

"Before we go any further, I'd like to go sit under that California oak," Andrea says. "I miss my tree and the grass between my toes. May I?"

"Of course."

Andrea moves toward the oak and its tree swing. "Nothing feels the same, yet everything feels familiar," she says. Mixed emotions fill the space, joy, and misery all at once. "I need to sit down; I need to practice breathing."

She sits on the swing and begins her breathing exercise, falling, as she does so, into a place of greater calm. She looks up into the thick branches of the tree and notices that the leaves have been stripped by the Santa Ana winds, which make it easier to see the perfectly round shape of the sun.

"We have one more house to see," the tigress tells her.

Andrea rises, and together they walked to the fifth house. It's nothing more than a framed-in shell. Nothing feels certain; it's like standing on shaky ground. At the front, held in by nothing more than framing, is a green door and sign that reads, "Knocking on Heaven's Door."

Andrea drifts toward the door, where she senses a distinct vibration. She reaches out to the knob but finds it locked. *That's strange,* she thinks. *There are no walls so we could actually walk around the door if we wanted.*

The tigress interrupts her thoughts. "Not really, we cannot pass into the house. Its energy will not allow us to go further."

"Why is the door green?" Andrea asks.

"In many cultures, the color green stands for growth, balance, and renewal," the tigress tells her. "Here, it represents an opportunity to find what is missing, to be transformed. By the time we end our visit to Relationship Row, you will be given a choice. And if you choose to trust, then you will be able to walk through the green door."

Andrea likes the idea of being transformed. "What kind of transformation?"

"All of the rituals you have been learning about will be available to you. You will spend time listening to music, dancing, and practicing yoga. You will have an opportunity to meditate, send intentions, or pray. The purpose of these rituals is renewal—so that you can begin to send your light out into the world again."

"What if I can't face the truth?" Andrea asks. "What if I can't fully trust? What if I revert back to believing everything is fine? Then what?"

"If you choose to go home, you will most likely continue to feel as if something is missing and that you are alone in your thoughts, actions, and choices," Tara says. "You will continue to sleepwalk as if nothing has happened, and you will cling to the belief that everything is fine."

Andrea frowns.

"You will remember this time, and it will remain precious," Tara says. "But you will have made the choice not to wake up. This is your final crossroads. Your choice. To wake up and move forward, or stay asleep and in denial."

"I wish I could just wave a magic wand and fix it," Andrea says.

"You are not broken, Andrea, and we are not here to fix you," Tara says. "If you choose this enlightened path, you will be preparing yourself to function from a higher level of consciousness, from your higher self. There you will find healing, balance, wisdom, harmony, calm, and tranquility."

"Sounds almost too good to be true."

"Life won't be perfect; you will have your challenges. But you will have new beliefs, perspectives, and tools to rely on."

Andrea looks at the green door and ponders what it really means: to walk through it is to embrace trust and acceptance.

Together, she and the tigress make their way to a small park across the street where there are a few wooden benches. Andrea sits and takes out her travel journal. She writes, "Forgiveness and love are key" at the top of a blank page, and her thoughts pour forth from there.

The tigress finds a comfy spot and begins to groom.

Andrea gazes across the street at the houses on Relationship Row and then looks back down at her journal. "I am in an ever-growing dream," she writes. The song "My House" by Flo Rida plays.

A healthy relationship, whether it's romantic,
brotherly, friendly, is when each person is
allowed room to grow, unjudged, and still loved.
—MAMA ZARA

Reflections for This Chapter

Integrate your thoughts by going through these activities now or coming back to them later. I invite you to listen to the song "My House" by Flo Rida. It's a catchy little tune that complements the themes.

When you read the dictionary definition for relationships what are your thoughts? How do you define the term relationships?

On a scale from 1–10, with one being the lowest and ten being the highest, how would you rate your relationships with the following and what would you like to see change if anything?

Spouse, Partner, or Significant Other
Parents
Siblings
Other Family Members
Friends
Colleagues
Pets
Money

What do you desire for your relationships? If you'd like for something to be different, think of one positive step you can take today in order to create a desirable change.

CHAPTER 14

Family Relationships

Today I will begin the process of setting myself free from any
self-defeating beliefs and perspectives my parents placed upon
me. I will strive to heal those places in me by setting appropriate
boundaries and by establishing new beliefs and perspectives.
I will no longer give my power away or be governed by someone
else's beliefs. I will take responsibility for what is mine and leave
the rest behind. Today, I desire healthy relationships.
—SUSAN M. TUTTLE

Andrea and Tara are standing before the gray and white house on Relationship Row. The one that looks like the house she grew up in.

She sighs.

"I understand your apprehension," the tigress says. "But this is how you will set yourself free. We will take a look at your relationship with each member of your immediate family, and those memories, no matter how painful, will become lessons."

"Will you be with me each step of the way?"

"Yes, Andrea, I will."

"This time, we will sit on the front porch and witness your experiences through the lens of this kaleidoscope."

An enormous celestial kaleidoscope made of lustrous brass appears overhead, lens pointing toward them.

"I used to love these as a child," Andrea says.

The tigress grins. "The symmetry of the patterns within represents harmony and balance. But they also are symbols of change and growth. What better way to visit this gray and white house and its inhabitants on Relationship Row?"

Andrea and the tigress climb up the stairs and sit on the porch swing, which seems remarkably like the one she used as a child. The swaying motion is peaceful and reminds Andrea of the lull of the ocean. She notices that she is already practicing her circular breathing pattern. Free of noise and distractions, her mind empties into pure silence and peace.

"We are going back to the day you were packing for college," Tara says. "Let's see what visualization the kaleidoscope provides. Look up, and in."

Mom

Together they look up and into the kaleidoscope's lens. Inside, a myriad of shapes and colors forms a pleasing geometric design. The kaleidoscope turns, seemingly of its own volition, and a mandala configuration appears in an array of vibrant colors in which red stands out. *Anger?* Andrea wonders.

As they watch, blue geometric shapes begin to take form, settling into a field of raindrops that look something like tears.

"'A heart filled with anger has no room for love,'" the tigress says. "I heard that from one of your kind, Joan Lunden, years ago."

Andrea thinks about those words—love and anger—and how the color red is associated with both.

"I want you to remember this because anything that comes out of your mother's mouth is coming from her angry heart," Tara continues. "Your mother tried, but her anger kept her from giving and receiving love. So no matter what hurtful words you may hear again today, know that none of it is a reflection of you. It is a reflection of her pain."

"I will try my best to take in what I need to hear so that I can heal and move forward," Andrea says.

Inside the swirl of the kaleidoscope, the scene clears to show Andrea's mom opening her daughter's bedroom door. Even before she speaks, her body language and facial expression say it all. Andrea resists her own wave of anger as she sees her mother's melodramatic pout, the way she's clutching at her chest. "If you go," her mother says, "I'll be so lonely! I just don't know how I will be able to go on."

"Ugh," Andrea says in disgust. "I've felt guilty about leaving my family behind, as she liked to put it, for decades."

Inside the bedroom, seventeen-year-old Andrea is standing amidst clothes and toiletries strewn across the floor. Shoes and boots predominate. Nana is there, too, filling boxes, whistling, and stopping frequently to reminisce. She reminds teenage Andrea to never forget to tend her inner garden, that her body is her temple, that she is a bearer of light, and to never stop shining the light. Present-day Andrea, watching, can now see that her nana's chatter was intended to distract her from her mother's theatrics.

Teenage Andrea is sweating profusely as she packs the remainder of her belongings. She calls out to the living room, where her dad is reading. "Dorm check-in is at 9 a.m., Dad, don't forget."

"Got it," her dad calls back.

"I am not supportive of this one bit," Andrea's mother says, seething in the doorway.

"What a surprise." Teenage Andrea rolls her eyes.

Nana fusses with a suitcase lock. "Hush now," she says. "This should be an exciting time."

Her mother's tormented expression turns frosty. "I want you to know, Andrea, that I always loved you. It was you who did not love me."

Teenage Andrea's face flushes. "Stop, Mom, just stop!" she yells in frustration. "If I hear about you losing another child one more time I ..."

Andrea's mother stiffens.

"All these years, all these years you hid out in your room hiding behind your alcohol and your pain," seventeen-year-old Andrea says. "All the years you ignored me. I worked so hard at trying to make you happy, trying to get you to become interested in me, interested in anything but your own suffering."

Now it is her mother's turn to roll her eyes.

"All these years I spent endless hours trying to get you to laugh, to help you find joy, to notice me. And yet nothing changed—you never changed. I wasted all these years on you!" young Andrea cries out.

Present-day Andrea watches as her teen self sobs and gasps for breath while her mother never once acknowledges her words. "I remember saying there was no way in hell I was going to let that woman guilt me, not that day, not ever," she says. "Then I snapped. I let myself become unhinged."

"Do you remember what you were thinking then?" the tigress says.

"I was thinking she was going to win," she quietly whispers.

In the kaleidoscope, Andrea's dad hears the commotion

and picks himself up from the chair. As he walks toward the hallway, he can hear the heated conversation escalating. But when he gets to teenage Andrea's bedroom doorway, he freezes. He stands apart, silent, watching as if from a distance.

"I needed his support and love in that moment, and he was unable to provide it," present-day Andrea says.

She watches Nana order her parents to leave. "Out, both of you!" Nana hollers, her face flushed and her body shaking. "This is Andrea's time, and you are no longer welcome in this room, out!"

Her parents leave, but teenage Andrea can't settle down. She helps Nana gather her composure then marches out of her room to finish what was started.

"I spent years watching my mother self-destruct," present-day Andrea says. "There was no way I was going to let her take me down on this day. No way I was going to let her win."

In the living room, teenage Andrea is confronting her mother. "How dare you, how dare you try and make me feel guilty for wanting to leave this Godforsaken place!" Accusations and insults begin to fly; the situation grows increasingly out of control.

"I will not be guilted into staying here, nor will I take on the responsibility for your loneliness or your life," teen Andrea snaps. "You never said thank you for all the times I tried to help you. You've never noticed all I do around here or praised me for being a good student. You don't seem to care that I'm a successful athlete. You don't even know all the community service work I do!"

Her mother throws up her hands as if helpless.

"You act like I don't even exist, so why on God's Earth would you miss me?" teen Andrea cries out. "Why?"

Andrea's mother is silent and unresponsive, something present-day Andrea now recognizes as manipulative.

Seventeen-year-old Andrea looks her mother straight in the eye and tells her, "I will not let your silence control me. I am going to college. I need a fresh start, and I am going to leave this house of horrors behind. And you, you are going to have to accept that."

Her mother doesn't even flinch. Her expression is impassive, almost bored.

This seems to fuel teenage Andrea's rage. "You are so self-absorbed you make me sick. Yes, I'm leaving. I'm leaving and I'm never coming back!"

Present-day Andrea begins to hyperventilate. She knows this scene isn't over yet, and she remembers what comes next.

Inside the kaleidoscope, the colors and shapes begin to change as the scene continues to unfold. There's another mandala forming, but this time there are little black poisonous arrows piercing the little red hearts.

"You selfish little bitch. Go, you little bitch," Andrea's mother spews. "I never loved you anyway—certainly not the way I loved your brother. Andrew is my blood, my heart, and my soul. He was the real angel given to me by God, not you."

Teen Andrea's mouth drops open. Watching, present-day Andrea's mouth does too.

"You will never be enough to make up for the pain I feel over the loss of your brother. You will never replace him. Go, you selfish bitch, go," her mother says.

Teenage Andrea flushes with anger and shame. Her mouth moves soundlessly, lips trembling.

"How do I ever forgive that?" adult Andrea asks. "How? Who talks to their child that way? Who tells their child she isn't loved as much as her dead sibling? Who does that?"

In the eye of the kaleidoscope, Andrea's mother seems to belatedly collect herself. "But ... that doesn't mean I don't love you at all," she says faintly. "I do love you. I love you the only way I know how, from a distance."

Teenage Andrea looks wary.

"I'm sorry, Andrea. I love you, but the loss of Andrew has been ... I did the best I could. You just can't go. You're all I have left ... I need you to stay."

"The best you could," teenage Andrea sneers. "That was the best you could do?"

Andrea's mother looks blank.

"You are quite the manipulator, Mom. You shut down, you use the silent treatment as a punishment, you reject me at every opportunity, you spew hateful words, and suddenly you're sorry? This is your best? This is how you show love?"

Her mother is silent.

"I know why you don't love me the way you loved Andrew, it's because I remind you of your failures," teen Andrea seethes. "I remind you of what you wanted so bad and couldn't have. I remind you of your own guilt over Andrew's death."

"Shut up, shut up!" her mother yells.

"You can't stand the sight of me because it just reminds you that he's gone," teenage Andrea persists. "And your idea of grieving is to blame everyone else and turn to the bottle. You're a coward, Mother. You're mean and hateful, and you can't face the truth about yourself, so you take it out on me and everyone around you."

Her mother remains still, but tears are rolling down her cheeks.

"I can never be enough for you because when you look at me, you wish it was me that had died instead of Andrew," teenage Andrea hisses.

"Shut up, shut up, you bitch!" her mother screams.

Seventeen-year-old Andrea raises her hands. "I needed you! I needed a mother, and you treated me like I didn't exist. That's not love, Mother, that's—"

"Abuse," whispers adult Andrea. "How do I ever forgive her?"

"You can and you will," the tigress says. "In time."

And so, for the second time, they witness Andrea's mother grasping her chest with one hand and placing the other on her forehead, crying brokenly. But this time, teenage Andrea's face falls in defeat. She no longer wants to fight this fight with her mother, at least not in this moment. She is exhausted and she gives in.

"You win, damn you, you win. I'll stay."

"I remember telling her that," Andrea says to the tigress. "And when I did, everything felt very dark, like the angel of death was around me. This was a defining moment for me."

"This is when you decided you were responsible for your mother's happiness," the tigress says.

"I believed that she would kill herself if I went to college, and I couldn't live with that. So I gave up my own dreams, knowing I would be the one dying inside," she says.

"No one should have to carry that kind of burden, Andrea," Tara says.

"That was supposed to be one of the happiest and most exciting days of my life, and it turned out to be one of the saddest. I've never talked about what really happened on that day. Thank you for sharing it with me."

The kaleidoscope vanishes, leaving Andrea and the tigress on the porch swing.

"The day my brother died, the day I lost both my mother and brother, was the day when I had to start proving my right to exist," Andrea says. "My teenage self didn't have a chance."

"What would you tell her if she were here, your younger self?" the tigress asks.

"I would say, 'I am so deeply sorry for not protecting you. I'm sorry for not respecting your need to be seen, understood, and valued. I'm sorry you felt you had to shut your emotions down. You have a voice, and you have the right to use it.'"

"What have you discovered from this memory?" the tigress asks.

"I can see how my mother's angry heart had no room for love. But I thought it was my fault she stopped loving me. So I abandoned myself and silenced my voice," Andrea says. "When my brother died and I lost my mother, a part of me died too."

The tigress nods.

"To this day when I feel threatened, manipulated, shamed, or blamed, I become small. I lose my ability to speak. I put my needs and wants aside, and I disappear. I dismiss the emotional part of myself and tell myself everything is fine."

The two sit together, swaying in the porch swing.

"I gave my light away to people who'd lost theirs, and then felt defeated when they wouldn't or couldn't embrace it. I can see that now," Andrea says. "I can see how I gave my power, love, and light away then and how I still do that now. I only wanted to receive and feel their love. I only wanted to be loved, and I still desire that now."

The tigress nudges her gently. "It is you who holds the light, Andrea. You had it all along, but you gave it away. Now it is time to reclaim it."

"How?"

"You must surrender your will, Andrea, your ego. You must allow the gifts from each of your guides in. Metatron's light, love, and guidance, the mother deer and her fawn's power of

161

nurturing and care, the wisdom and strength I carry, you need to allow all of this in. But most of all, you must forgive yourself so you can begin to love yourself again. So that your light can return to your soul."

"I don't know if I can do any of that yet," Andrea says. "What I do see is that when I tuck away all of my trauma, pain, shame, and guilt in my wooden box, I only hurt myself. I'm feeling discomfort for a reason, and I need to lean into what that means, so I can let it all go and heal."

The tigress smiles.

Andrea feels somewhat more grounded and confident to move forward. "Who's next?"

"Your dad," the tigress says. "Are you ready?"

Dad

Andrea crosses the porch and looks up to where the kaleidoscope has reappeared. Inside, the colors are swirling and twirling, with blues representing sadness, greens representing envy, and yellow representing sunshine. The patterns form and reform. In the center of them, Andrea's father sits in his brown leather recliner. It is positioned to command the living room, but he is silent behind his newspaper.

"That pissed me off and broke my heart all at the same time," Andrea says. "I wanted to light a fire under his ass as he sat there in silence day after day."

Then the kaleidoscope shifts, moving forward a few minutes to young Andrea in room, crying. There is a knock at her door.

"Can I come in?" says Andrea's father from the hallway.

"This is a good part," present-day Andrea whispers.

The door opens slowly. Andrea's dad is obviously nervous, yet he makes his way to her bed and sits down. He hugs teenage Andrea, and they begin to have a murmured conversation. Although Andrea can't hear it word for word, she remembers the hope her father extended that day.

"I found out later that Nana read him and Mom the riot act," she says. "I don't know what she said, but it finally got through to him."

"Andrea," her father says to her younger self, "you are going to college tomorrow, so you need to finish packing. We will leave as scheduled. I will help you pack what we can in the car this evening so we can get you there by nine as planned. Any questions?"

Young Andrea is in awe. The kaleidoscope turns as she finishes packing, sleeps peacefully, and wakes up to the sun shining through her blinds. Her room is empty, and the car is packed and ready to go.

One more turn of the kaleidoscope and teenage Andrea is ready to say her goodbyes. When Nana hugs her, she slips a picture of them both into teenage Andrea's pocket. Andrea smiles, blows her a kiss, and then turns without looking back. Her mother is nowhere to be seen.

The kaleidoscope shifts again, pink and white brightening the colored pattern. Andrea and her dad are unpacking the car, and their energy is high. It's move-in day. Parents and students are moving about in combined chaos and progress. Finally, Andrea's room is all set up. It is awash in pink, yellow, and white.

"I love this room," teen Andrea says with glee.

The scene shifts to a restaurant. Andrea and her dad at lunch. There are big smiles, gentle touches, some shrugs of the shoulders, but most of all a sense of peace. Andrea and her dad talk about her classes, the food plan, budgeting, softball, parties, and, of course, boys.

It was the perfect day, present-day Andrea remembers. *But we never spoke about what happened the day before. It was as if it had never happened.* She watches as her father leaves the campus, but not before he gives teenage Andrea a huge bear hug. He drives away, leaving teen Andrea with tears in her eyes. Teen Andrea wipes them away, gathers her composure, and heads back to her room where her roommates await.

"Ready?" They say in unison.

"One final detail," teen Andrea says. She picks up the picture Nana gave her and places it by her bedside.

Present-day Andrea winces. "I look so happy. But not even three years later, I was in a psych hospital detox unit."

"You took the loss of Nana very hard," the tigress says. "I believe she was your angel."

"She was."

Together they look up and into the kaleidoscope where the pieces of colored glass are coming together to form tiny lanterns, hundreds of them, all beaming light. As the kaleidoscope rotates, the lanterns radiate a white light from their center from them, guiding them back to Andrea's bedroom in the house where she grew up.

"Right back where I started, after rehab," Andrea says. "I thank God every day that I got a second chance."

"You thank who?" the tigress raises a furry eyebrow.

"I know, I know."

In the eye of the kaleidoscope, there's a knock on teenage Andrea's bedroom door. Her father enters. He's quiet, as always, but this time, it seems to present-day Andrea, there's something different about him. He exercises confidence and humility. He sits on her bed just like he did the day before she left for college and asks, "How are you doing, honey? And please don't tell me everything is fine. I no longer use that phrase, and I know you and Nana dismissed it years ago."

Present-day Andrea raises an eyebrow, and the tigress twitches her nose.

"I'm okay, Dad," young Andrea says.

Her father is twiddling his thumbs, something present-day Andrea remembers he always did when nervous, but she can also see that he has positioned himself so that he can have direct eye contact. "I should have said what I am about to say the day you left for college, Andrea, and I didn't."

Young Andrea looks uncomfortable but waits for what's next.

Her father's head is cast down, but he raises his eyes to meet hers. "Okay. I ..." his voice is faint.

"I can barely hear you, Dad," Andrea's twenty-year-old self says.

"I ... I ... I am so sorry for all the grief and pain I've caused you and our family, Andrea. I am sorry for not being there for you when you needed me most. I am sorry for not handling the death of your brother well. I abandoned you then. I am sorry for letting you take on responsibility for managing your mother. She was and is my responsibility, not yours."

Twenty-year-old Andrea gently touches her father's hand.

"But most of all, I'm sorry for not being available to you. For not telling you each and every day how much you are valued and loved."

"Do you hear him taking responsibility?" the tigress asks.

"Yes." Present-day Andrea has tears in her eyes. "Why didn't I use what he said to help myself then?"

"You did absorb and accept his apology," the tigress says. "And for a while you stayed the course and practiced recovery. Let's see how the rest of this unfolds."

Andrea's father looks at his hands. "Like you, I learned early on to avoid my feelings. I never acknowledged my own pain—sometimes I didn't even know I *was* in pain. You learned that from me, Andrea."

Present-day Andrea closes her eyes. Her lips twitch slightly, but she remains calm as she listens to her dad make amends to her twenty-year-old self.

Her father takes her younger self's hand. "I haven't used drugs, but I've used denial. I used it to shut down all of my senses. My feelings. Your light. I let Nana be your rock, and she was a great one. But I want to be that for you going forward."

Twenty-year-old Andrea hugs her dad.

"I love you, Andrea. I am so sorry for teaching you to pretend that everything was fine when nothing has ever been fine. Can you find it in your heart to forgive me?"

"I forgive you, Dad," whispers present-day Andrea.

Andrea's father tells her younger self that he's been attending meetings not unlike hers for the last year and that he has been learning how he's used denial as a coping mechanism and a survival tool, a way to protect himself and his family. "Especially you, Andrea," he says. "I was overwhelmed, and I left you to endure your mother's chaos. You took it all on yourself, and I allowed it."

As they watch, twenty-year-old Andrea takes both of his hands to her mouth to kiss them. "I forgive you, Dad, I forgive you."

Present-day Andrea steps away from the kaleidoscope with a renewed perspective and a sense of peace. She remembers this conversation with her father, but it means even more this time around. Hearing once again that none of that chaotic mess was her fault reminds her that she is a loving human being. She has her own permission to exist.

"I forgave my dad that day, and today our relationship is good," she says. "Together we faced our need to latch onto denial. We attended meetings together for a year or so."

The tigress stirs a bit.

"It helped, as did the twelve-step program I worked through. But I thought I had arrived at recovery, and I've only recently come to see that recovery isn't a destination, it's an ongoing process. And I have sunk back into denial over and over again," she says.

"Never underestimate the ability denial has to cloud one's vision and blur the lines," the tigress says. "The reality is that you did begin to recover. You attended meetings, embraced insights shared by others, and you began to heal. You not only completed your degree, but you also graduated top twenty in your class. Your parents were so proud of you. You were proud of you. You did move forward in a positive manner; you just have more lessons to learn. That is why we are here today," the tigress says.

"If I began to recover then how did I end up here? Why do I still feel like something is missing?"

"Your life with James, which we will get to later, led you down a narrow path to your old familiar habits. By pretending your circumstances with James are something other than what they really are, you have been choosing to live in denial and avoidance."

"Huh. I've been sleepwalking through my life to the degree that I walked myself right into a void."

"This is the void you have been feeling, living between two worlds. There is a part of you that is busy creating a fantasy version of reality. And then another part of you yearns to know and accept the truth. That cognitive dissonance has kept you feeling that something is missing."

Andrea shifts uncomfortably.

"For now, I want you to focus on this memory, and on the possibility of continued recovery and healing."

As they lean back into the kaleidoscope, Andrea asks, "Who's next?"

Inside the kaleidoscope, tiny bits of reflective glass twist and turn, connecting to form a small house of mirrors.

Andrew

The scene takes place around back, where young Andrea is sitting in her favorite rocking chair whose worn, curved wood absorbs the last rays from the sun. The chair was passed down from generation to generation. For Andrea, it's a symbol of the magical years of her childhood. A place to rest, a place to play, and the place from which she used to sit and watch Andrew practice baseball.

Her brother Andrew walks into view with a ball and bat. "Hey sis. Ready to take a crack at this?"

Thirteen-year-old Andrea moves swiftly as a cat to the lawn, eager to start their practice session together. No crowds, only the sound of the ball and bat coming together as one.

"Good eye, great arm," Andrew calls out as he pitches, and

she swings. "You're going to be a star athlete one day. Don't let anyone or anything stop you!"

After a time, he tosses the ball onto the ground. "Gotta go. See you later tonight at the game. Love you."

"Love you," present-day Andrea says quietly. "Those were his last words to me."

"We both know what happens next," the tigress says.

"Andrew went off for a ride in Greg's new car," Andrea says dully. "I was getting ready for the game when the phone rang."

The tigress nuzzles her wet nose into Andrea's hand. They both know that phone call carried the news of Andrew's fatal accident.

"It was a tragedy no one fully recovered from," Andrea says.

"Your relationship with your brother is about more than how it ended, Andrea," the tigress ventures.

Andrea pauses, thinking. "We were very close. Despite our age difference, we had fun together. He never treated me like I didn't belong, or like he wished I didn't exist."

In the eye of the kaleidoscope, young Andrea and her brother are sitting on the back porch now, sipping milk and eating freshly baked chocolate chip cookies from Nana.

"He loved teaching me things, especially softball. I adored him. I loved it when he came to my games. His excitement for me just filled my heart."

"Hey sis," Andrew says to Andrea's younger self, "remember it's not always about winning. Winning isn't everything. It's about being part of a team. It's what you learn from your mistakes and successes. It's what you take away and bring back to the game. It's about how you treat your teammates and yourself. It's about valuing and loving the game and the people you play with. It's about family and trust. It's about heart."

Young Andrea smiles around a bite of cookie. She listens avidly, absorbing each of his teaching points into her memory bank and into her heart. Brother and sister clearly share a love for the game—and each other.

"He was always passing along life lessons," Andrea says. "He'd say, 'Look, Andrea, we live in a chaotic environment, but that doesn't define who we are. You deserve happiness, and most of all you deserve to be a kid. Now go out there and be a kid who loves the game.'"

"Your brother loved you," the tigress says. "And what happened to him was tragic. His loss left so many scars. But I want you to know that though he may be physically gone from this Earth, he never left your side. He is with you today."

Andrea watches as she and Andrew share moments of laughter and love on that day his life was taken. The visualization ends with them hugging one another for the last time.

"I often feel guilty for surviving," she says to the tigress. "I feel like I have to earn my right to be here by being responsible for everyone's happiness. I've spent a lifetime trying to prove my worth. Mostly to myself."

"Trying to prove your worth is exhausting, Andrea. You must let go of these coping mechanisms of denial, control, and avoidance. None of this is in your control."

"I guess I wanted to think it was," Andrea muses. "When I took on everybody else's feelings, if I could deny my own pain, I felt like I was in control. But I never really believed I deserved to live, never mind live a rewarding and fulfilling life. I guess I've been living out my own self-fulfilling prophecy, the one that keeps telling me I'm not worthy of happiness or even existing, but somehow, I'm still in control. That's pretty messed up."

"You were always supposed to survive, Andrea."

"But why? Why was I chosen to survive, to have a second chance at life? Why now have I been chosen to have this opportunity to have a fuller life?" Andrea asks.

The tigress responds softly. "This is a good time for that power greater than yourself to share a few thoughts. Are you able to listen?"

Andrea takes in a breath. "I believe so."

At that moment, the bells from the church down the street ring out. With their chime comes a sense of comfort, peace, and ease. A light breeze lifts Andrea's hair from the back of her neck. The rays of the sun part the clouds.

"Trust asks that you accept that you have been chosen, even if you do not know why," says a voice filled with love and compassion. "You can choose to feel guilty for surviving and continue to carry the misery, guilt, shame, and denial others placed upon you. Or you can choose to live awake. The choice is yours."

Andrea lifts her head.

"You need to be willing to grieve your losses and work through your sadness and shame so that you can take the necessary steps toward believing that you are deserving. Deserving of happiness, health, being valued, being heard, being loved. It starts with you, Andrea."

Andrea turns to the tigress. "I feel like a cat. How many more chances do I have to fully trust, to fully surrender, to fully let go, before I reach my ninth life? I hear the message, and I understand the choice is mine. But I don't want to rush into what's next. I need more time. Do I have more time?"

"Time is not measured here in this place, so yes, you have time. You have one more person to meet before we move on to the next house. Are you ready?"

"Yes, I am ready."

Together, Andrea and the tigress look into the kaleidoscope.

Nana

As the kaleidoscope rotates, the stained-glass shapes form into magnificent flowers. A fireplace mantel lined with family photos comes into view. There are a few of very young Andrea and Andrew, one of Andrea in high school, a few from her time in college, and then one or two from her wedding to James. But the one that stands out is one of Andrea and Nana in the garden. It radiates love, light, and joy.

"I never properly grieved the death of my nana, either. I see now that this is something that needs to be completed on this journey."

The scene shifts and they see Nana and ten-year-old Andrea in the beautiful garden. They are kneeling side by side next to a bed of richly turned soil. Nana's wide, friendly face glistens with perspiration, and though Andrea can't feel the heat of the day from her adult perspective, she can see the trees and the grass shimmering in the sun.

"Come on, now," Nana says to ten-year-old Andrea. "We need to get all our supplies in order."

Present-day Andrea watches with bemusement as her ten-year-old self eagerly hangs on to Nana's every word. "I loved her so."

"You did," agrees the tigress. She leans in a little closer. "You do."

"Feel the soil between your fingers, isn't that nice?" Nana asks ten-year-old Andrea.

"The dirt isn't hot! It's all fresh and cool!"

"Soil, not dirt," Nana says. "But it's fun to get our hands dirty and not worry about it, isn't it?"

Present-day Andrea watches as Nana beams down at her giggling younger self.

"Being in the elements and tending to your garden is the best therapy of all," Nana declares as she picks up a tender seedling and deposits it gently in the soil. "Just listening to the birds sing, watching the bugs crawl, feeling the sun and the breeze on your face all at the same time—it's priceless."

"Priceless," present-day Andrea whispers.

"Living in harmony with nature is the key," Nana says. "And you, my dear, are a natural."

Ten-year-old Andrea is beaming with joy as she carefully handles each succulent.

Present-day Andrea smiles, remembering that Nana taught her the importance of connecting with nature, meeting the elements, paying attention to omens, and how to learn from all that is around her. She taught her to learn from the spirit of the trees, plants, animals, birds, insects—all of nature, even rocks. She taught her that the spirit within her lives in all things. And that it was important to cultivate her inner garden, so she could always have a rich inner landscape to reach into even after Nana was gone.

Why did I let all that disappear?

"Over here," Nana says. "We need to plant each one separately in their own little pot. When we're done, we can sit and have a nice chat over lemonade."

Young Andrea puts her hand on top of the soil and gives it a soft pat.

"How does that feel?" Nana asks.

Ten-year-old Andrea's eyes widen. "I feel the coolness of the soil, and when I pat it down, I can feel that it protects the plant."

"Ah," says Nana. "Protecting the plant is necessary to its safety and survival. When each succulent finds its home, when it feels safe, it exerts confidence and radiance. It contributes to the beauty of our outer landscape."

Ten-year-old Andrea looks at all the planters with admiration. "Each one is lovely, Nana; I love the choices we have made. These are the perfect homes for our succulents."

"All living things need to feel safe in their environment—even you," Nana says, poking young Andrea in the tummy.

Young Andrea laughs.

"I want you to know that, even when it may not feel safe here, I'm here for you. I am here to help you protect your inner landscape. You can create your own safety, and I will help you."

Ten-year-old Andrea flips some dirt into the air and then focuses back on her nana.

"It's your job to maintain your inner landscape so that you and your beautiful green eyes can continue to radiate light and joy."

The scene fades away.

"I loved my nana and all the wisdom she shared with me," present-day Andrea says. "Even after my brother died, when my mother checked out and my father stayed small, I remembered what my nana told me. I tried and tried to radiate light and joy."

"And you did a great job at that, Andrea," the tigress says. "But when someone rejects the light, the light bearer can feel defeated. You, my dear, felt defeated."

"The day Nana died—and the day I almost died—that was when I felt so defeated that I lost my light altogether. I think this is what has been missing—my light. I want it back. Can you help me get it back?"

"Your nana was a wise soul," the tigress says. "She gave you unconditional love, and she taught you to be strong, confident, and aware of your gifts and talents. She reminded you of your purpose."

"She used to tell me I had been born into a family of light bearers. I felt and still feel that it's the greatest gift of all," present-day Andrea says.

"She encouraged you then, and she is with you now. She wants you to radiate and shine your light no matter what. She wants you to stop putting your life on hold. She wants you to tend to your inner garden."

Andrea breathes quietly. She knows she's been neglecting and abandoning herself for years.

The voice of the power greater than herself returns. "You have been putting your life on hold for a very long time, Andrea. You can't continue nor can you afford to wait for someone else to fulfill you, make your life better, or be who you want or need for them to be."

"How do I do that?" Andrea asks. "How do I own my power to take care of myself, my garden, my light, despite what my parents or James or my kids or my friends do or say? I need help."

"In order to care for yourself, you must manifest love for yourself. You need to give me, and all your teachers and guides, permission to send you love."

She smiles as she thinks of Metatron, the deer, Tara—even Ruthie and Rae.

"When you can let go of the need to control and learn to accept love, you release the coping mechanisms and painful beliefs the black hearts revealed. Surrender to your higher power, the Universe, or what entity you choose. And you will find all you need to tend your garden and take your life back," the voice says.

Andrea stands up and looks at the yard, where the once-beautiful garden has not been tended for years. "I have so much more awareness of what happened to me," she says. "I can see that I wanted control over others, but took no responsibility for myself. This is a lot to process—I'm so tired!"

"Rest here, my child," the tigress says. "You have been through a lot. We can go to the next house once you feel rejuvenated."

The song "The House That Built Me" by Miranda Lambert plays softly in the background. Listening, Andrea hears the story of a girl who goes back to the house she grew up in to help heal the brokenness inside her.

"This is a beautiful song," Andrea says. She pulls her travel journal from her bag, and the healing begins as the power of words flow gracefully from her pen.

Today, I will let go of my guilt, shame, and fear
around my past and present circumstances.
I will trust that where I have been and
where I am right now is for me.
—MELODY BEATTIE

Reflections for This Chapter

Integrate your thoughts by going through these activities now or coming back to them later. I invite you to listen to the song "The House That Built Me" by Miranda Lambert. It is a beautiful song, and the words are very touching.

List the negative narratives you repeat to yourself in your mind. Try to come up with a minimum of eight to ten. For example, Andrea's list consisted of: "I am a bitch. I am not loveable. I am unworthy. I do not exist."

Think of someone you respect and love, like a child, friend, or family member. How would you feel if you knew they were saying these sorts of negative things to themselves? Cross out all the things that you wouldn't want someone you love thinking about themselves. You don't deserve to think those things of yourself either. You are worthy of being accepted and respected by yourself just as you accept and respect your loved ones.

What type of story are you creating about yourself? Are you ready to change the negative narrative? Own the narrative. Change the narrative.

When we deny the story, it defines us.
When we own the story, we can write a brave new ending.
—BRENÉ BROWN

CHAPTER 15

The Children
at the Beach House

*There is an endearing tenderness in the love of a mother to a son
that transcends all other affections of the heart.*
—WASHINGTON IRVING

Andrea and the tigress walk together down Relationship Row.
The sun bears down, but the heat feels welcoming. They head
toward the back of the second house, the one that resembles the
beach house she and James rented when the kids were young.
In the back yard there are four brightly colored beach chairs
next to a few Turkish cotton beach towels. There's a picnic table
with a tall glass of refreshing iced tea for Andrea and, under the
table, a metal bowl filled with fresh water for the tigress.

"Wow, this feels so familiar," Andrea says.

"Yes, it should," says the tigress. "You have been here before.
Shall we get comfortable?"

She directs Andrea toward the beach chairs and motions her
to sit down. "Before we get to why we're here, it is important
for you to think back to the time when Ben went to baseball
camp. Can you do that?"

"Yes, I believe I can do that."

"Breathe and visualize that day, like we've been practicing."

Andrea breathes, and the flashback begins. There she is at forty-something, waiting in the school parking lot waiting for the bus to pull in. When it does, twelve-year-old Ben, loaded down with his gear, steps down. He looks tired, worried, and a bit disheveled. Ben has been away at baseball camp for a week. Watching, Andrea remembers she couldn't wait to wrap her arms around him.

"Over here!" Forty-something Andrea waves excitedly.

Ben looks up with his bright blue eyes and smiles. He throws his gear to the ground and runs to give her a great big bear hug. She is his safe space.

"How was it, Ben? Was it as fun and as fabulous as you hoped it would be?" She helps load his gear into her SUV.

"It was okay. I did all right." He hesitates. "Some of the older boys were … never mind."

Forty-something Andrea seems to ignore Ben's discomfort, but as they get in the car, she clucks, "Put your seatbelt on, Ben. Safety first."

"Mom." Ben rolls his eyes.

Andrea watches them drive home, and sees when her younger self can't restrain herself from probing. "What about the older boys?" she hears herself ask. "Did something happen?"

Ben is silent, and she can see forty-something Andrea ramp up and start pushing. "I'm your mother, Ben, you need to tell me. You need to trust me."

Present-day Andrea thinks how her mother would badger her as she watches her younger self do the same to her son.

Ben doesn't answer at first, sniffling audibly. "It was kind of like a hazing. They made us pee in the field at night after everyone was asleep. They had us run laps around the bases naked, and they made us eat dog food. It was pretty disgusting."

Forty-something Andrea audibly takes in a deep breath.

"And the names they called us, Mom, they were stupid and humiliating. Baby Butt Face. Fatty. Willie Wonky. Dumbo. They yelled at us, and they even pushed our faces into the dog food. Some of the kids cried. But I didn't."

Andrea and her younger self can both hear Ben gulping and hyperventilating. The car pulls over, and Ben darts out to retch by the side of the road.

"You, okay?" Forty-something Andrea calls from her car window.

He spits one last time before getting back into the car and closing the door. He turns away from Andrea and faces the window. "I'm never going back," he mumbles.

Forty-something Andrea reaches over for her son's hand and grasps it tightly, sending the message that she is never going to let go. Her heart breaks into a million little pieces.

"My heart hurts now just revisiting this memory," present-day Andrea tells the tigress. "The abuse he endured while away at baseball camp sickened me. What's even worse is, that kind of abuse wasn't new. Ben heard it at home whenever James started in on me. We never talked about it."

The tigress nods slowly.

"Ben was my protector. He stayed close by me, and yet we never talked about it. I see that he needed to protect me, but he also needed me to protect him. I see how the patterns and sickness travel from generation to generation. It needs to stop."

"It does need to stop, Andrea, and that's one reason we're revisiting this moment.""

The visualization continues. Andrea watches her younger self drive Ben home, and she sees the moment forty-something Andrea decides she needs to set up a meeting with his coaches.

Ben pulls his hand away as if he knows what his mother is thinking.

"Don't, Mom. I'm begging you, don't say anything to the coaches, or Dad, or Sophia, please Mom, I'm begging you." Tears run down his face.

"He didn't want to be known as a snitch." present-day Andrea winces. "I told him I wouldn't go to the coaches, or file a complaint, or tell a soul. He trusted me."

"What happened can be repaired," the tigress says. "But understanding and forgiveness start with you."

"When I dropped him off at practice a few days later, he had to force himself out of the car. He didn't even want to play anymore. He'd lost interest in being part of the team. Worse, he'd lost his confidence."

"That was hard for you to see, wasn't it, Andrea?" Andrea is silent, remembering. Ben loved baseball just like Andrew had. Just like Andrea herself loved softball. She hadn't wanted Ben to feel like a snitch—the very word she'd screamed at her roommates when they'd revealed her drug use—but she'd also wanted to fix it for him. Her heart had ached at his humiliation and lost innocence.

The visualization picks up as forty-something Andrea and her family head for the beach house. Alice Cooper's "School's Out" plays on the car radio. Andrea's hair is trying to escape her pink and yellow scarf as she bounces up and down to the music in her seat. James's flicks his cigarette out the window so that he can tap his fingers to the beat of the music. Ben and Sophia sit back enjoying the cool breeze blowing through their hair. Everything seems to be fine.

"We're here," James yells as they pull up.

The family walks up the overgrown pathway toward the front door with a load in each hand. James turns the key and opens the door, and they all drop their belongings smack in the middle of the floor. There are boogie boards, surf boards, paddle boards, coolers full of food, snacks, and drinks.

Andrea and her younger self watch as James and the kids make several trips back and forth to the car, bringing in Yahtzee, Scrabble, Cribbage, and dominos and other games and adding to the mess of a pile on the floor. Within seconds, the kids are in their rooms donning bathing suits and flip flops.

"Let's hit the beach!" James is elated. They all are. "We'll clean up this mess later."

"We had a great day at the beach," Andrea tells the tigress. "Then we came back and roasted hot dogs and marshmallows and ate s'mores. We sat around the fire pit and told stories, and James and Ben had a burping contest. It was perfect."

"And then?"

"And then the next day, my friend Samantha arrived with her family. Ben and her son were on the baseball team together. We all went to the beach, and I thought it would be another great day."

"Let's take a look," the tigress suggests.

They watch the two families head for the beach, chattering happily. Once there, the kids dart toward the water, their voices full of enthusiasm and excitement. Forty-something Andrea and Samantha hang back to set up the food tables, beach chairs, and umbrellas. They toast with wine coolers as their husbands huddle in their corner, drinking beer and shooting the breeze. The men's job is to barbecue and then clean up after the day is done.

"Did you hear what happened at baseball camp?" Samantha whispers.

Forty-something Andrea is wary. "What did you hear?"

"I should never had asked that question," present-day Andrea says in disgust.

"But you did," the tigress says.

"I know. And as you said, it all needs to be revealed in order for it to heal. I hope you're right."

The two women gossip, heads close together. Samantha says, "I heard the coaches are going to be fired. And I heard those older kids are kicked off the team. I heard some of the moms baked the coaches cookies and substituted chocolate chips with Ex Lax. Me, I plan to file a complaint."

"I would," says forty-something Andrea. "But I promised Ben I wouldn't."

The wine coolers continue to flow, and Andrea is careful about how much she consumes. Two are her limit. Present-day Andrea watches her younger self get looser and less circumspect. Feeling free to kick back, laugh, and dismiss her own concerns. But as the day wears on, the high from the wine coolers wears off. Forty-something Andrea begins to have second thoughts about gossiping.

"Hey, I told Ben I wouldn't say anything," she says to Samantha. "You have to leave me and Ben out of it."

Samantha smirks and assures Andrea that she will.

Present-day Andrea knows better. "In my recovery meetings, they told us that gossip destroys intimacy and trust. For years, my motto was to keep my conversations free of malicious gossip. But I got sucked in that day."

The tigress nudges her gently. "You can make amends for this even today."

The conversation she shared with Samantha haunted her the rest of that summer. That feeling of walking on eggshells, waiting for something bad to happen, was horribly familiar from her childhood.

The visualization picks up as the family arrives back home, a couple of days after Samantha and her family had left. Their mood is different. They only have their memories now. Reality is what's next.

When they walk through the door, forty-something Andrea notices the red light blinking on the answering machine. She hits the play button and there is a message from Ben's coaches, something about a little league meeting with the baseball managers, coaches, and parents for the next night. She quickly erases the message, but it's too late.

Ben looks at her with bewilderment, tears welling up in his wide blue eyes. "You didn't."

Present-day Andrea can hardly bear to watch. "He looked at me like I was the biggest traitor in the entire world. James didn't know what was going on, but that didn't stop him from glaring at me. He knew I was keeping a secret."

When James hears what's going on, he looks away from forty-something Andrea, and crosses his arms, fists clenched and lips pursed. The more he fumes, the smaller she makes herself. Eventually, he is pacing up and down the hallway making threats and spewing obscenities. "You idiot! You liar; you gossip! You only made things worse!"

Ben hovers in the corner of the living room covering his ears, just like Andrea used to when she was a child.

"Breathe, Andrea, breathe," the tigress murmurs. "I know this isn't easy to relive."

"James went to the meeting alone," Andrea says. "He didn't trust me to go, and neither did Ben. The older kids who were involved in the incident at camp were suspended for the first week of school and had to take a class for bullies at the police station under James's supervision. He'd used his position as detective to make that happen."

"It seems the punishment fit the crime," the tigress says.

"The older boys were also suspended from the team for the first few games at the beginning of the new spring season. The coaches had to scramble to find new players, and it messed up the usual team building that usually took place in the fall."

In the visualization, Ben and Samantha's son Donny are walking quickly, heads down, through the school hallways as the other kids whisper and stare. "Snitch," one of them hisses.

"You wuss," a girl sneers at Ben. "Having your daddy fight your battles for you."

"Yeah, you Baby Butt Face," one of the boys cuts in. "No one likes a butt face."

Present-day Andrea can't fight back her tears as she watches her son being bullied and teased. Seeing for the first time how badly Ben was ridiculed because his dad, the cop, went to bat for him and his mom, it was believed, had told on the older boys.

The scene shifts to Ben at the first practice, where the coaches turn their backs, unsupportive and unprotective, acting as if nothing had happened and ignoring that Ben was being teased and harassed.

"Tattletale," one of his teammates says.

"Baby," another teammate snarks.

"When Ben came home from practice, he acted a bit strange. He then told his mom tiny snapshots of what happened at school that day, only snapshots because he did not fully trust her. She asked a few questions and was able to put two and two together. Ben was being bullied and ridiculed,"

Andrea tells the tigress. "At first he said everything was fine, and then he found a tiny piece of his voice to share the little bit he did."

"He must have felt very alone," the tigress returns.

"I shared with James and Ben what I thought happened, and Ben confirmed with a nod. The three of us made a decision, and we pulled Ben out and enrolled him in a new school. He quit the baseball team and little league altogether. That one conversation with Samantha turned my life and Ben's life upside down. And my relationship with my son changed forever."

"He didn't fully trust you, but he did find his voice."

In the visualization, young Ben confronts forty-something Andrea. "Mom, I trusted you. Why did you tell? How could you?" Ben chews on his lower lip, speaking in a monotone and avoiding eye contact. "I can never fully trust you again, that I know."

Forty-something Andrea reaches out for her son, but he steps back. Shaking his head, chin trembling, shoulders slumped, he says, "I used to love talking to you. But you betrayed me, Mom. I still love you, but I don't really trust you. I can't fully trust you ever again."

Present-day Andrea grimaces. "I listened to my mother defend herself and make up excuses for her behavior for years. I didn't want to do that, but I didn't know what to say instead. Instead of offering compassion and love, I froze. My silence wasn't a peacemaker, it was an intimacy-breaker. I'm just like my mother."

"You are not your mother," Tara says. "You made mistakes. But repairs can be made, forgiveness can be extended, and relationships can mend."

"Ben doesn't share things with me to this day. I don't want to pry, so I walk on eggshells. I miss his tall tales and silliness. I want him to know how much I miss him, how much I love and respect him." Andrea places her hands over her heart. "I want him to know I can be trusted. I want him to know the truth behind the mess that caused him so much embarrassment, pain, and suffering. But most importantly I want him to stop carrying that burden, and I want him to know how much I want our relationship to heal."

"I hear your heart. What do you see as the real lesson in all of this, Andrea?"

"The lesson? I don't really know." Andrea stands and paces restlessly. "I just want it to get better."

"Think, Andrea. What else do you know?"

"I know I wasn't a snitch, but I was a gossiper, which is equally hurtful. I know Ben wasn't the only one betrayed. I know how that feels and how sorry I am. I know holding onto this has only made things worse."

Andrea drops to her knees, her arms stretched out wide, and speaks to the cloudless sky. Her voice is thick with tears. "I want to repair our relationship, and I need help. I do not want this to go on for another twenty years. Too much damage has been done already. Can you help me find my way?"

"I am here, Andrea," says a familiar voice outside of herself. "I will guide you if and when you invite me in. I can show you how to keep your communications clean and free from malicious gossip and from omissions of the truth."

Andrea wipes the bitter tears from her cheeks. "Thank you, thank you, thank you." She rises and walks over to Tara. "I am getting closer to fully trusting." Her eyes mist over.

"I am pleased for you, Andrea," the tigress says. "Before we go, we have one more person to reminisce with."

"Yes." Andrea sighs heavily. "Sophia."

A boy needs his mother's respect.
Not only her love, but also her respect.
—EMERSON EGGERICHS

Sophia

The overgrown pathway that leads to the beach is the perfect spot to collect one's thoughts. Present-day Andrea walks to the edge of the yard, looks to the left, and sees endless sand and ocean. Tiny pieces of driftwood have made their way to the seashore. There are hundreds of sand crabs, and seashells of various shapes, sizes, and colors, blanketing the shoreline. To the right she sees the sand dunes embedded with grassy patches. *The kids liked to play hide and seek in those dunes,* she thinks.

As she walks back toward the beach chairs, she finds that the iced tea has been replaced with a tall glass of lemonade. Next to the pitcher of lemonade sits a paper plate covered with snicker doodle cookies. *My favorite.*

"Let's see the next time your family came back to the beach house, a time when your children were fourteen and sixteen," the tigress says.

"I'm ready," Andrea says, not entirely convinced this is so.

"Breathe in and allow your breath to flow. Breathe out steadily as if your breath were a circle. Nice and steady now."

Andrea does so.

"The school year has ended, and you and the kids are gearing up for summer fun at the beach house."

The visualization begins.

Present-day Andrea can readily see how different it is this time. Her younger self is packing the car alone. She remembers how James's drinking made him more erratic and unmanageable. He was disconnecting from her, from the kids, from life.

"I think this is when I started to feel married and alone," she says.

The tigress confirms and says, "I believe you are right."

It's summer 2004. There's fourteen-year-old Sophia, looking cute in her Daisy Duke shorts, her hair in a messy bun and her golden curls framing her face. She is racing around the house and getting ready to go hang out with friends. She seems so grown-up, but she's still innocent, vulnerable. Watching, Andrea remembers that not too long after this scene, Sophia would disappear into a whirl of teenage fun and drama, and Andrea herself would feel even more alone.

"Heading out soon," Sophia yells from her bedroom.

"What time will you be back?" forty-something Andrea asks.

"Don't know, I'll text you." Andrea and her forty-something self watch as Sophia blows through her beach house bedroom like a tornado, tossing the clothes she was wearing to one side and digging through a laundry basket in search of something new.

"What are you looking for, Sophia?" her forty-something self asks. "Maybe I can help you find it."

"That pink and white strapless sundress. And it's Sophie."

"Found it." Forty-something Andrea hands it over. "Um, Sophie."

"And if we see each other later, do not dare embarrass me because if you do…" Sophia glares at her mother with her gigantic hazel eyes. "If you do …"

They both laugh.

"Kidding, Mom. Mostly. My friends and I are going to a bonfire on the beach tonight, Mom. I should be back by 10:30. Will that work?" Sophie's curfew is 10 p.m.

"That should be okay. Please text me though when you leave the bonfire."

"Thanks, Mom, you're the best."

"Oh, and by the way, your dad is scheduled to be arriving around eleven, so don't be late."

Sophia heads for the door, turning and blowing her mom a kiss. Present-day Andrea and her younger self can hear her daughter chattering with her friends before they move off, and there is silence.

Ben follows close behind. The screen door creaks. "Bye Mom, love you."

"I thought Ben would never let anything happen to Sophia," Andrea says to the tigress.

Forty-something Andrea, now with the evening all to herself, plays her music loud, dances around the living area feeling spirited and free, drinks half a glass of wine, and then collapses into her oversized comfy chair. Within a half hour, she falls asleep with one of the Outlander books in her hand and the TV on.

"Looks like a nice evening to yourself," the tigress says.

"It was," present-day Andrea responds. "But then the shit hit the fan."

In the visualization, forty-something Andrea wakes up to see it's 11:30 p.m. As she rubs her eyes, she sees the red light blinking on the answering machine. The message is from James, calling to let her know he won't be there until the morning and apologizing for that.

"That was his first nice gesture in weeks," present-day Andrea remembers.

Her younger self heads to Sophia's room to kiss her goodnight only to find out that she isn't there. She quickly marches over to Ben's room to find him crashed out, his snore steady and loud. Panicking, she shakes him awake. "Where is your sister?"

"I—I don't know," he says groggily. "The last time I saw her was around 9:30, she said she was going to get ice cream with her friends and would head home after that. I thought she was here."

Ben gets out of bed, throws on his shorts and a t-shirt he grabs off the floor, and retrieves two flashlights from a drawer. He hands one to his mother, and they both run out the door.

"Terrible things went through my mind," present-day Andrea remembers. "The stories I'd heard, the ones James would come home with—they made my skin crawl. I ran to the beach, and Ben headed in the direction of the ice cream parlor."

Forty-something Andrea falls to her knees when she reaches the end of the pathway between their house and the beach. She looks anguished, lost. But then a sound in between the waves crashing and the air against the palm trees: giggling. She walks toward the sound, and comes to a bonfire where teens are gathered, drinking beer and smoking pot. The air reeks.

"For Christ's sake," forty-something Andrea hisses under her breath. She moves closer past the empty beer cans and through the haze of weed and wood smoke until she recognizes one of Sophia's friends. "Where's my daughter, where is she?" she yells in a shrill voice as she runs to the girl and shakes her.

Sophia's friend steps back and stares at Andrea as if she were a crazy woman. The girl points up toward the dunes.

"Both children were subjected to my crazy," present-day Andrea says to the tigress. "No wonder they feel the way they do toward me. I can't be trusted."

Forty-something Andrea scrambles frantically up the sand dune, tripping and falling over herself as if she were drunk. She calls out to her daughter as she looks frantically, but sees nothing. Finally, far off to the left, she sees two long legs in the air, and she gasps. Then up pops Sophia's head, her curls full of seaweed and sand.

Anger turns to rage. Sophia's clothes are still on thankfully, but her sundress is sideways. She got there just in time. Andrea yanks Sophia up by her hair with one hand and tugs on her dress straps with the other, spewing all kinds of unkind words.

Sophia freezes in humiliation as her mother heaps accusations. Then her mother drags her down the dune right past her friends. It's clear she's mortified.

"She came along quietly," present-day Andrea says. "She didn't want to attract any more attention."

"Understandable," the tigress says.

"The walk of shame back to the beach house was … quiet. But when we got back, I called her a drug addict and a slut. She told me I was a crazy bitch and a terrible mother."

"You both certainly know how to hurt one another with your words."

"We went at it for a good ten minutes, and then she picked up a magazine and threw it at me. She stormed off to her room, slammed the door, and sobbed. I did too."

"This pain has been bottled up for decades," the tigress observes.

"I also threw a magazine at my mother. That was the day I became vulnerable to the power of words. I felt like the worst daughter ever. I wonder if Sophia did too."

"Shame is insidious," the tigress says as she places her left paw on Andrea's hand.

"I cried myself to sleep that night, but Sophia never knew that. It was that night our relationship changed, and our bond was never the same. It felt like our souls were torn apart. I never shared that with Sophia either. How would she have ever known what I was feeling, what I still feel?"

"Souls can be reunited, Andrea. This is a temporary separation."

"The one thing she asked me not to do was to embarrass her, and I just could not help myself because of my inability to express my true feelings. I was scared to death, and I didn't know how to tell her that I was scared she would end up like me, a promiscuous drug addict. She doesn't even know that happened to me. Instead, anger took over, and I ruined everything in a split second."

"You acted from your emotions, Andrea. Any mother would have been frantic, angry, and scared."

It's early morning in the visualization. The sky is gray with mist, like a gentle blanket intended to comfort the humans inside the house. Andrea and the tigress watch as the house comes alive. James rolls in. The smell of bacon swirls through the air. The pancake mix is ready to be poured into the red-hot frying pan. Containers of fresh fruit, maple syrup, and powdered sugar line the table. Orange juice and coffee are ready to be poured. Everything looks perfect in an imperfect world. Breakfast is served.

"Ready, Dad?" Ben gets up from the table while swallowing the last bite of his pancake.

"Sure, am, son." Off they go.

In the kitchen, Andrea watches through the window as the two amble down the pathway toward the beach with surfboards in hand. Sophia comes into the room, reaches carefully past her mother for a banana without meeting her eyes, and says politely, "I will be at my friend Casey's house all day, so please don't disturb me."

Forty-something Andrea is unable to respond.

Sophia leaves a piece of paper on the kitchen island with an address and a short note saying she'll be back for dinner. She leaves, and the bang from the weathered screen door punctuates her plea for independence.

Present-day Andrea sighs. "From that day forward, Sophia sought her independence. I was left alone with my thoughts, and they got uglier each day. I yearned to talk with her. I wanted to beg her for forgiveness. But when we crossed each other's path, we were polite and the mood was frosty—no, icy, really. I found myself walking on eggshells. Again."

She remembers that the remaining weeks at the beach house were unbearable. No more girl talks, or teasing each other over silliness. Trust had been broken, and of course what happened between them was never discussed again. Silence took up all the remaining space.

"The anger between us was chilling," she says. "I knew I couldn't undo the trauma I'd created, so I chose to say nothing and act like everything was fine."

"And was it? Fine?" asks the tigress.

"All seemed to have been forgotten, but it never really was. We did heal our relationship some during her high school years. She let me in a little, and for that I was grateful. But we were never the same. I could tell she still didn't fully trust me. She was just waiting for the opportunity for me to embarrass her again."

"And now?"

"She fills me in with what's going on, but only on her terms. She's cautious. She doesn't want to be judged, controlled, accused, or embarrassed. Nor does she ever want to be victim to her mother's wrath. Can you blame her?"

"If you could go back in time and say something to Sophia, what would you say?" the tigress asks.

"I would look into her hazel eyes and say, 'Sophia, I know I embarrassed you and disappointed you, and I'm so sorry. I can't undo what's been done, but I want us to find a way to repair our relationship. Please forgive me. I made a mistake, and I will do whatever it takes to win back your trust.'"

"Go on."

"'Please don't shut me out. I apologize for my mistakes, and I want to do better, be better. I miss you; I miss our relationship. Can you forgive me?'"

"Is there more?"

"There is one more thing. When Sophia's twins were born, she invited her mother-in-law to help her for the first two months. I was devastated, but I acted as if everything was fine. I told her I understood."

The tigress nods.

"I saw the twins briefly when they were born, but I wasn't invited back until they were three months old. My heart still aches. I need to let her know how I feel so I don't blame her for my discomfort or remain resentful."

"That sounds like an excellent plan, Andrea."

Andrea begins to cry in despair. "They're a year old, and I barely know them. I regret that I allowed the wounds of my childhood to affect my relationships with my children. When I stand in denial and avoidance, I use blame as a weapon, and I create distance between us. I push away the people I love the most because I'm afraid of rejection. It keeps me safe, but it keeps them at a distance."

The tigress nudges her to continue.

"Those black hearts I have been introduced to on this journey—I've been wearing them like armor. I've been wearing them for a lifetime. It's time to let them go."

"As you learn to recognize your pain and that of others, as you see how you have contributed, you will see clearly what needs repair. You will be led to forgiveness, where growth and true healing exist."

Andrea wipes her face with her hand. "I would like to work toward forgiveness."

"The lessons bestowed upon you are lessons to help you surrender and trust. This journey has been an arduous one, but it is also acting as a catalyst to bring back the light you lost. Your willingness to surrender will help you heal all of your relationships. We are here for you when you are ready. You are not alone."

"I am so tired. May I rest?" Andrea asks.

The tigress nods her assent.

Andrea sits back down in one of the beach chairs. The back-yard is still, the sky a bright blue. The birds are singing, and the midday clouds are just beginning to roll in. Suddenly, a great California oak like the one in her own backyard, like the one in the meadow, appears.

"Wait, I don't remember this oak tree being here," Andrea says. "How did it get here?"

"It's your dream," Tara notes mildly. "Anything can happen. In fact, I think before you rest a bit you may want to reach into your bag. There is something special inside for you."

Andrea reaches in and pulls out a pair of jeans, a fresh t-shirt, clean underwear, toiletries, and a brush. "What's all this?"

"It's time to get out of your pajamas. Refresh yourself for the next leg of your journey."

The tigress and Andrea get up and walk toward the oak, where a brilliant ray of sunlight shines through the thick branches. At the base of the tree, Andrea finds her soft silky blanket just waiting for her to sit upon. Her journal and pen are lying on top of the blanket just waiting to be picked up and used.

She sits down gratefully and listens to the sounds of the waves and the repeated calls of the seagulls in the distance. Overhead, she sees pelicans swooping in to catch fish. It is a quiet afternoon at the beach, and the ocean air is fresh and cool. She allows herself to become one with the tree. This magical tree that whispers words of wisdom, this tree that is sturdy representing stability and safety provides her a sense of connection with the tree. Andrea takes up her pen, lets her words flow freely onto the pages of her travel journal.

"In this moment," she writes, "I accept my imperfection. In this moment, I see situations and people as they truly are. In this moment, I embrace the lessons in the memories of visiting these homes. In this moment, I accept where I have come from, and I accept where I am today. In this moment, I feel hopeful."

Time is of the essence, but it is not measured here in this place by the ocean. Andrea begins to drift, knowing there is hope. In the back of her mind, she begins to prepare herself for the next stop because she knows it will be a painful one: the bungalow. As she practices her breathwork, a sense of tranquility falls upon her. Resting peacefully by the tree. The song "I'll Always Be Your Mom" by Aimee Zimmermann plays quietly.

A mother's and daughter's love is never separated.
—VIOLA SHIPMAN

CHAPTER 16

James

A tongue has no bones, but it can break a heart.
—UNKNOWN

Leaving the beach house behind is difficult. But Andrea's dream shower and a fresh set of clothes helped. In a split second, she's refreshed and ready to go. Her heart feels a certain heaviness from the previous two houses, but the aha moments have provided a glimmer of hope.

As Andrea and the tigress draw closer to the next house, she feels trepidation. They approach the bungalow, and a massive sign that reads "NO TRESSPASSING!" drops from the sky. They look at one another, shrug their shoulders, and proceed as if nothing surprises them at this point in the journey.

"We won't be entering this house," the tigress says.

Andrea notices a metal security door in front of the actual front door, which is beaten up and scarred and does not look inviting. The silence and stillness in the air feel eerie, as if something is lurking about. *Those tiny demons, perhaps,* Andrea thinks.

"I collected your blanket and a few pillows to sit on," the tigress says. "There is a small yard with a bench on the side of the bungalow. We can sit there if you would like."

"Thank you." Andrea strategically lays out the pillows.

The house before them stands in the sunshine, but still appears as if it is constrained by a shadow of disappointment and despair. The windows display rusted bars that look like they block the light. The exterior paint peels; the natural elements are taking their course.

"This place gives me the creeps," Andrea says. "Who lives here?"

"We'll get to that," the tigress says. "For now, let's go back to when you began to feel married and alone. Breathe in and exhale, just keep breathing, that's right. Summer vacation is over, the kids are back in school, and you and James are in your home. Keep breathing steady, that's right, keep it going."

Andrea's visualization resumes. She can see her younger self fussing around James, who's sitting in an overstuffed armchair. "Is everything okay? Do we need to talk?" her younger self probes.

"Not now, Andrea, I'm busy." The armchair is James's throne and his cocoon at the same time. He sinks deeper into the cushions, clearly hoping Andrea will leave him alone. He shows zero interest in conversation.

"James, James, are you hearing me?" forty-something Andrea says anxiously. "I was at that beach house for weeks. I was scared for Sophia. I didn't handle that well, but I did my best. Why won't you talk with me?"

"What is wrong with you?" James snaps. "Can't you see I'm busy?"

"I was just trying—"

"Yeah, you're always trying." James scoffs in disgust, and Andrea storms out of the room feeling unheard, dismissed, and hurt. The push-pull pattern is in play. The push is when she

200

just wants to be heard and understood; the pull is when fear of being alone creeps in. It's a terrible cycle.

"We had some good times together," present-day Andrea says. "But he became so dismissive. These last few years have been rough. If he isn't insulting me, he's ignoring me, shaming me, or punishing me with silence. I've learned to welcome the silence. It feels painful at times, but on some strange level it's also a relief."

"You experienced a lot of shame as a child, Andrea, and the shame carried into your teens and adult life," the tigress observes.

"Shame taught me to repress my feelings," Andrea agrees. "It's been how I've survived."

The tigress's whiskers twitch.

"There are times when I feel like I physically leave my body when the shame and pain become too much."

"That is called disassociating. You unconsciously leave your present situation because your reality becomes too painful," Tara tells her.

Andrea shudders.

"Feelings such as sadness, grief, loss, joy, and love never fully registered with you because of the trauma you experienced. But we are here to heal this so that you can feel all of these things without having to disassociate."

"Rehab was a safe place where I could get in touch with some of my repressed feelings and emotions," Andrea says. "I started the process to get to know the real me while there. But then I met James, and I decided I was all healed. So I put a hold on my recovery work, and I acted as if. We dated, I fell in love, and we married. I took on so many new roles."

"You did," the tigress says.

"I became a wife, a mom, a human resource manager, a confidante, a volunteer, a daughter, a daughter-in-law, and a pet owner. I let all of that stop me from taking care of myself. And I lost the me I was just getting to know," Andrea says with regret.

"What do you think happened the night you exploded at Sophia?" the tigress asks.

"The message of being a failure was powerful and so shame overcame me. The adrenaline rush from the shame I felt coursed through my entire body, and it felt like a high. That high led to anger, and the anger led to the explosion. And when it was all over, the shame came full circle," Andrea says.

The tigress gives her a penetrating look.

"I felt shame for my marriage falling apart, shame for how I handled things with Ben and Sophia, shame for not standing up for myself and having a voice, shame for feeling married and alone, shame, shame, shame."

"I know this must be uncomfortable to discuss, Andrea, but acknowledging how shame and anger have helped you survive is growth." Tara pauses. "I would like you to revisit another bonfire that took place that summer."

"Ah," Andrea says. She knows what's coming, but she breathes deeply, and a visual of the last of the bonfires appears. She sees her younger self and remembers that she hoped she and James would connect under the moonlight, beneath the stars. "I wanted so much to feel connected with James. Damn that magical thinking."

The tradition was for all the vacationing families along that strip of beach to get together to have a bon voyage barbecue and bonfire. The theme for that particular year was Hawaiian luau. As the scene unfolds, they can see candlelit paths to the barbecue site and tiki torches standing tall around an area designated for dancing. There are colorful leis piled on each table, coconut drinks and Mai Tais with little paper umbrellas at the beach bar, and soft drinks for all the kids. The full moon softens the scene and allows the starlit heavens to shine. It's a magical night.

Most people are dressed casually in beach attire, while others sport their most outrageous Hawaiian outfits. The younger kids are running around in excitement, ready to roast hot dogs, grill hamburgers, drink Kool-Aid, and make s'mores. The older kids are already dancing, lit up like fireflies to the music Ben's band is playing. Ever since he gave up baseball, Ben has devoted himself to his music, and he's a gifted guitarist.

"Looks like you are enjoying yourself," the tigress says.

They watch forty-something Andrea swaying to the music. Her eyes shine with anticipation. Present-day Andrea remembers thinking that she and James might have some adult time and how great that would be.

A few of the men stand around drinking beer and shooting the breeze while they cook up the hamburgers and hot dogs. The smell of grilled meat wafts through the ocean air. The women scurry around placing condiments and sides on picnic tables lined with white plastic coverings. The tables are overflowing with food. The coolers are filled with beers from around the world, wine coolers, bottles of wine, and champagne. A second cooler is filled with soft drinks and water for the kids.

The partygoers wolf down the food and guzzle the booze. Their voices grow louder, the dancing a bit riskier, and a few guests are already passed out. *I guess I never realized what a hard party scene it was*, Andrea thinks. *So much potential for something to go wrong.*

Ben's band takes a break, and someone turns on a boom box. "Summer Breeze," a song by Seals and Crofts, begins to play. Andrea and James used to love to slow dance to this one under the moon and stars. Forty-something Andrea looks around for her husband, thinking it's the perfect moment to connect. Then she freezes. James is over by the sand dunes flirting with Samantha.

This was not the first time, present-day Andrea remembers, watching her younger self watch them. It's obvious they're both drunk off their asses—but it's also obvious something more serious than flirting is going on."

Samantha is in a tight Hawaiian-themed dress and has three leis stacked around her neck. She is leaning in toward James, giggling like a schoolgirl and tugging playfully at the hem of his Hawaiian shirt. *I hated that shirt and those ugly tan cargo shorts,* Andrea thinks. She watches her younger self and sees James reaching to grab one of Samantha's leis to pull her in for a kiss.

"What the hell?" she says.

Forty-something Andrea is similarly shocked and somehow ashamed. Her instincts send her marching over to confront them both. But then she stops in her tracks, as if an angel taps her shoulder and says, "Wait, this is not the time. Take a breath. Step back. When you feel calm, just quietly walk toward them, take James by the hand, and then walk as far away as you can so that you can begin your dance. Tonight is not the night to talk about this."

Present-day Andrea turns to the tigress. "So that's exactly what I did. That angel saved me from embarrassing myself, James, Ben, and Sophia. I sauntered over in my own tight little Hawaiian dress, which took James and Samantha by surprise. They stepped apart from one another. James took my hand and winked at Samantha, and then we walked away to dance to "Summer Breeze." The rest of the night was magical. We reconnected and everything was fine."

"Let me guess: you never talked about it," the tigress says.

"We never talked about it. But we actually did well for a few years after that. It wasn't until both Ben and Sophia were away at college and empty nest syndrome set in, that we began to live our separate lives again."

"What do you think changed?" asks the tigress.

"I began to feel lonely again, so I busied myself with work, the gym, lunch and happy hours with friends, painting, and of course my garden. James busied himself with work, golf, his woodworking projects, and his Wednesday nights out with the boys. We grew apart."

"You began to feel that something was missing," notes the tigress.

"Yes! We barely spoke. It was becoming apparent that we had nothing in common and nothing to talk about anymore."

"That must have felt very lonely and disappointing, Andrea, I am so sorry," says the tigress.

"Years went by, and it was as if I was living with a stranger. We never went on dates, we never danced by the pool under the moon and stars, and we hardly ever went out at all together unless it was with other couples from the neighborhood."

The tigress raises her eyes.

"He used to love it when we went out with Samantha and her husband. Watching them flirt hurt my heart because they didn't even try to hide it. But I thought I could trust James. He was my husband. And I thought she was my friend."

"These memories you buried so deep need to come to the light in order for you to heal," says the tigress.

"The other night, James and I had one of the worst fights ever. I was so upset and disappointed. And of course, angry and ashamed. It was horrible," Andrea says.

The visualization shifts to the night James went out "with the boys." Andrea's past self is upstairs listening to James banging around in the kitchen. "Are you okay?" she calls.

"I'm fine," he mumbles drunkenly, pouring himself a glass of Jack Daniels and grabbing a handful of pretzels before heading toward his armchair. Just as Andrea comes downstairs, his phone vibrates on the counter.

Watching, present-day Andrea takes in a breath.

James snatches up the phone, but not before her past self can see. She watches her own face as she reads the name that pops up: Samantha. Both Andreas stiffen and their hearts race.

"I thought Samantha was my friend," present-day Andrea says. "I felt small before, but this just devastated me."

The tigress looks at her with compassion.

They both watch as present-day Andrea screams at James. "You cheating bastard! You coward! You always had trouble keeping your peanut-sized penis in your pants! I've been keeping the peace so no one—especially our kids, James!—knew what's really going on. I've been catering to you for years, and putting up with your bullshit and your sorry drunk ass ... for what? For this?" Her body shakes, and she seems out of control.

"I sound like my mother," present-day Andrea says. "Everything I was holding in for years just came spilling out. I knew how cruel and emasculating I was being, but I couldn't stop. I wanted him to hurt like he hurt me."

James responds in kind. "You're a hateful, angry, ungrateful bitch, Andrea! At least Samantha knows how to appreciate what she has. She knows how to be happy!"

"Blame shifting," the tigress says.

"I hear it," Andrea replies.

"You are not responsible for James's choices or indiscretions, but you are responsible for your responses, reactions, and

206

decisions. I am here to help you figure those things out."

In the visualization, Andrea's face is red with rage. She picks up the closest thing to hand—a vase her mother had given her for her sixtieth birthday—and hurtles it across the room. Decades after her softball career, her arm and her aim are still good. The vase smashes into James's chest and shatters onto the floor.

James is across the room in seconds. He grabs Andrea by the arms.

"Please let go, James, you're hurting me!" Andrea pleads. He digs in deeper. "Let go!" She kicks him in the groin so she can break free. As James falls, he takes Andrea with him. On the floor, they both weep.

Watching alongside the tigress, Andrea is horrified. "This is not what people who are in love do," she whispers. "This is not how people who love each other treat each other."

Tara looks impassive.

"This is not who I am," present-day Andrea repeats. "But it's who I've become. I'm a critical, angry, ungrateful bitch. James is right."

"Watch," Tara says.

In the visualization, James tries to help Andrea up, but she pushes him away. He makes an attempt at an apology, but this only enrages her more. "Get away from me, you filthy piece of shit!" she screams. "I hate the sight of you!"

He looks at her with his sad blue eyes, seizes his phone, and walks out the door.

Both Andreas watch James leave for the second time that night. No more screaming, no more ugly words, no more high-intensity emotions. Past Andrea looks blank, exhausted, numb. She heads to her bedroom.

"I still wanted to believe that somehow everything would be

fine," present-day Andrea says, shaking her head. "Even though his actions broke my heart—and my words broke his."

The tigress's tail twitches.

"You know what's really twisted? I'd gotten a call from Samantha just a few days before, and she came over to chat. She cried for hours about her broken marriage. I listened, and she thanked me that day for being such a good friend. Can you believe that?" A wave of emotion washes through her.

The tigress waits, listening.

"I thought she was my friend. I thought James and I were reconnecting. My life is all a big fat lie!"

"You are a victim of circumstances, but not a victim, Andrea. Not if you decide not to be."

"The next day, I couldn't stop crying." Andrea stands and moves restlessly about. "So many things raced through my brain: my adoption, my mother, my drug addiction, my kids, the slow death of my marriage. The emotional part of me that I'd shut down years ago sprung a leak. That night, I crawled back into bed and fell into a deep sleep. I think that's when I entered this dreamscape."

"I know you think that, but it was not that night you left your ordinary world to come to this one."

"It wasn't?" Andrea is confused.

"You and James talked the next day," the tigress says. "You were extremely hurt, but surprisingly calm. You were able to listen. Watch."

The visualization shifts to the next morning, and a knock at Andrea's bedroom door. When past Andrea opens it, James asks, "May I come in?"

She stands aside for him to enter.

"Andrea, I'm so sorry for hurting you," he says. "You don't

deserve any of this. I'm here to tell you the truth about what's been happening between me and Samantha."

"Go on," Andrea says stiffly.

"Samantha and I have been seeing each other off and on for a few years." His voice is barely audible as guilt comes off him in waves. "I tried to end it a few times, but she is a master manipulator," he says.

Andrea glares at him and shows him her palm. "Don't you dare blame her for your choices, James, don't you dare."

"Fair enough," James says. "She and I were in an off season when she called last night out of loneliness and desperation. You and I have been connecting more, so I told her I didn't want to meet. But she pleaded with me, and I went to see her. I told her it was over. That's why she called again. To try and talk me out of it."

"So I'm supposed to just forgive everything?" Andrea is unmoved.

"I'm sorry!" James repeats. "I love you!"

The visualization ends.

Present-day Andrea sits silently for a moment. "Why don't I remember that part?"

"You disassociated, Andrea," the tigress says.

"I'm good at that."

"You are."

"Do I want to know what happened after that?"

"Together you agreed to separate. James called a friend and arranged to rent his bungalow. This bungalow. He was already packing to leave. That was the day you left your ordinary world to come to this one."

Andrea sinks back into the beach chair, allowing herself to feel her sadness, her disappointment, and her grief. "I tried so hard to be the perfect daughter ... wife ... mother ... human.

But no matter what I did to try to please everyone, I only hurt myself in the process. No wonder I needed to escape my ordinary world and enter this one."

"You reached a kind of bottom," the tigress agrees.

"All I can see is that my relationships aren't what I hoped they would be, and the only common denominator is me. What's wrong with me?"

"As I've told you before, Andrea, you're not broken, and you don't need to be fixed. But what if you don't have to know all the answers right away? What if insight comes naturally when you are open to it?"

Andrea bites her lip.

"The plan, if you will, your personal growth journey, will reveal itself when the time is right. It's a process, and you are not completely in charge," the tigress says.

"But that means I would need to feel my feelings, let go of control, stop people-pleasing, and release perfectionism," Andrea says almost jokingly.

"Perhaps the lesson is to let go of outcomes and to come to trust yourself, and that power greater than yourself. Perhaps it is time to surrender."

"Ugh." Andrea is on her feet again. "I still want to control, perfect, please—and, oh yeah, sleepwalk. It's so much easier to just sleepwalk through life."

"Is it?" The tigress stretches herself out by the bench outside the bungalow and Andrea sits back down beside her.

The tigress says, "A man named Tom Bodett says that a person just needs three things to be truly happy in this world."

"Yes?"

"You need someone to love, something to do, and something to hope for. Hope is something you can carry in your back pocket," the tigress says.

"Literally or figuratively?" Andrea.

The tigress grins. "Both, I think. You can take hope with you everywhere you go. You can embrace it when you are becoming one with the tree. You can hold it while talking to me, one of the other guides, or your higher power. You will always find a living hope in your higher power."

"I never thought of carrying hope in my back pocket."

"Envision yourself taking one more step toward loving yourself by placing hope in your back pocket, Andrea. When you do that, your love will extend to yourself first and then others. From there forgiveness will flow."

"This sounds like a beautiful way to live," Andrea says with humility.

"Have patience with the process," Tara continues. "As you pick up those pesky black hearts one by one and face them head on, you set the process of healing in motion. Committing to that process and learning to love self is critical. When you do, self-care, recovery work, and finding something to hope for will follow."

"I love the idea of exchanging despair for hope."

"Together we will witness your transformation and healing. Walking the path of recovery will lead you back to yourself and to your heart and soul."

Tears roll down Andrea's cheeks. "I see how my need to control and my expectations around perfectionism have affected my relationships. They keep me in that familiar state of panic, anxiety, and frenzy. I act out on the familiar and cause harm to myself and others. Control is an illusion. Whenever I am trying to control something, I see how it is really controlling me."

"Control is a powerful coping mechanism, used when everything else feels as if it is out of control," says the tigress.

"Awareness is also powerful, and it can free you from the need to control."

"Me trying to control how others think and behave is a mistake. Me looking at others and thinking it's their job to make me happy is a false truth."

The tigress's tail twitches in affirmation.

"Even if I could control others—and, I see clearly, I cannot—it would still be an illusion. I need to learn to deal with my feelings. I can see that now."

"Ah, this is key," says the tigress. "Working on these things will bring peace and calm. Then you can find true happiness for yourself.

"I see that. I also see how perfectionism has affected my relationships with myself and others. It sets me and others up for situations that are uncomfortable. It makes me and others feel uptight. No wonder I feel as if I am walking on eggshells all the time. I create that environment for myself and others in my expectations around perfectionism," Andrea says.

Tigress places a thick white paw on Andrea's shoulder.

"I need to stop expecting perfection from myself and those around me. I can see how I do horrible, irritating, and annoying things to myself and others when I expect perfection."

"Expectations and perfection are a dangerous mix."

"I wonder if I can learn that imperfections are what makes me and others unique. I wonder if I can learn to laugh at my imperfections, nurture them, learn from them, and find acceptance in them."

"This is the work on finding your Inner Goddess, making your own personal internal inventory," the tigress affirms.

"While in rehab I had an opportunity to search within. I think I only reached the surface," Andrea says. "I see more work needs to be done."

The tigress waits.

"Even though I've been clean from drugs for years, I've lived in that 'pink cloud' somewhere between being sober, then euphoric, and then crashing when my disappointments become too much."

"Do you remember when you first experienced what is called the pink cloud"? asked the tigress.

Andrea considers. "After detox. I felt euphoric. It's a natural high, but it usually doesn't last because of unrealistic expectations. When that pink cloud began to dissipate for me, anxiety and depression took its place."

"What happened, do you think?"

"I thought I was cured," Andrea admits. "I went back to my life of deferring to my ego, living off my will, back to believing everything was fine. I became a dry substance abuser. But it's clear to me now that my emotional scars still affect my heart and soul."

"It takes courage and a willingness to look at all of this, to face your messes, your realities, your truth, and a way back to your soul," the tigress tells her. "How about we get out of here and take a ride? Let's go Beauty Gazing."

"What's that?"

"A mindfulness exercise I picked up from a woman named Jennifer Pastiloff who called it beauty hunting. I amended the term. Come, let's practice restoring joy."

"I love that thought, restoring joy."

"As we venture into the skyway, notice the beauty. It can be a person's outfit or smile, a place, nature, animals, a child jumping in a puddle, whatever is beautiful in your mind."

Andrea climbs onto Tara's back, and they prepare to hit the skyway. The song "Joy," by Bastille, begins to play.

Find out where joy resides,
and give it a voice far beyond singing.
For to miss the joy is to miss all.
—ROBERT LOUIS STEVENSON

Reflections for This Chapter

Integrate your thoughts by going through these activities now or coming back to them later. I invite you to listen to the song "Joy" by Bastille as you do so. Let the song flow through you as you answer the questions.

Have you ever taken the time to Beauty Gaze? It's an amazing experience, and it brings me joy. I encourage you to carve out some time, whether it's for an hour, half a day, or a full day, to search for beauty. It could be anything—people laughing, sunrises, your pet. It could even be a sign.

Journal about whichever beautiful things you can recall from this time you carved out for yourself.

If you were to do this daily, every other day, or once a week, how might Beauty Gazing shift your awareness and perception?

Do you take the time to appreciate your ability to see and sense the beauty life has to offer?

Jot down two things you are grateful for today.

CHAPTER 17

Self

The relationship you have with yourself is the most complicated
one because you can't walk away from you. You have to forgive
every mistake and deal with every flaw. You have to find your
way to love you even when you are disgusted with you.
—Unknown

Andrea has found Beauty Gazing exhilarating in a way that exchanges loneliness and despair for comfort and hope.

"You are responsible for your own happiness," the tigress reminds her.

Andrea closes her eyes and breathes in the clean, fresh air that surrounds them.

"This next house might be the most difficult visit of all. It is your house within the dream, and also the house you will return to upon awakening. Here we will further investigate the relationship you have been having with yourself. The relationship with self is perhaps the most complex of all, and one you can never walk away from."

Andrea smiles. "I'm beginning to understand that."

Back on Relationship Row, Andrea and the tigress walk toward the fourth house, which looks almost exactly like the house Andrea lives in when she is awake. In the backyard, where the palms and cacti thrive and the pool sparkles, there are a few additions. The firepit is surrounded by the ceramic bowls, balls of yarn, and sticks she was introduced to earlier. *Rituals,* she thinks. *My guides have been busy at work, I see.*

"You're getting closer to returning home and opportunity to live awake, Andrea," the tigress observes.

"I'm grateful for this experience, Tara. But I'm also anxious about leaving this world and returning to my ordinary one."

"You have much more knowledge and many tools to take back with you, you know. Your ordinary world will no longer be ordinary."

Andrea considers this. She knows she has a better understanding of why her life has felt so empty, of what's been missing. She's come to accept that her life has been unmanageable and that she is powerless over others. She sees that she's been sleepwalking through life. And yet …

"I see how I've contributed to making my life more complicated," she says. "But I still need help putting it all together. The battle between my ego and the spirit has gotten in the way. I see that."

"This visit will give you an opportunity to put the puzzle pieces together. Remember, you do not have to instantly experience total faith and trust in your higher power. All you have to do is welcome one in."

Andrea takes a huge breath in and then exhales with relief.

"Just for today, ask this divine power for healing and direction, to help you open up so you can heal these wounds. Invite love in, so it can flow through you."

"Thank you," Andrea says. "I can do that." She takes another deep breath, places her hands over her heart, gazes up into the gorgeous sky above, and silently meditates on those words. She immediately feels a release. Her fears, reservations, and concerns subside, and she feels a divine power enter her space.

The tigress is beaming.

Then the voice of her divine power speaks. "I accept the invitation, Andrea. And yes, I am happy to show you the way."

Andrea feels herself relax into knowing that her higher power is a reflection of herself, and that she is part of the divine. That this is a spiritual journey, not a religious one. She sees that she doesn't have to follow specific dogma, but instead simply open to possibility and allow the rest to unfold.

"Thank you," she says gratefully to her higher power as the tigress walks with her to the blue front door of the house.

"Blue is a healing color," her divine power says. "It represents serenity and stability. In some cultures, it represents loneliness and sacrifice. You may experience all of this once you walk through the door."

Tara takes over. "The healing that can take place here today will be lasting, Andrea. But this journey is not a time to be faint of heart. You are strong, and your desire to leave the void is strong. Embrace this moment."

Andrea takes in a deep breath and holds it to a count of seven, holds it for seven, then releases it for seven. She repeats this seven times. "You are strong," she tells herself. "You are worthy. You are enough."

Together, Tara, Andrea, and her divine power approach the door, from which Andrea can feel a strong energy emanating and hear a faint sound. As they approach, the door opens, and they enter.

"Come, sit here on the couch," the tigress says, placing a paw on top of the TV remote. To Andrea's surprise, the television turns on. It makes a crackling sound, and then a picture comes into view. It's a meeting room. On the screen, Andrea can see that the chairs are set up and the coffee is on. She can hear the murmur of voices as women begin to enter the room.

"It's the community center," Andrea says. "The meeting for women seeking their inner goddesses." On the screen, she can see that the tree painted on the meeting room wall is covered with the black hearts that were once at its base. "What are those pesky black hearts doing there?"

"They are here for you to notice and perhaps relate to. If you see or hear something you identify with, please jot it down in your travel journal," the tigress says.

Andrea pulls out her travel journal just as Rae appears on the screen. After telling the group how happy she is to be there, Rae walks over to the tree and pulls some of the black hearts off. "These behaviors and beliefs stand in my way. They are not who I am spiritually; they are made up of my negative thoughts and codependent behaviors I've been using to survive."

Andrea listens avidly as Rae, clutching a handful of black hearts, reads: "We relied upon these shortcomings for many years, and because of that we have struggled to let go."

"I struggle to let go," Andrea says.

Rae continues. "It's challenging to let go of 'old friends' like fear of change, obsessing, perfectionism, and self-criticism." She pauses. The room is silent but for the scratching sound of the ladies busily taking notes in their Goddess Within handbooks.

Damn, I have a lot of "old friends," Andrea thinks.

Rae shakes the hand holding the black hearts. "These hearts represent what I am now ready to release. And so I will practice letting go as I move toward the next step, which is to humbly ask my divine power to help me exchange these survival skills for new ways of thinking and coping. Today I choose to love myself."

"What would you add to that list, Andrea?" the tigress asks.

Andrea writes: "manipulation, self-abuse, self-abandonment, wanting others to do it my way, isolation, believing I need to act on my feelings." She had already noted "perfectionism, people-pleasing, addictions, resentments, guilt, shame, and neglect."

On the screen, the meeting facilitator asks for a volunteer to go next. Ruthie stands, walks to the tree, and pulls off her own black hearts. She reads aloud, softly but with intent: "Food addiction, compliance, staying too long in unhealthy settings." Ruthie looks up. "With the acceptance of a loving divine power greater than ourselves, within ourselves, we become willing to believe our shortcomings can be released. We take responsibility for our lives, we do the work, we take the risks, and we move gracefully into living life rather than surviving it."

There it is, Andrea thinks. *That's the way toward release: acceptance of a divine power and asking that power for help.*

Ruthie says, "There are consequences for giving up one's truth to gain the approval of others. There is power in accepting oneself without being controlled by what others say, think, or feel about you. Today I stand in my truth and maintain integrity even when others don't agree or approve. I do this even if it means making difficult changes in my life. Because I matter."

This hits Andrea square between the eyes. "My entire life has been based on what others say, think, or feel about me."

The tigress quietly says, "Isn't it time to let go of that?"

Andrea looks down.

"It's time to look to yourself for approval, not others. It's time to stand in your truth, to walk with integrity, and to make those difficult decisions. This will help you build a trusting relationship with yourself."

Andrea looks up at the tigress with deep appreciation.

"Your higher power has seen all you have done and loves you just as you are, Andrea."

Andrea's eyes fill with tears. She knows these self-defeating beliefs and practices have not served her well. "It's time for me to take responsibility for me, to accept myself as I am, and to love myself without being controlled by what others think of me."

"Yes, that's right, dear one," the tigress says.

Ruthie reads the next, last few sentences from the goddess handbook. "It's up to each of us to accept the messes we created, because we tried to do it on our own, and with humility allow a power greater than ourselves to guide us. We must allow this divine power to do for us that we cannot do for ourselves."

The women listening nod appreciatively.

Ruthie holds her black hearts up high in her right hand and closes with, "For today I am willing to let go and let my divine power take these shortcomings. I thank you, higher power, for your wisdom and strength."

"Humility, not humiliation," Andrea says in wonder. "It's humiliation I have been carrying, while believing what others say, think, and feel. For today, I can exchange humiliation for humility, and in humility I can ask my divine power to do for me what I cannot do for myself."

The facilitator thanks everyone and closes the meeting with a prayer.

This time Andrea joins in.

As the TV clicks off, a welcoming silence, a stillness, fills the room.

Andrea thinks about the harsh way she's treated herself over the years. Believing that she is unlovable, unworthy, without value. She sees that it has been she, not others, who has been getting in the way of her experiencing happiness and being present. She sees that not only has she contributed to her own suffering, but she has also contributed to others' suffering.

She looks up, as if she can see her divine power hovering overhead. "You have always been there for me. I've been the one who's pushed you away. But I feel your presence now. And I know I'm no longer alone." *Actually,* she thinks, *I was never alone.*

A beautiful light fills the room. "Suffering and despair are never the end of the story, Andrea," her divine power says. "I have always been here for you, and I always will be. There is more to be done, but we will pause here. Thank you for your courage and vulnerability."

A cool breeze wafts through the room.

Andrea closes her eyes in gratitude, then cuddles up next to the tigress on the couch. Together, they rest.

• • •

What feels like hours might have been minutes; time is not measured in this place. Andrea stretches her arms toward the ceiling and notices the tigress is already up and about. "Tara, where are you?" she calls.

The patio door opens. Tara's glowing amber eyes are almost invisible as she enters with the rays from the sun. Her tail swishes back and forth and her grin widens as she approaches Andrea. "I think you might be ready for a healing exercise. It's a little ritual I enjoy teaching, and it uses the items that have been placed by the firepit."

"Ah, the bowls and yarn! I've been wondering how those will play a part."

"We'll be doing a fire ceremony to release painful beliefs that block you and hold you captive. Once we release them into the fire, they can be transformed into love and light and you can feel more peaceful and content."

Andrea heads out into a beautiful spring day. The birds are singing, the bees are buzzing, the hummingbirds are making flickering noises while dipping their beaks in and out of the flower bushes and beds and innocently stealing the pollen. Ladybugs are flying through the air, while butterflies flutter about gracefully. Lizards dart back and forth from the garden scurrying behind the firewood against the wall. The sun is shining with only a few clouds scattered above. The flow of life, harmonious and precious. It's a perfect day for a ritual.

Andrea stops in the middle of the yard. "I see we have company."

"Yes, the spirit animals," Tara says, coming up behind her and nodding to the chipmunks, squirrels, and rabbits who are gathering up black hearts from the wooden box. "They will take part in today's ritual."

The little animals approach and, using the small black hearts, create the shape of a larger heart on the patio. Her old "friends," her old beliefs and coping mechanisms, sit boldly in plain sight. Andrea exhales.

"I want you to choose one old belief and one coping mechanism. I want you to hold them in your hands but close to your heart," the tigress says.

With some anxiety, Andrea walks over to the large heart and looks at each of the small black ones. Curiosity kicks in. She picks one up, places it down, then picks up another, and then another. "There I have my two. What's next?"

"Which did you choose?"

"I chose not feeling loveable or worthy of life as my old belief, and people-pleasing as my coping mechanism," Andrea says.

"Tell me what comes up for you when you consider these two hearts."

Countless examples of people-pleasing go through her head. The times she tried to please her mother, her father, even Nana. The times she tried to please her teammates and coaches; year after year taking on the task of fundraising and Vegas Night. Innumerable times she tried to please her co-workers by planning company picnics and the annual Christmas Party, spearheading fundraisers and community events. She sees herself being pulled in a hundred directions, never having time to stop and do what she wanted or needed to do. And then there were all the times she tried and failed to please James, particularly that last night at the beach barbecue when she interrupted James and Samantha's little interlude. It has all led to her not feeling loveable or worthy of living a fulfilled life.

The tigress flicks her tail, and the spirit animals remain still.

"I ... I don't feel so well," she says. "My thoughts, they've been consuming me. I see how I lost pieces of myself."

"Go on," Tara says.

"My mother and James told me self-care was selfish, another lie I believed. So I neglected myself and abandoned myself." Andrea shakes her head. "I get now that self-care is not self-indulgent or selfish. It just means 'me first,' or 'me too.'"

The chipmunks, squirrels, and rabbits step out of their stillness and twirl in a circle. Their little animal noises sound like cheers.

"Most of all, it means me learning to take care of myself, being responsible for myself, and learning to love myself," Andrea says. "Believing I'm not loveable and that I don't matter has only damaged me and my relationships. Today, I would like to humbly ask my higher power to remove these shortcomings."

"Beautifully said, Andrea," the tigress notes.

Andrea looks hopeful. "I will continue to focus on self-love and self-care. I will begin to treat myself positively because I do have value, and I am enough."

Tara steps forward. "There is one more step for you to take. Close your eyes and listen closely. Follow the rhythm of the drum."

As soft drumming music plays, the tigress directs Andrea to think of the elements—wind, fire, water, and earth—and encourages her to sit with them for a few minutes. "Now choose one of the elements and visualize it cleansing you, cleansing the toxins from within you. Relax into the beat of the drum."

Andrea chooses fire because Tara has told her fire is used to release blocking beliefs. As Tara gives her step-by-step direction, she opens her eyes, takes the two black hearts over to the ceramic bowls, and picks up two of the healing herbs covered in cloth. The sound of the drum enters through her soul as she secures the hearts around the bundle of herbs using the colorful yarn to tie it tight and wraps the bundle around the two longest sticks. She uses more of the colorful yarn to create heart energy and promote synchrony.

"There," she says. "What's next?"

The tigress encourages her to walk toward the fire. The spirit animals lead the way, their tiny voices encouraging her. "Blow gently on the bundles, Andrea, blow on the bundles, say goodbye to those old friends," they chatter.

Andrea blows and blows, and blows, and whispers, "You no longer serve me. It's time for you to go."

The beat of the drum is steady and strong, unlocking her heart energy and allowing what no longer serves her to be released into the fire. She holds the long thin sticks over the firepit and tenderly drops both bundles in. She watches the flames leap, releasing the blocks and their toxins into the air. The black smoke disappears, but the blazing colorful flames remain, each color shining with strong, dazzling light. Healing and transformation have begun.

The chanting and drumming begin to slow as the air fills with the smell of sage and other spices. Together, Andrea, Tara, and the spirit animals give thanks to those who assisted in carrying out this ritual and those who have acted as protectors. Thanks to the sun, moon, and stars. To her guides, divine power, and to all who act in the spirit of love. When they are done, they fall silent, relishing the stillness.

"I feel like a piece of me has been returned," Andrea says slowly. "I'm so very grateful."

The tigress closes her amber eyes in acknowledgment. "Come, sit under the tree and rest. You can write about this adventure afterward."

Andrea walks over and sinks comfortably onto her soft blanket placed over the roots of the tree. The spirit animals busy themselves cleaning up the remaining black hearts, placing each carefully back in the wooden box. As they scamper about, the song "Learn to Let Go" by Kesha begins to play.

Andrea falls into a deep sleep, a dream within her dream in which she processes the ritual and its long-lasting effects. She does so unaware that the black hearts she bundled up and released to the fire have been replaced. There are two new colorful glass hearts sitting like royalty in two of the ceramic bowls. The words on the blue heart say "self-care," and the white heart says "loveable and worthy." The ceremony is complete, and magic has transformed the space.

Some people believe that holding on and hanging on
are signs of strength. However, there are times when it
takes much more strength to know when to let go and do it.
—ANN LANDERS

CHAPTER 18

Reflections

Step into your authentic truth,
because your truth will light up the world.
—GABBY BERNSTEIN

Andrea "wakes" under the great oak tree in the backyard of her house on Relationship Row. She asks herself: *Is this me being led around aimlessly by a cast of characters who only help because they feel sorry for me? Or is this me learning to take charge of my life through a dream in which each character represents a part of me that couldn't see the truth in my ordinary world?*

She ponders.

Suddenly the little spirit animals gather around her. They are chattering, fussing, they seem like they're in a hurry.

It's so complicated, Andrea thinks. *Why have me looking into the sky to watch a movie, peering through picture windows and kaleidoscopes, watching big screen TVs? Why couldn't I just see all I needed to from my own bed?*

She doesn't know. She returns her attention to the spirit animals who, it becomes clear, are getting ready to leave and are saying goodbye. She tenderly pets each one and thanks them for their help, kindness, and love. "Will this be the last time I see you?"

"You are never alone," they sing out, and scamper off into the distance.

She feels bereft for a moment, then a noise interrupts her thoughts. Looking up, she sees there's now a note hanging in the thick branches of the tree. "Tara? Tara the tigress, are you here?"

There is silence. Andrea considers a moment and then plucks the note from the tree. It reads:

You are in charge of your dream, and there is a greater purpose in you visiting each separate location. All will be revealed in due time.

Andrea sighs. *I keep hearing in due time.*
The note continues:

There is more work to be done, more truths to be told, more that needs to be discovered and explored. These truths will be powerful ones, and you will need this dream time to digest all this. You must decide whether to fully wake up, or continue to live asleep.

Andrea takes in a breath while counting, repeating this exercise several times before taking in the deepest breath she has taken all day. When she exhales, she lets out a tone from her mouth, a sigh of deep relief. A sense of calm washes over her.

She notices the note has writing on the back. She flips it over:

This stop on the adventure will help prepare you to go home to Serenity Court.

Andrea feels a wave of joy move through her body. She sees clearly that she's being given an opportunity for a new beginning, a new way of life. She also understands the alternative. If she chooses not to stop sleepwalking, she will awaken from her dream back in her ordinary world, but she will be alone with her thoughts and still carrying her burdens. The stakes are high and she knows it.

She looks at the note again and whispers to herself, "I know there's risk in choosing to wake up, and I don't like taking risks. But if I don't truly start to live awake, my life will not change."

A woman's voice floats from the near distance. "The challenge is in seeing clearly that you hold the key. When you accept that, the gates to freedom will swing wide open."

Andrea looks around, seeing no one. The wind picks up and the breeze delivers an invitation. It reads:

Be sure to bring your journal, pen, and the wooden box. Bring your blanket as well. Walk across the street to the park, and there you will see a lake. You will meet your new guides at the water's edge.

New guides! she thinks and feels a jolt of excitement. She closes her eyes after peeking once more at the instructions, then takes a deep breath. Ready. She walks down the street to where the water meets the sun. The two come together as one, an eternal dance bringing calm and hope.

There is no one in sight. The lake begins to ripple, its deep blues and greens offering a shimmering reflection of the sky above. Andrea leans over and gazes into the water, seeing herself in this window within the lake.

As she watches, the ripples begin to take shape, and an image she knows as the Lady of the Lake appears.

Andrea gasps.

The Lady is a vision of beauty, her hair is silvery gray in color. Most of her hair sits neatly upon her head, but there are small, soft strands that fall like wild waves down the side of her delicate face. Her electric green eyes are a reflection of her personality. She exudes positivity, balance, and light. She has a tendency to get jealous easily, but mostly because she possesses large amounts of love. She is a symbol of mystery and magic. She is curious, passionate, and she has a creative outlook on relationships. This is why she has been chosen for this leg of Andrea's journey. She holds her hands close to her heart and speaks. "Andrea, my name is Aurora, and I am one of your guides for this leg of your adventure."

Andrea unconsciously places her hands on her own heart too.

"My mission is to help you reflect and exchange old beliefs for new ones," Aurora continues. "I am here to provide wisdom, strength, and courage. I am here to help you through a transformation of a lifetime if you so choose."

"Hello, Aurora," Andrea says.

A second Lady appears, with what looks like pure white feathers surrounding her body and head. Her hair—long, wild, and loose—dances in the wind. She exudes confidence, energy, femininity, and love. Her eyes are deep brown in color, also a reflection of her personality. She is determined and exerts independence and confidence, all traits she wants to help Andrea expand. She is humble, trustworthy, and possesses immense mental strength, characteristics she wants Andrea to embody. She holds her arms out wide with her palms up as a sign of welcome. "Andrea, I am Viola, and I, too, am one of your guides."

Andrea holds her arms out as if to accept the welcome.

"I am here to help you gain and maintain clarity, and to redirect and sustain your conscious energy from the darkness into the light. I am to assist you with being more attuned with yourself and others," Viola says. "I am here to assist you with getting reacquainted with your femininity, with your body, heart, and soul. I am here to help you choose love, freedom, and passion over anything and everything else, if you so choose."

Both goddesses are powerful. Both embody the supernatural. The depths of the water surrounded by concentric rings of color appear to keep both goddesses afloat. For beneath it all is a lake of mystical conjuring. There is a gentleness about them, about the lake. Andrea is acutely aware of her surroundings because water is often used as a symbol of healing. Andrea takes a breath; she is in awe. She recognizes she is right where she is supposed to be.

"Do you accept our guidance?" they ask in unison.

"Yes! Yes, I do."

"We will be using the lake as a means to reflect," Aurora says. "Together we will see reflections of your past experiences that still need healing before we head back to your awake world."

Andrea is hungry with curiosity.

"The words written on those pesky black hearts take up space in your soul," Viola says. "They will be shaken out of the darkness and brought into the light. It is then your Universe will begin to change its course."

"Do you have the box?" Aurora asks.

"Oh, yes." Andrea reaches into her bag and pulls out the box.

"Please set it on the bank," Viola says.

Andrea complies as a breeze blows through, and the mingled scents of sage, lavender, rosemary, vanilla, and cinnamon fill the air. The weeping willow trees and the clouds create a sense of protection. There is a strong presence.

The box makes a creaking sound as it magically opens. From under the lid, a gigantic beam of light bursts into the air as if angels were filling the sky with love. The goddesses look up with apparent joy.

Andrea can hardly believe her eyes. The white light takes shape of a big, gorgeous white heart, which releases seven single hearts. They float gracefully one by one, landing softly in the lush green grass below. Four of the seven hearts are black. The fifth is a mixture of colors, the sixth one is yellow, and the seventh is bright white.

Andrea's eyes fill with tears and her face flushes. Her body seems to know what might lie ahead.

Aurora picks up the four black hearts and says, "We will revisit specific times in your life where each of these have shown up. We will look at the impact they had on you; times you may have felt affected negatively or even possibly traumatized."

"Look at this one," Viola says. "The one with a mix of colors. It says, 'Grief.'"

"Yes, grief," Andrea says. "Something I will need help processing."

"This yellow one," says Aurora. "This is no stranger to you."

"Yes, forgiveness," Andrea says. "I will need help with forgiving myself too."

The white is still lying on the ground. Aurora and Violet look at it, and then say, together, "Stillness."

"Stillness is something we will teach you," Aurora says.

"From a place of stillness," Viola adds, "you will walk into the light holding love, peace, and freedom."

"Sounds fascinating. And frightening. Will I need my journal?" Andrea asks.

Aurora nods, and Viola says, "You may want to take out your blanket, too, it's time to get comfortable."

The Ladies of the Lake, these goddesses sent to guide and protect, spread their arms wide and together form what seems like mirror. "This mirror," says Aurora, "contains the past, in perfect reflection."

Andrea looks in the mirror and sees a fetus, floating in a womb. *It must be me*, she thinks. She is tethered to her mother by her umbilical cord—theoretically supplying whatever she needed to survive—and yet present-day Andrea can feel, almost physically, that something key is missing. She senses the mother—*my birth mother*, she reminds herself—and the woman's feelings of anxiety, guilt, and shame. *She is not emotionally connected to me*, she realizes.

"You were impacted by anything and everything she experienced while carrying you," Aurora says.

Andrea is trying to understand what this means when the mirror's reflection shifts. Now it shows a very pregnant woman—she knows without ever having seen her before that this is her birth mother, so that must be Andrea herself inside—and someone else she recognizes quite well. "Nana! What is Nana doing with my birth mother? And why is she holding a baby?"

"That baby is your older sister," Viola says. "Your birth mother had just given birth two months before getting pregnant with you. This is why she is so upset. She feels unable to keep you, and she hasn't known what to do about it. Her emotional detachment, her reaction to this trauma, was passed on to you. Unintentionally, she was not creating a safe place for you to reside, so you learned to survive, even then."

"So …" Andrea feels her away along. "So, this feeling of being unlovable, of having no right to exist, has been with me since the womb?"

Aurora nods. "These subconscious memories created an emotional imprint, a conditioning, if you will. It set the course for how your body and mind would respond to the outside world."

"You came into the world feeling unsafe," Viola says. "You have been surviving ever since."

"What about Nana, what is she doing there?" Andrea asks.

"She knew your birth mother," Aurora says. "Nana saw how distressed she was and knew how much your parents wanted another child. So she arranged for your parents to adopt you."

Nana orchestrated my adoption. Andrea finds this oddly shocking.

In the mirror, Nana is kissing the belly of her birth mom, talking to her belly. *Talking to me,* she realizes. She tells Andrea how special she is. That she comes from a family of light bearers. She sings Andrea a song about angels.

Viola, who has been humming softly along, says, "The love your nana extended to both you and your mother was beautiful."

"But you couldn't feel that love yet," Aurora says. "You felt disconnected from the woman who was carrying you, and you knew instinctively that you would be abandoned by her."

Andrea is speechless. A few minutes go by before she looks up at and says, "No wonder I feel anxious all the time. No wonder I believe people are inherently untrustworthy. No wonder I feel everyone else's stress and unhappiness."

"Abandonment and trauma are woven into your birth story," Viola says.

"And your birth story has impacted your entire life," Aurora adds.

The familiar lump forms in Andrea's throat, but this time she is able to swallow past it. She feels an emotional wave surge through her at the sound of what she knows deep in her heart to be truth. "None of it was my fault," she says in wonder.

She streams her most significant memories and realizes how so many of them were influenced by this trauma she experienced in utero. She doesn't know whether to curl up in a ball and cry for that fetus or to stand up tall and tell her she survived and she will heal. She looks down to see that she is holding cupped hands out, as if cradling a tiny baby with compassion and love.

"Nana stood by your birth mother her entire pregnancy," Viola says. "She talked to you every chance she got."

"Nana is the angel who helped bring you into the world, Andrea," Aurora says. "Nana arranged it all."

In the mirror, a montage of memories shines: adoption papers being drawn up; baby Andrea being handed to her parents. Andrea sees for the first time her mother's smile and her father's pure joy. Even Andrew looks happy. Nana beaming. The new family of five, content and grateful.

"Shortly after you were born," Aurora says quietly, "she and her 11-month-old moved far away. You felt that loss, too, but at the time, adoptions were closed, and it was thought best that you not learn anything about your birth mother.

"This is one of the reasons Nana was always telling you about your light," Viola says. "She knew your losses better than anyone. But she also knew you were meant to shine."

Andrea is still for a moment and then makes a decision. "What do I need to heal my body from this memory, this loss?" she asks.

"Heal through the breath." The Ladies of the Lake speak as one.

Aurora and Viola guide Andrea through a breathing meditation, offering her nurture, comfort, and healing as she lies quietly on her blanket. Their words are soothing, loving, and kind. They guide her to let go of the negativity and trauma she felt in the womb and then tuck them away in her memory bank. They guide her out of utero, that place of emotional darkness, and into the light.

"It's time to let it all go," Aurora says.

"Let go of the guilt, the shame, the emotional trauma you have carried," Viola says. "Let go of your sense of abandonment and loss. Let it all go, Andrea. It is no longer yours to carry."

Together the Ladies of the Lake cradle and rock her like a baby as they encourage her to allow herself to heal. Their steady back and forth motion goes on for a while, along with their soft chanting and the sound of soothing music. The meditation closes with the sounds of flutes and the thrumming of a drum.

Andrea's eyes open. She can feel that the energy emanating from her is pure light—light that had been muted, blocked, almost lost. She can feel the trauma she has been carrying her whole life—the story she has told herself—begin to fade. She can see how her beliefs and stories took up residence in her body and how they showed up in her relationships.

"What you experienced in the womb and early childhood impacted how you saw humanity," Aurora says.

Andrea places her hands over her heart. "They impacted the way I responded to the whole world."

Viola says, "In a system that is broken, it's easy to lose connection with yourself. But you survived."

Survival Andrea thinks. *Sleepwalking through life has been a means of survival.*

The Ladies of the Lake stand and hold out their arms to form the magical mirror once again. Reflected in it are four-year-old Andrea and her dad. They're sitting on the floor with her dolls and having a tea party.

"We had a tea party almost every day," Andrea remembers. She marvels at how full of light and laughter she is at this age, and how her father so obviously dotes on her. But something bothers her. Her dad also looks a little anxious, even desperate. The thought comes from deep within her: He counts on my light to help him maintain what little of his own he has left.

She sees her mother appear in the doorway. She looks unhappy. *She feels threatened,* Andrea realizes. *She doesn't like Dad being light when she is not.*

"Give that here," her mother says, grabbing the teapot away from her roughly. "Don't you know how to pour tea? I've shown you a million times. What's wrong with you?"

Four-year-old Andrea sits up very straight, trying to not cry, trying to pay attention.

"It's not like there's anything in this pot anyway," her mother says witheringly. "But here, once again, is how you pour *imaginary tea.*" She slams the empty teacup down, scoffs, and walks off.

"She won," Andrea tells the Ladies. "She stole our joy, our fun, our light, our game."

"And your father, without healthy boundaries, didn't know what to do about it," Aurora says.

In the mirror, her father is pretending to sip tea while pretending nothing has happened. He appears not to notice that little Andrea is on the verge of tears.

237

"This is just one incident. There were many others," Viola says.

"Times when you were criticized and punished," Aurora says.

"Times when she clung to you while she hid in her room and times she pushed you away," Viola adds.

Andrea doesn't realize she's rocking back and forth on her blanket in agitation.

Aurora: "She created situations in which you could never feel secure. She would often ask you to come in and play cards and then criticize you for not playing the game correctly."

Viola: "She would roll over in bed with disgust and dismiss you as if you did not matter."

Aurora again: "You just kept trying over and over to please your mother, and nothing seemed to please her. Do you remember?"

Andrea suddenly remembers a time she and her mom were playing cards. "Gin!" her mother yelled out with glee and put down her hand. Then she laughed and called Andrea a loser.

Loser, Andrea thinks. *I always felt like a loser around her.*

"Even when you would bring her the cookies you and nana baked, she would find a way to criticize or embarrass you," Aurora says.

"One time, she threw the cookies back at me and told me they tasted like shit," Andrea says. "At times I felt like nothing made sense, like my life was fragmented and disorganized."

"You wanted so much to feel love from your mom, yet she was unsafe," Viola says. "That presented conflict, of course, and so nothing made sense."

"I carried this way of life into my adulthood," Andrea muses. "I want to be close to people—but I'm afraid of it too. I don't trust them."

"It is what stands between you and shining your light," Aurora says.

"I tried that!" Andrea says. "I couldn't lift my parents up!"

"And so you felt worthless," Viola says gently.

"Unlovable and worthless," Aurora says. "Two painful and untrue beliefs you have subconsciously carried your entire life."

Andrea and the Ladies look back into the mirror of the lake to see Nana with four-year-old Andrea in the garden.

"Plants need light for energy, Andrea, and so do people," Nana says. "You are a light bearer. It's your mission to shine the light."

Young Andrea grins as she digs her fingers deep into the soil, beaming with pride to be part of a family of light bearers. "All living things need light," she repeats.

Nana smiles down at her. "Light bearers are quite ambitious, and they are fueled by the light. Never forget that you are a light bearer. You are quite ambitious and deeply capable of spreading love and light. Never stop shining your light, Andrea. Onto people, nature, animals, onto all living things."

Four-year-old Andrea dances upon the garden floor, and a light, joined by the rays of the sun, fills the scene with energy, warmth, and love.

Present-day Andrea speaks up. "I did feel like it was my job to spread love and light. But my father clung to my light in ways that made him my job to fix. My mother was jealous of my light, and uncomfortable with the attention my father gave me. It was confusing."

Aurora and Viola concur, raising their arms high.

"Nana poured love and light into me, but I wasn't getting anything from the people I was supposed to trust the most," Andrea says. "And yet I still felt responsible for my parents. I would have done anything to help them be happy. It didn't feel normal, but it felt so necessary."

The Ladies nod and form their arms to shape the mirror once again. In it, fourteen-year-old Andrea is in the living room. She's wearing headphones and doing her homework while standing and dancing in place to the music of her favorite bands.

In his chair in the corner, her dad is staring off into space, as he often did in those days after Andrew passed. Present-day Andrea watches her teenage self put her homework aside so she can comfort and support her dad. She watches him soak it up. He loves the attention, but he doesn't notice she's set aside her responsibilities—herself—to focus on him.

"Night after night," present-day Andrea murmurs. "This was a regular routine. I felt so sad for him. But taking care of him took a toll on my grades."

Aurora says, "Your brother had died. Your mother wasn't emotionally available. He felt empty and alone. He turned to you, to your light. It wasn't fair to you."

"Your mother's emotional demands were placed upon you as well," Viola says. "She relied on you for comfort and love even though she couldn't return them."

Tears roll down Andrea's cheeks. "This has been a lifelong pattern—trying to get love from people who can't give or receive it. It's what's kept me stuck with James."

"It's also what almost killed you," Aurora says.

"Yes, it did." Andrea is newly aware that it doesn't matter how much she achieves on the outside if she's empty on the inside. The consequences of numbing out and sleepwalking through life have taken a physical, mental, emotional, and spiritual toll.

The Ladies of the Lake cradle Andrea in their arms and encouraging her to practice her breathing, steady and strong, as they help create a safe space between the breaths. For the first time, Andrea is able to grieve the old beliefs, the loss of them, and even the challenges in her mission of being a light bearer. The lake takes in the darkness from the memories in her dream and transmutes those memories with a light that brings calm and exudes love and healing.

Andrea feels her body's reaction to her unfolding truth. She can feel the weight of all the toxic beliefs and trauma leave her—especially the belief that she was unlovable.

"It's time to rest now," Aurora says.

Andrea lays her head down on her bag, a perfect pillow atop her soft, silky blanket spread at the edge of the lake. She thinks, *Keeping hope in my back pocket will provide new pathways to peace. I can find peace here by the lake.* She begins to drift into a deep meditative state.

Meanwhile, something magical is happening back home on Serenity Court. An exchange is taking place as the shiny ceramic bowls begin filling with colorful glass healing hearts. The first exchange is the black heart that stands for abandonment, which turns into a deep purple heart representing protection. In the second exchange, the black heart for trauma turns into a red and gray heart representing healing. The black heart for attachment patterns is exchanged for an aqua heart representing emotional connection. And last black heart, for parentification, is exchanged for a heart full of a mixture of vibrant colors of red, yellow, and blue representing parenting.

The entire back yard lights up. Butterflies fly freely overhead. All this will be waiting for Andrea upon her return home.

As the Ladies of the Lake continue to help her move through her sadness and grief, a song begins to play softly: "Healing Hands," by Elton John. Aurora and Viola hold out their healing hands. They provide safety, nurturing, clarity, love, wisdom, and strength. They help her exchange fear for courage and provide healing and comfort as Andrea sleeps. She will need all of it in order to move forward.

Everything you ever wanted is on the other side of fear.
—ANONYMOUS

Reflections for This Chapter

Integrate your thoughts by going through these activities now or coming back to them later. I invite you to listen to the song "Healing Hands" by Elton John as you meditate on the questions below and answer them. May your healing begin.

Do you sometimes feel, as Andrea does, that something is missing? If yes, feel free to journal about it.

Did any of this information resonate with you? If so, write a few sentences about what resonated most and why.

Do you feel like you might need further information about any of the specific topics mentioned? If so, what steps can you take today to seek this information out? What can you do for yourself to start your journey to freedom? (See references in the back of the book for starters.)

CHAPTER 19

The Path to Forgiveness

Grief never ends...but it changes. It's a passage,
not a place to stay. Grief is not a sign of weakness,
nor a lack of faith ... It is the price of Love.
—UNKNOWN

Loss and grief together as one
Awkward, Confusing, Chaotic, and Daunting
It hovers like a big black cloud
We wear it like a cloak
It's Heavy, Draining, Disruptive, Sad
It's a process ... It takes time to heal
Gentleness, Kindness, Compassion, Patience
Archangels of Grief bring comfort, protection, warmth
Archangels are filled with healing and light

Andrea is beginning to feel the stillness within, but she is reminded that she needs to deal with her losses. Her grief feels limitless.

Aurora and Viola ascend from the lake, their movements synchronized in a way only their creator could orchestrate.

Aurora asks, "Are you ready to embrace this glorious day and all it has to offer?"

Andrea stands up and says, "I believe so."

"Today we will be looking into the mirror to face some of your most significant losses. Together we will process the grief you never were able to process," Viola says. "From there, we will walk down the path of forgiveness in order to wholeheartedly greet the light."

"Let's start with you writing in your journal the losses you remember," Aurora suggests.

Andrea thinks back upon her losses and realizes she has a new one to add: the loss of her birth mother and the sibling she never knew.

The list is lengthy and enlightening, beginning at birth and continuing through the loss of her brother, her mother's love, her father's happiness, Nana, her own serenity. There was a miscarriage, loss of love between her and James, loss of her children's trust, loss of faith, loss of her own confidence. In trying to please everyone so she could feel loved and accepted, she lost parts of herself.

"I feel a great deal of grief," Andrea says. "But I buried my feelings for so long that it's a relief to feel them start to slowly seep out."

"We've covered a lot of memories and moments around your birth, childhood, and teen years. It's time to move forward and look at the more recent past. Are you ready?" Viola asks.

Andrea hesitates. "Yes," she finally says.

The Ladies of the Lake invite Andrea to step closer to the water as they prepare to reveal a piece of her soul that was lost. They raise their arms to shape the mirror, and its reflection reveals time and time again where Andrea is giving in to James's temper tantrums.

He shifts blame. "Damn you, Andrea, look what you made me do." He is self-righteous. "Andrea, only an idiot would think that. Now, experts like me ..." He objectifies her. "Love the cleavage showing in that dress, it's just the right tease."

The Ladies move their arms, and the mirror turns around. On the flip side, Andrea sees a montage of times when she allowed James to bribe her. "Just do it, Andrea, do it for me," he says. "I'll take you to see Adele in Vegas ..."

Watching all this, Andrea shudders. *I lost myself. I traded in my truth for lies, I accepted the bribes and fantasy, and ignored my reality, my existence.*

The reflection shifts again to show her growing disconnection from her children, the way her yearning for connection overrides boundaries. She sees herself not speaking up when she should; arguing and pushing when she shouldn't. Saying yes when she means no; saying no when she means yes.

"Everything I ever wanted is on the other side of fear, or so it's been said," she whispers. "Why couldn't I step away from the fear?"

The mirror shows her that in losing her relationships with her children, she has lost those with her grandchildren too. She sees that when her feelings have been hurt, she either freezes or runs. She regresses to old behavior and gets angry, then blames, shames, and goes silent. She sees her part with her struggles with her children and the loss that is a result of her choices around fear. This breaks her heart.

Andrea shakes her head. "No more," she says quietly.

The reflection shifts one final time so that she can witness the biggest loss of all: the loss of self. Incident after incident flashes by as Andrea sees herself losing her voice, losing respect for herself. She witnesses the uncaring way she treats herself, how she abandons herself, how she continues to believe everything is fine when nothing is fine. She sees herself struggle with asking for what she wants and needs because she is so lost, she does not even know what she wants or needs. These flashbacks end with a vision of Andrea looking in a mirror and asking herself, "Who are you and where did Andrea go?"

The reflection disappears.

"I feel suffocated by all of this loss!" Andrea cries out. Tears pour from deep inside her. Her pain has at last found its way to the surface. "Is this what true grief feels like?"

"Yes!" a new voice cries out. "This is what grief feels like."

The Ladies of the Lake raise their arms toward the sky, and down from the sun's rays comes an archangel.

Metatron? Andrea thinks.

"This is Azrael," Viola says as the angel descends. "He is the Archangel of Grief. He is a heavenly helper sent by a power greater than yourself.'

"He is here to help you move through your grief," says Aurora. "With his assistance, you will learn to accept what is, so that you can move forward without continuing to carry this unfinished business with grief."

"Hello, Andrea," the archangel says.

"Hello, Azrael," Andrea says as she focuses on his every move.

Azrael's physique is nothing like Metatron's. Azrael is a bit stocky yet sturdy, like the trunk of the great oak tree. His wings are not as wide as Metatron's, but they appear to be strong and comforting. His hair is dirty blond and short, unlike Metatron's. Azrael is neatly shaven, yet he sports a tiny goatee, which he twirls when pacing back and forth. He wears a robe made up of a mixture of bright colors, just like the heart that represents grief. And he has flip flops on, not sandals like Metatron. He is a character indeed, yet he exhibits a kindness about him, a softness.

"I am here to guide you through this part of your journey, but I am also here to console you," Azrael says. "Come, rest your head inside my wings." His voice is soothing.

Andrea is a little afraid of feeling even more than she does right now. She looks to the Ladies for reassurance, which they give her with their nods. Then she walks toward Azrael, who enfolds her gently in his soft, comforting wings.

"Relax into the breath," he says. "Just breathe."

Andrea hangs her head, and her breathing relaxes into her familiar pattern: inhaling for seven, holding for seven, exhaling for seven. She repeats this several times as Azrael murmurs to her. He calls her "dear one," and she smiles, reminded of Metatron.

Finally, she is able to raise her head, though memories of her losses continue to flash by, and her heart feels heavy. *Grief is draining, disruptive, and sad,* she thinks to herself. *Grief is here.*

"Grief is the price of love," Azrael says. He invites Andrea to sit back and relax and advises her to get out her journal, as he has plenty to share about grief. A fresh breeze from the north blows her hair around and rustles the leaves around the edge of the lake. The wind is light and pleasant.

"Grief is more than just sadness," Azrael shares. "It can be shattering. It can affect your thoughts, your ability to make decisions, even your body. It can take up more energy than you can imagine."

I can imagine, Andrea thinks.

"Even when grief feels insurmountable, it is possible to heal. I will teach you how to process grief so that you can recover from it."

"It feels like I'll never get over it," Andrea says.

The Ladies of the Lake from a circle with their arms once again, creating a mirror image as they hover over the clear, fresh water.

"There are many ways to process grief," Azrael says, "but I find the seven-stage process to be most helpful."

"What are the seven stages?" Andrea asks.

"The first stage is shock," Azrael says. "The second is denial. The third is anger. And the fourth is bargaining."

I have made many bargains, and I have taken many bribes, Andrea thinks.

Azrael continues. "The fifth is guilt. The sixth is depression, which includes reflection and loneliness."

Andrea thinks, *There it is. I have felt so very lonely.*

"Then there is the upward turn. A phase of working through our feelings, of reconstruction. Ultimately, this leads to the seventh stage: acceptance and hope."

"This is a lot to take in," Andrea says. "But it makes sense, and I can see that I've never allowed myself to move through all the stages."

The Ladies and Azrael encourage Andrea to journal about what she's just learned, so she sits on her blanket by the lake and writes out one incident, one memory, at a time, breathing in the emotions around her grief. She nurtures herself during the process, and then exhales any toxins left behind. She breathes in as she counts to seven, holds for seven, and breathes out for seven. She repeats this process seven times, releasing the grief she has held onto in her body. She gives herself permission to let it all go.

"You are doing well," Aurora tells her.

"We can see the light you are breathing in, and the blackness that escapes your body as you exhale," Viola says.

Andrea completes the breathing exercise and begins to journal about letting go of her grief. As the ink flows from her pen, that place inside her where she tucked away all her emotions loosens. She thinks of the wooden box. *It's time to spring the top of that box wide open.*

"Yes, Andrea," Azrael affirms. "Imagine that when you spring that top open, you will step into a new space, into an emotional landscape with less pain and more joy."

Andrea smiles.

Azrael and the Ladies watch with excitement as Andrea gets closer to stepping into new possibilities of living and loving. They can see her heaviness and weariness beginning to be shed. They can see her finally breaking free of the burdens she carries.

"Be gentle with yourself, Andrea." Azrael says. "Give yourself the time you need to fully grieve. We are here to help you with your transition from grief to acceptance and to walk you toward a light-filled space of love, peace, and freedom."

"How will I know when I am ready to fully surrender?" Andrea asks.

"You will know when you feel yourself fully coming alive," the Archangel of Grief tells her. "You will know when you cherish your ability and capacity to transform, and when you believe it is all possible. It is then you will be awakened. It is then you will feel anything inauthentic fall away. It is then you will be ready to fully transform."

"I feel like I'm moving closer and closer to this place of mystical potential. Like I will become one with the divine, with what Ruthie and Rae would call my Inner Goddess," Andrea says.

Azrael hands her a little affirmation card that reads, "Grief is a passage, not a place to stay." "My time here is coming to an end for now, Andrea, but I will be with you in spirit as you continue down the path of healing. Stay the course. I will be back, and together we will cross over into the light. May you continue to be blessed."

"Wait, don't go, wait, I have questions, wait…" Andrea calls out. She stands and watches in awe as the archangel slowly glides away. When she can no longer see Azrael, she sinks down onto her knees as if to pray and notices he left behind pouches of lavender, heather, and rosemary. She smiles in delight.

"It's time for another ritual," Aurora says. "You don't want to miss the invitation."

"Invitation to what?"

"An invitation to come into closer contact with courage," Viola says.

"We will create fire within the lake, and you will begin the exchange process. This is where your healing will continue," Aurora says.

Andrea takes a few fragrant handfuls from each pouch and gently tosses them into the fire.

"Here, we will exchange fear for courage," Viola says.

Andrea pinches more petals from the sachets and the aroma of each spice thickens in the air. She feels a different energy, and opens her arms, twirling around enough times to make herself dizzy. She can feel the exchange, and it feels like freedom.

It is a heavenly way to move through the losses,
let go of the grief, and move toward the light.
—MELODY BEATTIE

Amends

Humility leads to strength and not weakness.
It is the highest form of self-respect to admit
mistakes and to make amends for them.
—JOHN J. MCCLOY

Andrea opens her travel journal to find unfamiliar writing there. "What's all this?"

"Sometimes lessons from our higher power appear via divine intervention," Viola says. "I have learned not to question them but instead to embrace them."

Andrea raises an eyebrow and reads: *Sometimes we find ourselves in the wrong place at the wrong time. You might have found yourself with the wrong partner, spouse, colleague, or friends. You may have been robbed, physically or emotionally harmed, lied to, betrayed, fooled, or taken advantage of. Bad things happen to good people all the time.*

"Huh." Andrea picks up what is left of the sachets and thinks about her family and its dysfunction. She can see more clearly how this dysfunction translates into other areas of her life and in most of her relationships.

"You did the best you could to survive, Andrea," Aurora says. "But when we use coping skills such as control, manipulation, minimizing, and anger, we end up hurting ourselves and others. This is why making amends is so important. Amends work both ways."

"Wait, I know I owe specific people amends. But when it comes to James, isn't he the one who owes me amends?" Andrea asks.

251

"You owe each other," Viola says.

"Open your journal and make a list of all the wrong done to you, especially by the people you may still have discord in your heart toward," Aurora directs. "But be careful to process the events that took place first because offering amends and forgiveness too soon can be damaging."

"Then make a second list of the wrongs you've done to others," Viola says. "It is time to make things right."

Andrea nods in agreement.

Viola smiles and continues. "This will not only free you from guilt but also allow you to take responsibility for your hurtful behaviors and actions and restore these relationships. Making amends is a gift."

"Often making amends to ourselves and forgiving ourselves can be the most difficult part of the recovery process," Aurora says.

"But if you want to recover from all the wrongs done to you as well as all the wrongs you did to others and to yourself, you are the one responsible for taking the steps forward to do so." Viola's voice is full of compassion.

Andrea scatters the last petals from the sachets and smells their fragrance, then sits down to work on her lists.

While she writes, the Ladies of the Lake prepare. They create the mirror in the lake, but this time a ring of fire surrounds it. Fire will serve as protection as well as help release blocking beliefs and transforming them into love and light.

Andrea finds herself enjoying making a list of the people who harmed her. James, Mom, Dad, Samantha … but when it came to making a list of those she has harmed, she pauses.

I have to be willing to make amends to them all, she thinks. She sighs, but resumes writing. She knows she has a responsibility to make amends to the people she has hurt.

"How is the process of amends going for you, Andrea?" asks a familiar deep voice.

Andrea spins around, heart racing, and spots Tara the tigress. She runs toward her animal guide, nearly tripping over her own feet.

The tigress welcomes Andrea by purring loudly, showing her affection as cats do.

Everyone settles in at the edge of the lake.

"This lake symbolizes strength, stability, endurance, justice, and honesty," Aurora says. "This is a time for all those attributes to shine. Making amends is not about blame, but is instead an opportunity to move away from blame. Making amends is about healing."

"In many ways, Andrea, you are the one who received the greatest injury," the tigress says. "Some done to you by others and some by yourself."

Andrea tears up.

"Nothing you did as a child warranted the abuse and neglect you suffered," Tara adds. "But it is important to recognize how you reacted to these injustices and the consequences of your reactions. We have established that rage has been a big part of that. This force needs to be reckoned with, but these steps will provide a pathway to peace."

Andrea thanks the tigress for the reminder.

"This next reflection will bring memories from the best of times and the opportunity to forgive the worst," the tigress says.

Andrea takes a deep breath. She wants to be ready; she doesn't know if she'll ever be fully ready. She gazes into the tigress's deep amber eyes and says, "Let's do this."

The group sits comfortably by the fire as the late afternoon breeze starts to roll in. The Ladies of the Lake take turns manning the fire, and together they all observe the vibrant flames jumping from one side of the ring to the other and dancing intimately as one. The glows from each and every angel contributes to the colors changing from red to orange to yellow to green to blue.

An image appears. There are Rae and Ruthie at their home group meeting, talking about their experience, strength, and hope.

"I see them, there they are. I feel like I have known them forever," Andrea says with excitement.

"Tonight is the night when the women share personal stories and make amends," Tara says.

Rae starts things off. "When I made my list of people I'd harmed, I put myself on top of the list. I knew I had to be willing to make amends to everyone on the list, so I felt it was best to start with me. God—the God I didn't believe in—was next on my list. Then the others."

Andrea realizes she needs to be at the top of her own list. She wonders if she will end up putting God on her list after herself.

"I feel like I'm far enough along in my program to make amends and forgive the people who've harmed me," Rae says. "But it takes a while to get there, so be patient with yourself."

Andrea makes a note in her journal.

"The second list, though … it was hard to recognize how I'd harmed others," Rae admits. "A form of denial, I suppose. Now I see that not only did my drinking affect others, but I also hurt others when I lied to them, or manipulated them, or when control and anger led the way. Others suffered because of my drinking and codependent behavior."

Several of the women nod their heads. One woman winked at Rae; another raised an eyebrow. A small voice from the back of the room said, "Amen."

"I didn't realize that my alcoholism and codependency had a partnership," Rae says. "A bad marriage, if you will. The abuse I placed upon myself, the neglect, how I abandoned myself, these were all means of punishing myself. And when I punished myself, anyone else in my path would also be punished."

Andrea places her hands on her heart.

"The people on my list of those I've hurt, after myself, are my higher power, then my parents, my siblings, and some longtime friends. I've carried a lot of guilt and sadness for many years, but I'm so grateful to be able to make my wrongs right. I have no room for defensiveness, victimization, or minimization. Only integrity, honesty, and humility."

Andrea cringes. She carries a lot of guilt and sadness when it comes to her relationships, and she sees now that she has used manipulation, defensiveness, and victimization to get her way. She knows she needs to make her wrongs right.

Rae brings her share to a close. "By owning my own behavior, choices, and attitudes, by taking responsibility for myself, I am making proper restitution. This is my means of making a proper amends and then asking for forgiveness."

All who are witness place their hands together in a sign of giving thanks.

"I will continue to ask my higher power for guidance and strength. I am forever grateful for the lessons I've learned and continue to learn," Rae says. "I am so happy to be one step closer to fully discovering the goddess within."

Andrea sits in awe of Rae and her share. She has so much respect for her. She wants to hold her and tell her she understands. She thinks about her use of drugs and alcohol, and her codependent behaviors and patterns. She thinks about the people she's hurt along the way. Tears well up as she sees how important it is to take responsibility for her own behavior and to clean up the messes of the past, so she can feel good about how she conducts her relationships in the future. The importance of seeking the goddess within is becoming crystal clear.

Ruthie is next. She tells the group she'll be sharing her experience, strength, and hope, as well as the process she uses when making amends and how she checks in with herself every day.

Andrea thinks, *I like that idea of taking a daily personal inventory of myself and when I am wrong to promptly admit it. This is huge!*

"Like my fellow goddess traveler, I, too, placed myself first on the list when making amends," Ruthie says. "Forgiving myself has been the hardest part of the process so far. It starts with giving myself permission to have feelings and emotions because I stuffed them for so long."

Andrea looks over at the box, the box that represents where she stuffed her feelings and emotions until just recently.

"I used food to numb myself, so I didn't have to feel. This realization has been painful, but I see now how unhappy I've been, and that I've blamed others for my unhappiness. This is a pattern," Ruthie says.

Andrea can relate.

"I had to learn to give myself permission to be alive and happy because happiness was not something I felt I deserved," Ruthie continues. "Being unhappy is a familiar feeling from childhood. Ever since I was quite young, I've questioned my existence and how I came to be."

Andrea gasps.

"I had to learn to re-parent myself, to be gentle and compassionate toward myself. This was the most difficult amends I had to make because for years I allowed others to mistreat and control me. As a result, I treated myself in the same manner."

Wow, wow, wow, Andrea thinks to herself. *It's like she lives inside my head.*

Ruthie speaks earnestly about knowing it is time to own her power, to start trusting her instincts again, and to value her own feelings and needs. She knew that when she could learn to do all of these things for herself, that would be the biggest amends of them all. "Taking a personal inventory on a daily basis is key for me," she says. "If I wake up not feeling my emotions, if my body aches, and if I feel my motives become about using food for comfort, then these are signs that I am out of touch with myself."

Andrea is rapt.

"So I give myself permission without blame and shame to accept where I'm at. I stop and breathe, I reach into my goddess toolbox, and I help myself get back on track. If I need help from others I reach out. Most of all, I ask myself what I need. For so long I had no idea what I wanted or needed."

Andrea writes feverishly in her travel journal: "What do I want and need?"

Ruthie ends with, "I used to keep myself from feeling love and joy in my relationships. I would deny myself the simple things. Today, I embrace all life has to offer. My divine power promises that there is hope in a new day, and for that I am grateful. I am so ready to celebrate the goddess within."

Andrea sits quietly with tears rolling down her cheeks, absorbing all that has been said. She sees that punishing, neglecting, and abandoning herself are all wrongdoings toward self. She sees how she has been substituting control for owning her own power, and how she has used fear to avoid being courageous.

The lingering fragrance of the petals tells so many stories, so many tales. Andrea glances over at the meeting room before the reflection dissipates and before the fire dies out, and she sees the tree on the wall with all the heart exchanges. There in the middle of the trunk she sees a yellow heart that says "forgiveness."

Viola asks Andrea if she has anything she would like to share. Andrea responds first with a smile because seeing the tree is comforting. Then she thanks them all for this experience. She acknowledges the importance of these visions and accepts where change is imminent.

"It's up to me to clean up my own messes and claim my happiness," she tells the Ladies and the tigress. "I must walk the path with humility. Then I can come from a place of strength."

"There is one more heart that needs to be addressed," the tigress says, holding up the yellow heart of forgiveness. "This is why fear has been exchanged for courage. It takes courage to truly forgive."

Forgiveness

Forgiveness is a virtue of the brave.
—INDIRA GANDHI

"Staying in resentment and blame only hurts you, Andrea," Aurora says. "Forgiveness is all about taking one's power back."

"If you continue to define your life by what others say about you, or by what others did to you, this will only cause you more pain and suffering," Viola says. "Playing unresolved pain over and over in your mind, reliving the offenses done by others, and being unwilling to make things right—all these things steal your dignity, integrity, joy, and power."

A vision of Andrea herself appears in the lake. Her fists are clenched and her mood irritable. She is stomping around, angry at the world and justifying the hate she holds in her heart toward James. She is ranting and raving, wrestling with feelings of indignation and distress. Her hurt overpowers everything else.

As the vision begins to fade into the ripples of the lake, Andrea says, "I don't like that person. How do I help her forgive? How do I forgive her?"

"Will you choose a clenched fist or an open heart, Andrea?" the tigress asks. "Will you continue to entrap yourself in a cage, bound by guilt, shame, and pain when there is so much more to see and discover?"

Andrea, eyes widen.

"It's time to expand your heart and fill it with joy," Tara urges her. "It's time to invite a loving heart in, one that will protect and guide you and allow you to receive and give beauty, creativity, and trust. The choice is yours, Andrea."

The vision of angry Andrea fades, leaving a playful light dancing on the lake.

"Your heart must remain open even if there are those unable or unwilling to hear your amends or say they are sorry," the tigress says. "Forgiveness is not for them, it is for you, for your healing."

"Forgiving does not always mean reconciliating," says Aurora. "It just means we stop punishing ourselves and the other person."

"Thank you for that gentle reminder," Andrea says. "It will be my choice as to how these relationships unfold, I know."

Viola says, "It is important to stay open to the idea of divine intervention so all that needs to can and will emerge. Then you will be able to reclaim yourself and your life."

"What a perfect gift to take home," Andrea murmurs in quiet gratitude.

The Ladies of the Lake spread their arms out to create a final reflection. It appears to be words of advice on seeking forgiveness. With each wavelet comes a new thought.

The first wavelet says: amends are a spiritual exercise in humility.

The second says: amends can be in writing, like a letter or a journal.

A third ripple calls for prayers or mantras. "This one, especially the prayer Ho'oponopono, is widely used," the tigress says.

"Ho'oponopono?" Andrea asks.

"Let's look into the mirror and witness someone you know who practices that particular mantra," the tigress says.

The Ladies of the Lake glide freely upon the rising air. In the mirror, Andrea sees soft white petals and …

"Wait, that's Sophie," Andrea says.

"I need help letting go of distrust," Sophie's reflection says, "especially of my mother. I am sorry. Please forgive me." Sophie breathes out, releasing the toxins as she cleanses her soul.

Andrea places her hands over her mouth.

"Thank you," Sophie says. "Thank you for helping me release these negative thoughts." As she breathes in deeply, she adds, "I love you, memories. I am thankful for the chance to liberate you. To free myself, to free my mother. I love you. Thank you." She breathes out as she cleanses and releases her memories of distrust.

Andrea hears the magic in Sophia's words, magic that she knows without question opens the combination lock to the Universe. She says, "I am here to open everything that is locked within me." She closes her eyes and throws her arms wide open, thanking the power greater than herself for her journey.

The reflection ends, the mirror fading into a swirl as the soft white petals continue to float above the surface.

The Ladies of the Lake speak in union. "This ends our time with you."

Aurora says, "May you take with you the wisdom, strength, and courage to live fully awake, so that your transition from this dream world to your real, waking world will be complete."

Viola says, "May you take with you clarity, love, freedom, and a passion for life, all gifts we bestowed upon you so that you can step out of the darkness and into the light."

Andrea thanks Aurora and Viola for their Inner Goddess beauty and spirit. Within seconds, they vanish.

"When you are ready," the tigress says, "we will move toward the green door."

"I'm not sure what awaits me there," Andrea responds, "but I trust you, in all of you. I trust that when you take me there, I will not be alone, and that my journey home will be one of freedom and redemption. Today I am feeling brave."

Then, just as they are about to leave the park and move on to the last house—the one with the green door—a gust of wind blowing across the water causes them to turn around and look at the lake one last time. There, right before their eyes, the black heart, the one from the box in Andrea's bag that was named fear, flies up and over the lake. There, it turns to emerald green, representing the courage to walk through the green door. The heart is whisked away by a gust of wind and dances ahead of them toward the last house on Relationship Row.

As they follow, Andrea feels warm summer rain on her body. In that moment, her soul connects to the sacred healing taking place. The enduring song "Forgiveness" by Matthew West plays on.

Forgiving isn't something you do for someone else.
It's something you do for yourself. It's saying,
"You're not important enough to have a stranglehold on me."
It's saying "You don't get to trap me in the past.
I am worthy of a future."
—JODI PICOULT

Reflections for This Chapter

Integrate your thoughts by going through these activities now or coming back to them later. I invite you to listen to the song "Forgiveness" by Matthew West as you do so. This song is a true expression of what it means to let go of grudges and bitterness. How to let it go and set it all free. It's a song about doing what seems impossible, yet is so attainable. Let this song guide you toward forgiveness.

Have you thought about loss and grief in the terms described? Did you learn anything new? Have you lost anyone you loved? How do you process loss? What steps do you take to heal when grieving?

Making amends is not just about apologizing. It's about changing a behavior. Have you ever made amends, and to whom? How did it go? Is there room for improvement? Can you think of any more people you need to make amends to? Feel free to journal about it.

If you have never made amends, did this chapter persuade you to at least think about it? Explain.

Forgiveness can be tricky. What are your thoughts on forgiveness? How can forgiving someone who hurt you benefit you? How can asking for forgiveness from someone you hurt benefit you? Remember, it's not about the other person. Forgiveness is about you taking responsibility for your healing.

What do you think about the Ho'oponopono prayer (I love you; I am sorry; Please forgive me; I thank you)? Have you used it? Would you consider using it? Feel free to look it up and play and practice.

CHAPTER 20

The Green Door

*It is this belief in a power larger than myself and
other than myself which allows me to venture
into the unknown and even the unknowable.*
—MAYA ANGELOU

*The Green Door
What's behind it?
Stillness …
It's intriguing, a mystery, a venture
Where does it take you?
Into the unknown and even the unknowable
Who guides you?
A Power Greater than Yourself and Other than Yourself
Who is this Power Greater than Yourself?
One of your understanding
What does that mean?
It means someone or something you feel safe with
surrender to, trust …
What does this Power do?
Guides you … loves you … shows you the way
How do I get there?
Through the Green Door*

A gentle wind blows in from the south, bringing the rain. The raindrops bring deep joy, prayers that are being answered, a sense of being alive, all perfect gifts from the skies. Each drop kisses the skin, steady and soft, the very essence of nature. Water represents healing.

The emerald green door awaits—vibrant, fierce, and powerful. There is a strong vibe, a spiritual vibe indeed. Andrea stares at the green door. It looks so inviting and frightening at the same time. While standing and staring she finds herself reminiscing about everything that has taken place so far on her journey, catching glimpses of the divine interventions that took place in order for her to face the green door. She remembers when she first entertained the idea of coming on such a journey, first having to admit her life was a complete mess and that she needed help to untangle it. Each visit and memory, each snapshot, each visualization, each lesson brought her here.

The tigress quietly and respectfully stands still beside her.

Each step along my journey has been in perfect synchronicity with the next, Andrea thinks to herself as she stands on the sidewalk regarding the green door.

She hears a sound and turns to find Metatron beside her. "Hello, dear one."

Together they walk up the path to the door. The door that once stood alone is now blessed with support. Waiting for her there are White Tara the tigress, the doe and her fawn, the Archangel Azrael, Andrea's spirit animals, the Ladies of the Lake, and a number of ancestors, including …

"Nana!" Andrea exclaims.

Each of them nod at her, a quick bow of humility. It reminds Andrea of the humility she has felt along the way, the humility she wishes to take home. She feels gratitude growing inside and gives each of them a loving smile.

The spirit animals hand Andrea the rest of the black hearts they gathered, the ones that have not yet been exchanged. Andrea tucks the hearts in the box she has carried inside her bag.

Because of her willingness, her open heart, and her courage, the healing has begun. But not knowing exactly what's on the other side of the green door still feels a bit ominous. She puts her feelings and skepticism aside and faces forward with enthusiasm and strength. The green door with the flat black wrought iron handle, still locked tight, emanates a sense of spirituality.

"Today is an important day," Metatron says. "It marks the day for you to make your final decision, your decision to wake up and walk through the green door."

Andrea faces the green door with hope.

"In that decision you will commit to live your life fully awake in your ordinary world. You will choose to take risks by walking away from resistance. You will choose to operate from a higher state of consciousness from your highest self. Life will not be perfect, but it will be greatly improved. Your truth is your freedom," Metatron says.

Andrea takes in a deep breath and counts to seven, holds for seven, and exhales for seven. She repeats this process seven times. "I will be taking all of my guides with me, right?"

Metatron nods.

She lets out a sigh of relief at the knowledge that she will not be alone.

"In this new kingdom loss, grief, and despair will be exchanged for joy. Self-loathing and self-doubt will be exchanged for self-love. Denial and avoidance will be exchanged for living awake," the tigress says.

"When you walk through the green door, you will no longer feel as if something is missing," the doe says. "You will feel whole."

Metatron steps to Andrea's side. "If you choose not to enter the green door you will not be alone, but that nagging feeling that something is missing will persist. It might leave you feeling paralyzed at times."

Andrea knows that if she chooses not to commit, the decision may cost her. She will not become the person she wants to be, but she will also have to live with that truth, since denial and avoidance are no longer her friends. She reaches for the heart that says "courage," and holds it to her chest. Within seconds a white heart lands at her feet. Andrea picks it up and smiles. It says stillness. She holds both hearts close to her own.

Andrea closes her eyes. "I, Andrea, want to have healthy, loving relationships in which there is no room for judgment, anger, bitterness, resentment, control, or manipulation," she announces aloud. "I want to live a life that is mine, to grow and mature into my best self, and allow others to do the same."

Her spirt animals scamper about with joy.

"I am willing to take the risks necessary to have that life. I know it won't be perfect, and I accept that. I understand I have more pain to face and release. I see how and why creating my lists and making amends is something I must do in order to walk in integrity."

Aurora and Viola spread fresh petals that flutter like butterfly wings, vibrant and alive.

Andrea looks at her spiritual team with love, admiration, and appreciation. "I will persist in letting old beliefs and perspectives go so I can make room for new, healthy ones. I will tend to my inner garden and landscape daily by taking a personal inventory. I will make my wrongs right. I want to thrive and live life, not just survive it. My ego is no longer in charge. I release ego and welcome the spirit in. I wish to walk in humility with each of you by my side."

The fawn pushes a wet nose affectionately into her hand.

"You all have given me a new outlook on trust," she says. "Trust that led to hope, hope that led to acceptance. I understand that I cannot do this alone, and I am grateful for each and every one of you. You accept and love me just as I am, and you taught me to accept and love me just as I am. You taught me that I am enough. Thank you!"

She pauses and looks at Metatron. "If I choose to walk through the green door, I'll leave the void behind, right? I'll have an opportunity for a new way of being?"

"Life won't be without challenges, Andrea," Metatron says. "But it won't be the ordinary life you have been living because in this new way of life, you will be fully awake."

Andrea feels a thrill of anticipation.

"You will have the tools, resources, love, and support you need when those challenges arise, and you will not be alone. Life will be fulfilling; joy and laughter will be present again. In acceptance there will be a sense of freedom, freedom from the bondage that you have carried, freedom from being stuck in the void."

"Thank you!" Andrea, says. "Thank you! Today, I choose to trust the mystery of what lies behind the green door. Today, I embrace the magic that acceptance can bring into my recovery and my life. I am ready to walk through the green door."

Time expands, and true happiness fills the air. The green door opens, and Andrea leads the way through. It is as if they are all riding upon the breath of divine grace. On the other side of the door is nothing but vast, pearlescent light.

Andrea takes the biggest breath of all; her soul and spirit are finally at peace. She is ready to live awake and ready for the rest of her life. "How do I get home?"

"Jump on," the tigress says. "You will be surrounded by stillness, but the messages you will receive will be many. Take it all in. Absorb it all as you leave the void behind and open to a new chapter. Close your eyes and relax into your dreamscape as you head home."

Andrea nods nervously.

Her higher power chimes in. "Allow your breath to become deep and slow, and if you wish, feel free to pause after each inhalation and exhalation. Allow this to become your new natural flow. Let there be a soft light that glows and expands bringing in a sense of peace and tranquility."

Andrea breathes and looks around to make sure her guides follow.

"Allow there to be a passage and openness to your heart," the tigress says. "Your awareness will eventually settle within the center of your heart, and you will rest there for as long as you need. You will stay centered in this place as you experience the stillness available in your breath. Are you ready?"

Andrea, already in a trance-like state, says "Yes, I am ready."

The green door closes behind her. Before her is a radiant, pure white light that feels oddly familiar, like a place of origin. She is riding on Tara's back through a space that feels still and calm, like the essence of nature. She sees white fluffy clouds begin to assemble, forming what looks like a pathway to peace.

"Do you remember when you asked how will you know when it's time to fully surrender?" the tigress asks?

"Yes."

"It is time now," Tara says. "It is time to move forward in love and light."

Andrea formally and silently releases all that she's been carrying. And as they continue to fly through the air, a change takes place. There in the skyway, a magnificent prism of colors illuminates the center of an enormous white heart. Little glass hearts dance freely through the air. The exchange has begun.

"What's happening?" Andrea asks.

"You are witness to your own awakening," Tara says.

She watches as right before her eyes, neglect is exchanged for cherish, which is a cool and sophisticated off-white with a subtle blue undertone. Resentment is exchanged for the magenta of contentment. Bitterness is traded for silver magnanimity. Judgment for deep green simplicity. Manipulation and resistance for glittery gold acceptance. Control for deep blue surrender. Self-doubt and self-loathing are exchanged for shocking pink self-acceptance and self-love.

Andrea is speechless.

The tigress circles them around just in time to see denial and avoidance exchanged for a vivid violet living awake. And, last but not least, grief and despair are swapped for joy, which is a mix of orange and yellow. The light continues to amplify itself reaching far and wide, into every dimension.

"The hearts will be waiting for you in the shiny ceramic bowls when you return home to Serenity Court," Tara says. "Do you now believe there is more to life than what you have been living?"

"The truth has been exposed, and I no longer need to protect myself," Andrea says. "I am precious, and it's time for me to create space for my for existence, the one I now believe I deserve. I want to be alive. I want to live awake."

This power greater than herself whispers, "This is the way back to your soul, back to living awake. May you come fully out of the darkness and into the light that is reaching out to guide you through the rest of your life."

Andrea reminds herself to stay present in her stillness. She can't help but think back on all the times she sat under the tree, where she became one with the tree. Her memories about all the strange and mysterious events that took place flash through her mind.

"Hold on tight," the tigress says as they glide through the continuation of life.

"Be still, dear one," she hears Metatron say. "Be still and open your ears, your heart, and your center. Be still in spirit, in self."

Andrea feels herself relaxing her grip on Tara's fur, content to enjoy the ride. She wanders in her stillness until her mind takes her to her safe place under the tree, free from anything that might cause her harm. The place where her journey started. The song "Almost Home" by MercyMe begins to play.

CHAPTER 21

Home Sweet Home

be easy. take your time.
you are coming home. to yourself.
—NAYYIRAH WAHEED

Andrea can hear music—it's the song "Home," by Daughtry. *I love that song* she thinks to herself.

She opens her eyes, fully awake, and gasps. She begins to inhale to the count of one, two, three, four, five, six, seven; holds for seven; then exhales for seven, a sequence she repeats seven times with the familiarity of having done it all her life. She senses something miraculous and magical has happened, yet she's not quite sure what.

She sits up, looking at the familiar walls of her bedroom and seeing the sunlight shining through the big sliding door. She's looking for clues to help her make sense of what she's feeling inside.

I think I've been asleep for some time, she thinks. And yet she has an odd feeling that she has left her bed. She looks over at the travel magazine on her nightstand and remembers the words "faraway places." If she went somewhere, where was it? And how did she get there—and back home?

From outside, she hears the birds singing, the crickets chirping, and the frogs croaking, all in perfect harmony. She gets up, walks to the sliding glass door, and looks down from her balcony into her backyard. There, the sun shines bright on what feels like a new beginning. She can see that there are a few scattered clouds here and there, but no rain in sight. The subtle waves of the swimming pool reflect the beautiful blue sky. It all looks normal, though it doesn't feel normal. There is a strange new energy to everything.

She can remember bits and pieces of her dreams. She remembers learning something, and … flying? Thoughts come unbidden to her mind: *Life is a generous gift. Sometimes easy, sometimes hard, but never does it have to be a struggle. Life can be joyful, precious, and free.*

Memories of her dreams—Metatron, the doe and her fawn, Tara the tigress, the Ladies of the Lake, Archangel Azrael—flood her mind. *What was that all about?* she marvels.

She sits back down, pulls her travel journal off the night-stand, and notices that the title on the cover of her journal says, "The Secret Dreamworld of Andrea Cooper." *How did that get there?* she wonders.. Then she begins to write. "What if," she writes, my dream was about learning to trust a power greater than myself so that I truly could let go of all the old beliefs and limiting perspective and self-sabotaging thoughts and live a more peaceful life? What if my dream was intended to turn me toward my higher power, my light, and my strength for guidance and healing?"

As Andrea writes these thoughts, she notices that many of the pages in her journal are already filled. She resolves to read them later, feeling an urge to focus on and live in the moment.

She takes a breath, as deeply as she can, and exhales with a lion's breath, stretching her arms out wide. *I'm home,* she thinks. She walks downstairs to her kitchen, over to the sliding door, and steps outside. *I'm finally home.*

She looks around to see that her pool is filled with clean, crisp, filtered water. She sees the tiniest of waves rippling and hears their swishing sounds. It reminds her that she is not alone. She looks up, smiles, and says "thank you" to her higher power, to the Universe, to the divine. "Thank you!"

The nearby firepit smells comfortingly of lavender, heather, and rosemary. She notices that there are shiny ceramic bowls placed around the pit, just like the ones in her dream. "Nah," she says. "Can't be." But as she walks slowly toward them, she can see that there are a great number of bundled sticks tied with colorful yarn, and the remains of what look like black hearts. She can also see glass hearts made up of a myriad of colors. *The exchange,* she thinks to herself as she picks up one of the hearts. The one she chose says retribution and punishment. She remembers with a start that it was exchanged for absolution and forgiveness. It is bright yellow.

"I have been forgiven," she says quietly out loud. "I have been forgiven, and I am able to forgive." She smiles and wonders if all of her guides are with her now.

Just beyond the firepit, her neglected garden is somehow mysteriously thriving. She walks toward it as two bunnies cross her path—they look a bit like the spirit animals from her dream. She looks up questioningly but all that comes back is the breath of a whisper, "Trust your inner self."

There are two signs pounded into the soil of her garden. The sign on the far end says, "Live Life in Full Bloom." *I want that,* Andrea thinks. *And I have all the tools I need to do it.*

What follows enters Andrea's mind like a download: *Self-care means choosing it as a way of life. Set and maintain healthy boundaries. Do the step work. Attend meetings. Read, journal, meditate, breathe, stay present. Practice mindfulness and yoga. Dance and be playful. Let go of all of it. This is what it is to live life in full bloom.*

The second sign says, "Bloom Where You Are Planted." Andrea pauses and feels a strong presence. She looks up and sees, in the wooded area behind her home, a black-tail doe and a fawn gazing at her with their huge brown eyes. She feels a comforting wave of understanding, compassion, nurturing, and grace—all the things the doe and fawn in her dream gave her. She smiles, places her hands on her chest, and calls out, "Thank you!"

The mother deer and fawn walk slowly toward her fence with their ears pricked up. She has been heard.

"I've been looking and looking for that something missing for so long I never stopped to look here," she tells them. "I never thought to bloom where I am planted. I couldn't see what was in front of me because of all the distractions and the lies."

The deer swish their tails.

"I've been neglecting and abandoning myself, my relationships—my garden," Andrea says. "But today, today I can make room, grow where I'm planted, and live life in full bloom."

The bunnies hop over near the deer and sit down next to a newly dug hole. Next to it is a box very like the one in her dream. The box is emitting light, and it emanates a presence she can identify as ... Nana. *I feel you, Nana,* she thinks.

Andrea opens the box and finds a note. She recognizes the handwriting: it's from Nana. It reads:

Dearest Andrea,

I am so pleased you took the opportunity to take the ride on the road we call life. The journey you embarked upon took willingness and courage. I am so proud of you. But your journey does not stop here. You will be given many opportunities to share your experience, strength, and hope. I am here to guide you when you need that extra shot of strength and courage, as your story is an important one and the messages are significant.

There is one thing I would like for you to add to your story, and that is the concept of honoring life. My wish for you is for you to find joy and acceptance in every facet of your life. Life is a precious gift, and I believe you understand that now. I want you to feel it, believe in it, and allow for the light in you to ignite gratitude for your past, present, future.

I wish you a life of good health, happiness, and abundance. An abundance of joy, spirituality, love, light, and peace. Go out there and share and shine your light. I believe in you.

I will love you forever.

Nana

Tears roll down Andrea's cheeks as she remembers her nana's unconditional love and support. She remembers all of the stories about how she was born into the soul family of light bearers and how the angels brought her to her mom and dad. Nana was Andrea's rock.

She feels a surge of gratitude for Nana—her first guide, she realizes—and for all her guides. She feels a powerful presence—the most powerful one she felt all day. "Are you here with me?" Andrea asks.

"I AM. I am with you, always," her higher power replies.

Andrea thinks about all of her spirit teachers and guides, angels, ancestors, spirit animals, and of course her higher power. She walks to the tree with Nana's note in hand and sits quietly on the swing. She closes her eyes and swings peacefully back and forth to the rhythm of the wind as she thinks about all there is yet to learn about her courageous self. About staying open to vulnerability, because it is in being vulnerable that she will access the love and wonder of the world and of her own soul. She gives thanks for her simple, plain, ordinary life—the new and improved ordinary life she now gets to live. She thanks herself—she loves herself—for being willing.

Her higher power whispers softly, "Keep your eyes closed, Andrea, and allow this recognition of who you are. Let that recognition be what you carry close as you rise and fall throughout your day. Let this recognition anchor you to the love that is yours. Let yourself be reminded that everything is a gift, and that this crazy ride we took together is one of the biggest gifts of all."

Andrea breathes deeply.

"This is a story of how you learned to explore and discover the immense beauty inside of you, the goddess within," her divine power says. "Allow yourself to be led by the wisdom of your heart and soul. Go forth, dear one. Your quest has just begun."

Andrea realizes that her life is hers to create and recreate and in that she gets to define her life's purpose. She feels immense gratitude for all the lessons, all of the glory, and all that still awaits her.

Andrea opens her eyes to see the spirit animals in her beautiful garden. The wind picks up, heralding the presence of the rest of her support team. She wonders for a moment if this was all really real, or whether the whole thing was her learning to take charge of her life via characters in a dream, each representing a part of herself?

Perhaps it's a combination of both, she thinks. *Today I can recognize how each character has been a part of me living within me. Each character plays a part in my healing. Each character will continue to guide me as I take charge of my life—and that feels remarkable.*

She speaks aloud. "Thank you all for your patience, kindness, and unconditional love. Thank you for loving me just as I am and for showing me that I have value and that I deserve to exist. I'm grateful I have the courage to travel to faraway places, places unknown. Today, I choose to live awake."

She gets off the swing and sits under the great tree where her soft, silky blanket awaits. Her pen is there, like a magic wand weaving her dream across the pages. Her travel journal is now there, too, filled with pages describing her journey into self, into untapped emotions, into truths, into leaps of faith. A dream upon the pages where her subconscious came out to play.

Her higher power whispers in her ear. "You are not alone Andrea; you will never be alone. You are a precious gift from the heavens above, and I thank you for your bravery, vulnerability, authenticity, and for your humility. I want to encourage and support you as you venture out there shining and sharing your light. Honor your life, Andrea. You are enough. I want you to see that you are enough. Be easy, and take your time as you continue on the majestic path coming home to yourself. Welcome home Andrea, welcome home!"

On the last page of her journal a message appears. It says:

"Dear blessed one,

I want you to know that here you are welcome. Here you belong.

Here you are enough. Welcome home!

Sincerely,

Your heart"

Reflections for This Chapter

Integrate your thoughts by going through these activities now or coming back to them later. I invite you to choose a song of your choice to listen to as you do so. May you be inspired to embark on or expand upon your own personal journey.

List everything you thought about when you woke up today.

List how you feel today in your body, mind, and heart.

Are you leaning in the direction of either beginning or continuing your own personal journey?

What path are you thinking of taking?

Who or what will help you get there?

One Year Later

Andrea walks into the Goddess Within meeting room and sees Rae and Ruthie waving her over to where they've saved her a seat. Tonight's meeting is focused on breathing, prayer, and meditation, things Andrea knows something about.

Today, Andrea shares authentically from her heart about the spiritual awakening that led her to this room and about choosing to live awake. She shares the struggles she still encounters along the way, only this time in empowerment instead of shame. She practices sharing her story as her way to give back. She serves as the secretary for her home group meeting, something she's gratified to find that she's good at.

Going out for ice cream after the meetings with her new friends Rae and Ruthie brings her joy. Rae loves to talk about the mysteries of life, which include the love she has for her cat Jaggy. Ruthie stays curious about life's mysteries as well. She also enjoys talking about how proud she is of her sons and how much she loves her pets too.

These two special friends will not allow her to stay small; together they are a growing force as they burst forth from the womb that binds them all together. They are a sisterhood of sorts, one where the bonds are tight, and the love is genuine.

In times of fellowship, they talk about their lives, their family, their pets. Even when they are talking about something sad—Andrea's own cat, Riley, passed, and she is still grieving—Andrea finds such joy in their stories. She sees more clearly now that grief is a passage and not a place to stay, and that she used to stay too long in her grief. She has a fifteen-year-old cat she adopted that she named Kayla Kitty, who she loves unconditionally. Kayla reminds her how precious all lives are: animal, plant, human—everything that lives.

Andrea has revisited the power of forgiveness and healing many times while working her recovery program, reading books, attending and participating in meetings, and chanting mantras and prayers of forgiveness. She understands that forgiveness is a two-step process: making the decision to forgive, and then actually doing the forgiving.

It took a while before she could consider forgiving James. She had to learn to let go of resentment and give up her sense of injury. She made a promise to herself that she would not keep revisiting what happened in their marriage, staying stuck in resentment and anger, and giving him and the events her power. Today she chooses to pray instead, praying for help forgiving James, her parents, Samantha, and all who have wronged her, including herself.

She and James managed to heal some of the hurt done to them as well as the hurts they did to each other. She has made some amends to him but she knows there is more to come. It's been a slow and difficult path, but a healthier one. Andrea has boundaries now, and she follows through with what she says. She stands strong in herself.

James is on a path as well. He attends Alcoholics Anonymous and is working his program. He is a willing participant, and Andrea is proud of him. Although they are not living together, they remain friendly as they work toward their next steps.

As for her children, she put her big girl panties on and met with each of them separately. She was able to make her amends and ask directly for her needs. She has learned that people feel safe around those who are direct and honest, who speak their minds and let others know where they stand. Being direct helps her own her power.

Andrea sees her children and her grandchildren at least two to three times a month, arranging to meet halfway between their two cities. Sometimes, now that they know her well enough to call her Nana, she has her grandchildren over for sleepovers. It is one of her truest joys in life. This year her extended family is planning a vacation, one she doesn't have to organize but can simply attend and enjoy.

She met with Samantha only to let her know she has forgiven her. They are no longer friends, but Andrea doesn't hate her or resent her. She prays for her.

Her parents are elderly now, and they seem to have mellowed in old age. Her mother, who had not touched a drink since the day Andrea almost overdosed and was hospitalized, has not changed much. But she's softer at times, and she tries to extend her love the best she knows how. Her mom has worked her own recovery program, but more on a superficial level. Life has been too painful for her to dig too deeply; she does the best she can. Andrea can accept that.

Her father also works a program of healing and recovery, but she thinks he attends meetings more for the fellowship than for his own personal recovery. He, too, volunteers and gives back, his way of being helpful and making sure "everything is fine." He tells Andrea how proud he is of her and lets her know how much she is loved and valued. She tells her dad how proud she is of him, for stepping out of his comfort zone, for exploring his need to have everything be fine, and to make room for when things are not fine. Today, he loves the challenge. Andrea and her dad continue to grow their special bond.

Andrea herself is living life in full bloom. She is blooming where she is planted. Her home and her garden bring her joy. In addition to attending meetings, she's taken up painting again. In fact she turned one of the spare bedrooms into an art studio. She obtained her yoga and breath work certificate, and teaches them twice a week. She also dances twice a week with her dance team called Tigress. Her relationships are beginning to blossom, and her codependency is beginning to dissipate. She knows she will always have her challenges, but she has many tools to pull out of her basket, and many people she can rely on when those old beliefs and thoughts creep back in.

When Andrea first fell into her dreamscape, she was at first seeking an escape. Then clarity. Finally, she knew she had to face her truth and to heal. As she often says, if you can't find your purpose, look for your passion—and let it lead you to what you're meant to do. In just this way, Andrea has been led to finding her passion, where she found strength, wisdom, clarity, and calm. She learned in her secret dreamworld that when she surrendered to a divine power, she was able to find true happiness in her awake life. She continues to shine and share her light, and to tell the story of how she had to journey to faraway places in order to be led back home to her heart.

Higher Power, please help me accept all the
life-changing experiences that I may have. Help me
to see the wonder in rebirth and to learn your lessons.
—paraphrased from MELODY BEATTIE

Conclusion

Life is a gentle teacher. She wants to help us learn.
—MELODY BEATTIE

We all have lessons to learn in life, lessons that come in all shapes and sizes. We may become frustrated, confused, conflicted, angry, or afraid. We may even feel hopeless at times. But the real truth lies within. As we explore who we are, fear is inevitable—and may keep us stuck. Surrender is when the exchanges take place: fear for faith, confusion for clarity, and uncertainty for wisdom, to name a few.

Andrea took one of many paths of exploration as she sought to repair and recover. No matter which road you take, the experience of surrender will be life-altering.

I believe that it's our individual responsibility to look at what is within, to clean up the messes we've left behind, to make amends, to forgive, and to take charge of our life. No matter how frightening that may seem, the benefits outweigh the fear.

Recovery creates space for new narratives and new relationships. Recovery warrants making peace with the past so that we are free to enjoy life free from worry and the "what-ifs." Recovery is about cultivating self-care, self-love, and inner peace. There is no secret map for self-care or recovery, but there is a path. You get to decide what you need to take care of yourself.

Recovery is made up of surrendering to a higher power, gaining trust in ourselves, and in collecting, correcting, and connecting the dots. Doing this deep work can be one of the best rewards that life has to offer on this side of the green door. It is about transformation. It is a journey of the heart that will lead you home to where you can live awake in the present moment.

What will it take for you to take your first step toward self-care and recovery?

In the end, only three things matter: how much you loved,
how gently you lived, and how gracefully you let go
of things not meant for you.
—JACK KORNFIELD

In gratitude,
  Susan M. Tuttle
  MS Counseling Education
  Certified Personal Life Coach/Breath Practitioner

List of Songs/Artists

Feel free to listen to the song at the end of each chapter.

Resources

Books

Beattie, Melody. *The Language of Letting Go: Daily Meditations for Codependents*. Harper Collins Publishers (A Hazelden Book), January, 1990.

Beattie Melody. *More Language of Letting Go: 366 New Daily Meditations*. Hazelden Publishing, September, 2000.

Carnes, Patrick J, PhD, with Bonnie Phillips, PhD. *The Betrayal Bond: Breaking Free of Exploitive Relationships*, Revised Edition. Health Communications, Inc., 2019.

Codependent Anonymous, Inc., Third Edition. CoRe Publications, 2016.

Fairchild, Alana. *White Light Oracle: Enter the Luminous Heart of the Sacred*, Guidebook, Llewellyn Publications, November 8, 2019.

LePera, Nicole, *The Holistic Psychologist. How To Do the Work: Recognize Your Patterns, Heal from Your Past and Create Your Self.* New York: Harper Wave/Harper Collins, 2021.

D'Simone, Sah. *5-Minute Daily Meditations, Instant Wisdom, Clarity & Calm*. Althea Press, 2018.

Seal, Moorea. *52 Lists for Calm: Journaling Inspiration for Soothing Anxiety and Creating a Peaceful Life*. Seattle: Sasquatch Books/Penguin Random House LLC, 2019.

Shriver, Maria. *I've Been Thinking . . .: Reflections, Prayers, and Meditations for a Meaningful Life*. New York: Pamela Dorman Books/Viking/Penguin Random House, 2018.

Stokes, Worthy. *The Evening Meditation Journal: Relaxing Prompts for Reflection and Relaxation*. Emeryville, California: Rockridge Press, 2021.

Terkeurst, Lysa. Forgiving What You Can't Forget: *Discover How to Move On, Make Peace with Painful Memories, and Create a Life That's Beautiful Again.* Nashville, Tennessee: Nelson Books/Thomas Nelson/Harper Collins, 2020.

Online

Admin. "Seven Stages of Grief – Going Through the Process and Back to Life," Recover from Grief, Home, Living with Grief, March 30, 2020, https://www.recover-from-grief.com.

Schulman, Lisa M. MD, FANN. "Healing Your Brain After Loss: How Grief Rewires the Brain," American Brain Foundation, September 21, 2020, https://www.americanbrainfoundation.org/how-tragedy-affects-the-brain.

Poole Heller, Diane, PhD. "Attachment Styles Test. What is your Attachment Style?" Trauma Solutions, https://traumasolutions.com/attachment-styles-quiz.

Lo, Imi, Master in Mental Health (Australia). "Did You Have to Grow Up Too Soon? Healing from the Trauma of Parentification.", Psychology Today, Living with Emotional Intensity, December 12, 2019, https://www.psychologytoday.com/us/blog/living-emotional-intensity/201912/did-you-have-grow-too-soon.

Ingerman, Sandra, MA. "The Healing Power of Shamanic Journeying: How to Access Inner Guidance from Helping Spirits," The Shift Network, https://www.theshiftnetwork.com.

Insight Timer App and online community for meditation, https://insighttimer.com.

Title 9 References, National Collegiate Athletic Association (NCAA), https://www.ncaa.org/searchresults.aspx?q=Title%209#gsc.tab=0&gsc.q=Title%209&gsc.page=1.

Oxford Learner's Dictionaries, https://www.oxfordlearnersdictionaries.com/us/definition/english/relationship?q=relationships.

Guha, Ahona, D. Psych. "The Parentified Child in Adulthood. Understanding the Psychological Impacts of Being Parentified as a Child." Psychology Today, Psych of Prisons and Pathos, July 31, 2021, https://www.psychologytoday.com/us/blog/prisons-and-pathos/202107/the-parentified-child-in-adulthood.

Acknowledgments

Thank you to my editor, Maggie McReynolds, whose words of encouragement and enthusiasm had much to do with getting this story told. She told me to go ahead and write the story the way I needed to tell it; that we'd worry about streamlining and tightening up later. Thanks to her skill, talent, and magic wand, we did just that.

I am grateful for my copyeditor, Sky Kier, who kept me honest. His fact-finding abilities, his keen eye for technicalities, and his reference-checking skills all assisted me with keeping my writing clean and clear. So much gratitude.

Thank you to my husband, who poked his head into my office from time to time and asked, "How are you doing?" I'm grateful for his caring and for also allowing me the time and space to think, write, and create.

Thanks to my family members for their continued support, especially my sisters Beth and Rena. They have been my encouragers and cheerleaders from the get-go, and I could not have done this without them.

Thank you to the women in my writer's circle: Stephanie Wild and Rebecca Cornell. I am so grateful for their kind words and support through and through.

I am so very grateful for all of my friends who checked in periodically to ask how I was doing and for their continued support throughout. I am especially grateful to those friends and supporters who read the manuscript early. Thank you for the reassurance to go for it and for helping me build the confidence I needed to actually put my message out there to the world.

I can't forget to thank my cat Riley, who has since passed but who used to sit with me on my lap, all sixteen pounds of him, purring as I wrote. I am equally grateful for my new senior cat Kayla, who looks up at me with her deep green eyes as she rolls in the sun beside me while I write.

I want to thank each of you who stood by me as I created this book from the bottom of my heart and from the depths of my soul. If I missed anyone. I apologize. Please forgive me.

Most of all, I want to thank my higher power, whom I call God, for making this all possible and for guiding me so that I have a safe space for sharing my stories with the world.

About the Author

Susan M. Tuttle is a certified personal life coach and breath practitioner with thirty years of recovery. She is also a public speaker, workshop facilitator, and popular podcast guest who practices mindfulness and considers giving back an integral part of her life's purpose.

When not focused on writing, Susan can be found cycling, painting, taking long walks surrounded by nature, and traveling with family and friends. She lives in the San Diego area with her husband and her beloved fifteen-year-old deaf cat, Kayla.

susanmtuttle.com
info@susanmtuttle.com
instagram.com/lifeofsusan24

Made in the USA
Las Vegas, NV
04 October 2023

78537937R00184